IAN SAYER and DOUGLAS BOTTING have co-authored three previous documentary accounts of hitherto unknown aspects of World War II and the Third Reich – *Nazi Gold: The Story of the World's Greatest Robbery, America's Secret Army*, and *Hitler's Last General: The Case Against Wilhelm Mohnke*.

IAN SAYER is the founder and owner of the most extensive private document archive and library on World War II and the Third Reich in the UK. He was publisher and editor of the monthly magazine *World War Two Investigator* and maintains ongoing research connections overseas, especially in the USA and Germany. It was his extensive research that cracked the mystery of the disappearance of the Reichsbank gold and currency reserves at the end of World War II, and it was his discovery and acquisition of the hitherto unknown papers of Walter Wagner, the mystery man at Hitler's wedding, which was the starting point for the present book.

DOUGLAS BOTTING is a Member of the Royal Institute of International Affairs and a Life Member of the National Counter Intelligence Corps Association of America (he was its historian). He was formerly a special correspondent for the BBC and Time-Life, and in addition to collaborations with Ian Sayer has written a number of books on Hitler's war in his own right, including *In the Ruins of the Reich* and *The U-Boats* (described by Hitler's successor, Admiral Dönitz, as 'really very good but a bit on the short side'). Other highly praised biographies include *The Saga of Ring of Bright Water – The Enigma of Gavin Maxwell* and *Gerald Durrell: The Authorised Biography*.

HITLER AND WOMEN

THE LOVE LIFE OF
ADOLF HITLER

IAN SAYER AND DOUGLAS BOTTING

ROBINSON
London

*The authors would like to dedicate this book
to their respective children, with gratitude and love –*

Kate and Anna Botting

Cara and Drew,
and Jamie, Kallum, Lana and Lilly Sayer

Constable & Robinson Ltd
3 The Lanchesters
162 Fulham Palace Road
London W6 9ER
www.constablerobinson.com

First published in the UK by Robinson,
an imprint of Constable & Robinson Ltd 2004

Copyright © Ian Sayer and Douglas Botting, 2004

The right of Ian Sayer and Douglas Botting to be identified as the
authors of this work has been asserted by them in accordance
with the Copyright, Designs & Patents Act 1988.

A copy of the British Library Cataloguing in
Publication data is available from the British Library

ISBN 1- 84119-918-4

Printed and bound in the EU

1 3 5 7 9 10 8 6 4 2

Contents

Contents

Part 3   Champagne – and Cyanide

Part 4   End Game

Contents

Part 5   Postscript – The Unsolved Puzzle

Illustrations

Illustrations courtesy the Ian Sayer Collection.
*The authors acknowledge the use of a diagram of the bunker layout by
Ray Cowdery, whom they have been unable to contact.

Preface

This is a new book about Adolf Hitler – his love life, his women, his strange proclivities – for a new generation of readers. Adolf Hitler was an enigma. Today historians still struggle to understand the intricacies of his public life and career – how he achieved power, how he used it, how he lost it. But if his public life is a labyrinthine puzzle, how much more so is his private life, above all his love life, which by its very nature was meant to be kept secret not only from public gaze but from the gaze of even his associates and those few intimates he ever had in his life. It is a subject of more than prurient interest, for it can be argued that Hitler's failure to find a mate lay at the heart of his destructive spirit. Hitler himself never intended that the world should know about the affairs of the heart or flesh of the man his nation reverently knew as the Führer. Anyone who did and was deemed untrustworthy, be they esteemed medics or responsible journalists or political associates or even past mistresses, were either summarily disposed of or fled for their lives. Nor, not surprisingly, did he let anyone past his bedroom door, especially when there was somebody else inside. My love is Germany, he would say. I am married to the women of Germany.

Investigating the private life and sexual inclinations of Adolf Hitler has been like trying to work one's way through an Elizabethan maze built on a tidal mudflat. Or perhaps more exactly – like trying to investigate a major scandal or crime, or

conduct a secret intelligence operation, where all the partici-
pants are dead, the main suspect never left a confession and such
evidence as exists (rather a lot, in fact) is variously contradictory
or partisan, based on the word of those against and those for, and
those manipulating the facts for their own diverse and devious
ends (including political ends and the Allied war effort). There
is no overwhelmingly damning document (though there are
many damning words-of-mouth), no smoking guns (no writs,
divorces, or even babies), though there *are* a lot of empty shell
cases lying around (figuratively speaking), and the broad picture
is relatively clear.

It is indubitably evident that Hitler liked women, both the
pretty and sexy young ones and also the warm and matronly
mother-figure ones, and it is equally clear that he had relationships of various sorts with several of them, including one he had
adored and one he even married.

The big question, though, is – did Hitler *do* it, at least in the
conventional sense of the phrase. His colleagues and contem-
poraries were constantly asking themselves this question. His
women friends – those that survived suicide – occasionally provided a conflicting medley of responses. Historians, biographers,
sexologists, psychopathologists, and specialist sleuths like Sayer
and Botting are asking it still. We believe we have provided the
right answer, but since we are aware that there may be more
than one we have examined and included the others.

This then is the inside story of Adolf Hitler – not in power,
not at war, but in love – three inextricable strands of the life of
the modern world's very own Genghis Khan.

Ian Sayer
Douglas Botting

PART 1

The Beauty and The Brute

A Walk on the Wild Side

He came to the foot of the stairs. There were four flights of stairs up to the top, thirty-eight steps all told. Like everything else in the place – floors, walls, ceilings, rooms – they were built of solid concrete. They needed to be. With every step he took towards the surface the percussive impact of the high explosives landing in the garden overhead grew ever louder, ever more unnerving.

For this 37-year-old, middle-ranking local city councillor and ad hoc Registrar of Births, Deaths and Marriages – an unassuming man in a brown Nazi Party uniform with a red Volkssturm (Home Guard) armband for whom there was now nothing much left in life but his sense of duty towards his country and his undying love for his young wife he had not seen for half a year and his baby boy he had never seen at all – the devastating tattoo of the shells landing above his head served only to underscore the phantasmagoria of the last few hours.

For he, Walter Wagner, a man of modest pretensions and a face hitherto unknown to most of the powers that be, had just played a crucial role in the penultimate rites of the supreme ruler of the greatest empire Europe had ever seen; he had participated in the end-game of a turning point in history – an insane ceremonial, a fantastical nightmare. And now, in all probability, he was going to die. It is not difficult to guess his state of mind. With his own eyes he had perceived that his supreme leader was a shambling wreck, that the game was up, that there was no longer even the faintest hope.

Confused and fearful, he heaved himself up the stairs to the emergency exit. With every step up the ear-splitting impact of the artillery salvoes grew louder, the walls trembled and cement dust rained down from the ceiling. From the distant room below – the room where the surviving elite celebrated the results of his handiwork in the final hours of the dying empire – he could still just catch the sentimental refrain of the last intact gramophone record, a popular ditty of the time ironically entitled 'Blood Red Roses Spell Happiness for You, Happiness for You'.

What exactly was in his mind we can only speculate. Wait till I tell Cordula about this, he might well have thought. Do you know the Führer's just got hitched, he'd say. And guess who got him through it? Me! It was me that married Adolf Hitler, he'd tell his wife. It was me that asked him if he was an Aryan, would you believe. I even asked the Führer if he was mentally defective, can you imagine? Not in so many words, of course. Cordula'd never believe it. He wouldn't blame her. Not long for this world, the Führer, by the look of it. Got the shakes. Could hardly sign the marriage certificate. And who was that pretty woman he'd married him to? Eva something. Eva Hitler now. Where did she come from all of a sudden? He'd never heard of her. Had anybody ever heard of her? Get on with it, Herr Wagner, she'd scolded him, time's running out. The cheek of it! After all he'd gone through to get there. Russians and whatnot. Now he'd got to run the gauntlet again. Shock to the system all this. Well, better up here than that hell-hole down there. How are they going to get away from that place in a hurry? And she in her silk black wedding dress and diamond necklace and all? Pretty lady, though. Sad, really.

4

He was near to the top of the stairs now. His mind probably began to dwell less on the bizarre nightmare he had just left and more on the all-too-real nightmare that now lay ahead of him. Finally he came to the top of the stairs. Two armed, jackbooted SS sentries still stood dutifully on guard there. They returned to Walter Wagner his camouflaged combat smock, his coal-scuttle steel helmet, his grenades, pistol and sub-machine gun. Then, wishing him luck, they opened the heavy steel doors of the Bunker's emergency exit and he stepped out into the Reich Chancellery garden – and into the next and final fantasy of his life.

It was well past one on the morning of 29 April 1945. The Soviets were just in the process of launching their all-out offensive against the city centre, and it was into this maelstrom that Walter Wagner was about to step. He looked briefly around, taking his bearings, checking if it was safe to proceed. What he saw was an unreal hell in an unreal city.

All Berlin was aflame. The sky was full of the deafening thunder of the heavy artillery, mortars and *Panzerfausts*, and from all around – and already alarmingly near – came the rattle of machine-gun and small-arms fire as the street fighting drew closer. The air was thick with fumes and smoke and a fine ash that sifted down like a dry drizzle; the night sky was livid and yellow, the colour of sulphur, from the sheer weight of high explosives that rained down, with here and there a lurid red glow as great fires gutted what was left of the capital of all their dreams.

Cautiously Wagner began to pick his way in the eerie, flickering dark eastward across the shell-holed, debris-strewn Chancellery garden to the street that would lead to his Volkssturm infantry company in the once-fashionable Potsdamer Platz in Berlin's besieged city centre. The capital's predicament, like Wagner's, was dire. Soviet forces now occupied all of the former Nazi capital but the inner government area – an area less than the size of Westminster or Manhattan – where Adolf Hitler and a few remaining top dogs of the all-but-extinct Thousand-Year Reich still had their being. The front line was now only 400 yards from the Chancellery Bunker and savage fighting was already in progress in the streets around.

Wagner was now in the midst of a nightmare, stumbling between life and death, from one to the other. He had never even set eyes on his little baby son Michael, hopefully safe and well with his mother Cordula on the quiet little island of Föhn far to the west of this terminal nightmare. Perhaps he would never see him now. Not long ago, in almost his last letter out of the doomed capital, he had written to his beloved wife of a year:

> Whatever fate may have in store for us, one thing we do know for sure is that we will be bound together in true love until we draw our last breath. With your love you have given my life a very special meaning, and you have made me very, very happy. In this hour, I want you to know my heart is yours forever, that I love you very, very much, and that I will always love you. My thoughts are also with our dear little Michael, who has made our lives richer still.

When he got to the Potsdamer Platz the situation there was apocalyptic. The whole broad expanse of the square was a waste of ruins, a mass of damaged vehicles and half-smashed ambulance trailers with the wounded still in them. The dead were strewn everywhere, many of them dreadfully cut up and mangled by tanks and trucks. The wounded who were not torn apart were not being taken in anywhere. The civilians in their cellars were afraid of them – too many of them had been hanged as deserters. There was no rest, no relief, no regular food, hardly any bread, and water could only be got from the canal and then filtered.

'My dear, good Cordula, our life together is yet to come,' Wagner had written to his young wife far away, more in grief than in hope. 'Sadly, at this moment, as you read this letter, I cannot be with you, but in my thoughts I am – now more than ever.'

So Walter Wagner – the mystery man in the last hours of Hitler and his court, the man who had shouldered the delicate responsibility of coaxing Adolf Hitler and Eva Braun through their desperate machine-gun wedding in the bowels of the Bunker – disappeared into the darkness, and the battle, and from history.

Where he had come from when he stepped centre stage into the Führer's presence at this dire juncture was never entirely clear. What happened next was not generally known. Years later, Germany's leading news magazine, *Stern*, reported – wrongly, it turned out – that Walter Wagner had been spotted alive and well and living near Frankfurt. Now, for the first time, the true story can be publicly revealed – the story of the man who married Hitler, of Eva and Adolf's love unto death, of four funerals and a wedding, and escape, death and myth – and much else besides.

A Room with No View

Once they had shut the gas-proof, flood-proof, sound-proof door she could hardly hear a thing in this cement cell they called a sitting room. Just the distant thud of an incoming high-explosive shell now and then, a faint jelly-like tremor down the concrete walls. But down here in the Bunker over thirty feet below Berlin city centre they had nothing to worry about. After all, they'd be dead in a minute or two, so that was alright.

She had dressed especially for the occasion – blue chiffon frock and frilly white collar, pretty and spring-like, and neat, fashionable shoes. After all, it was a *very* special occasion. The very *last* occasion, in fact, the big goodbye. And she did so much want to be a pretty corpse. So no gun and bullet, no blood and brains, not as far as she was concerned. Just a quick, quiet nodding off. Well, so she hoped. *He* was going to do it differently, of course. But *he'd* been in the war, been in two wars come to think of it – fought in one and waged the other – and anyway, he was a man; men knew about guns and things. But she was dreadfully afraid.

She had kicked her shoes off and curled herself up at one end of the blue and white brocade sofa with her legs tucked up to make herself more comfortable, more relaxed. Her husband of a few hours was sitting rather stiffly and upright at the other end. He looked quite smart in his brown Führer's dress uniform. No food stains on his tunic today. She'd cleaned off the tomato ketchup and mustard spots herself specially for the occasion. Not that it mattered, but it was best to keep up standards, especially at historic moments like this.

What was he thinking, she wondered? After all these years, the power and the glory, the pomp and the circumstance, the salvation of the Fatherland, the adoration of millions – and for it all to end up like this, in a concrete hutch in a hole in the ground, the bare cement walls a dull battleship grey, or rusty looking brown or orange, or moist or even mouldy, the air stinking of old boots and disinfectant and blocked drains. Betrayed right, left and centre – the ingratitude of it all, it was enough to make the worms weep.

There was a little framed photo of his long-dead mother on the side table beside him. How proud she would have been of him if she had lived. Her little boy, so timid and shy – and look what became of him, King, Emperor, Dictator, Führer, God – call him what you like. But she was worried. His hands shook so violently these days, she was undoubtedly afraid he'd miss and just blow his ear off or perhaps even put a bullet through the head of his hero, Frederick the Great, whose portrait hung on the wall.

She wasn't going to use the pistol they'd given her, not if she could help it. 'Wait till you hear the shot,' the experts in this sort of thing had advised her, 'and then bite on the capsule.' She fingered the capsule in her hand. It was quite a pretty little thing really. It looked like a rather flashy copper lipstick holder and inside it was a glass phial containing a golden liquid. Crush the phial between your teeth and the cyanide would cause a rapid progression from breathlessness, through paralysis and unconsciousness to death in seconds.

She could remember it as if it was yesterday, the day they first met. He wasn't the Führer then, just another politician, but on his way. Half her lifetime ago. She had loved him always, through thick and thin, through nothing and everything, and she loved him still, here and now, even down here with a minute to go and eternity to live through. What times they had been since then – revolution, war, conquest, and then a world on the wane, the enemy at the gates, their own curious switchback love affair, and now this: a cyanide capsule between her teeth, a Walther pistol on the table before her, waiting for the shot that would end her lover's life and signal it was time to clench her jaw to end her own.

9

It could be worse. She was with the man she loved. He would not be going away again. No one could take him from her now. And it would not hurt, she would not cry, she was home – a concrete pen the size of a bathroom in the middle of a catacomb, but for her the centre of her world. And they would remember her.

Remember me!

Wait till you hear the shot . . . wait till you hear the shot.

She heard the shot.

'This character was looking at my legs'

It was curious, the chain of events that led to this concrete, gas-proof cell, to these final minutes of a life no one would have guessed could go down this route and end up here. She could always remember only too well the day she first met him – the defining moment that led to all this, the room she was in all those summers ago that led step by step to the room she ended up in that last late spring. It was September 1929 and she was seventeen years old, just out of convent school and working as an assistant in Heinrich Hoffmann's photographic shop and studio in Munich.

'I had climbed up a ladder to reach the files on the top shelves of the cupboard,' she recounted to her sister later. 'At that moment my boss came in accompanied by a man of uncertain age, with a funny moustache, a light-coloured English-style overcoat and a big felt hat in his hand. They both sat down opposite me and I sensed that this character was looking at my legs. That very day I had shortened my skirt.'

Now if she hadn't shortened her skirt that same day it is possible the man with the funny moustache, who called himself

Herr Wolf in those days, would never have started staring at her legs – and for that matter her bottom – and she would never have met him again. But one thing led to another.

Noticing Herr Wolf's fascination with the girl, Hoffmann sent her off to fetch some sausages and beer from the tavern on the corner. It didn't matter that Herr Wolf was normally a vegetarian who almost never ate sausages and only rarely touched mild beer. That wasn't the point. The point was to have Eva at the same table as he was. She was round faced, fair haired, blue eyed, pretty, blonde, lissom, youthful, full of life, physically desirable, intellectually unchallenging – or as the future valet of the man Eva called the 'elderly gentleman' was to put it more bluntly the first time he saw her: 'good legs, firm breasts, well-rounded bottom', an ideal Aryan Fräulein. Herr Wolf was quite smitten.

'I was starving,' Eva told her sister afterwards. 'I gobbled my sausage and had a sip of beer for politeness' sake. The elderly gentleman was paying me compliments. We talked about music and a play at the theatre, with him devouring me with his eyes all the time. Then, as it was getting late, I rushed off. I refused his offer of a lift in his Mercedes, but before I left Hoffmann pulled me on one side. '"Haven't you guessed who that gentleman is? It's Hitler! Adolf Hitler!"' Hoffmann should know. He was Hitler's photographer.

Here he was, this 'elderly gentleman', approaching middle age in fact, funny-looking toothbrush moustache under his snouty nose, lick of black hair plastered across his forehead, eyes bulging like a possum's, face lean and haunted and fanatically intent, and excited like a part-time psychopath's, 'face and head, bad race, crossbreed, low retreating forehead' (as one Nazi racial hygienist described his non-Nordic, pro-Aryan, racist, future

Führer), tightly buttoned up in a dark leather overcoat with a hippopotamus-hide whip in his hand and the faintly quaint makeshift uniform of the early Nazi streetfighter or boy scout leader imbued with a grudge – Charlie Chaplin to a tee. Surely this could not be God's gift to womankind?

Adolf Hitler was still a struggling, up-and-coming politician at that time and not yet a household name. Eva had never heard of him and when she got home she asked her father, 'Who is that character, a certain Adolf Hitler?'

'Hitler?' her father replied. 'He's a jack-of-all-trades, an imbecile who thinks himself omniscient and wants to reform the world. He thinks he imbibed wisdom with his mother's milk. I cross to the other side when I meet him in the street.'

There was a time in his life – indeed much of his formative years and early manhood – when the whole world seemed to pass Adolf Hitler by on the other side of the street. A loner, an eccentric, a young man morbidly fearful of women and the sins of the flesh, he would never have dreamed of staring at a young girl's legs as he had just that afternoon stared at Eva's. He wasn't like that now, of course. That was all thanks to Dr Krueger.

'A somewhat dishevelled man'

Dr Kurt Krueger remembered his first encounter with the future Führer of Germany and conqueror of Europe vividly – or so a controversial author of that name, who claimed to have been Hitler's medic and psychiatrist until he was forced to flee from Germany in fear for his life, was to allege in a book first published in New York in 1941 under the title *Inside Hitler* and again in 1942 and 1943 under the title *I was Hitler's Doctor*.

It was in the twilight of a day late in August 1919, the doctor claimed, that the door of the doctor's humble residence-cum-surgery in Munich was pulled open and a stranger stood in front of him – 'a medium-sized, slender, somewhat dishevelled man,' Dr Krueger alleged, 'with a sparse, curious little goatee decorating his weak chin.' Hitler, it seems, was not a very prepossessing figure as he stood there, clad in an old trench coat, probably to hide the shabbiness of the rest of his attire, so Dr Krueger guessed. The doctor went on:

> Left alone with the man in the trench coat, I confess that I felt not a little ill at ease. Aside from his bizarre presence, he seemed, despite a verbal show of self-confidence, profoundly unhappy with me, as well as with himself, and kept straining within his clothes as if it would have greatly relieved him to scratch himself. But there was no way I could communicate this assurance to him, so he sat in misery, pulling away at that curious goatee of his in the manner of old Polish Jews I had met on the Eastern Front.

This was almost the first recorded description of the apparent non-entity – who before long would electrify the world and destroy a race and a continent – as he was at almost the very beginning of his political career in the first months of the postwar era. Historians have tended to scorn the apparition of Hitler in a beard as suspiciously inauthentic, though at this particular time, it has to be said, Hitler was working as an undercover spy for the German Workers' Party in Munich and may have grown a beard as part of his undercover disguise, and the OSS (America's Secret Wartime Intelligence Organization) also record the existence of a beard at around this time. In any case, as the doctor was to observe, the beard was soon replaced by 'an abbreviated growth of hair several inches higher up on his upper lip'.

Hitler that first evening presented an image that Dr Krueger described as 'tragically human' – a helpless softness beneath a crust of hardness after four years of war service as an infantry corporal on the Western Front in World War One. 'His face looked both fear-driven and disease-hounded,' Krueger noted, 'with a pair of wild suffering eyes and lonely and secret pain.' Physically he was not at all impressive. Psychologically he was still on the battlefield, nervously clenching and unclenching his fists as if he were constantly preoccupied either with attacking or being attacked. Krueger went on:

> But most of all he was fearful of being ambushed by Life. He was a soldier of misfortune who could not be demobilized, his shattered nerves driving him to an eternal combat with himself, which he mistook for the hostility of the world.
>
> He placed both his elbows on his side of my desk, and let his head sink into his two open hands, in a gesture of utter weariness and despair. Then, looking up at me suddenly, quizzically, he said:
>
> 'I guess I've nothing more than the old French sickness.'
>
> I smiled.
>
> 'You mean syphilis?'
>
> He nodded.
>
> 'Suppose we go into my laboratory?' I suggested.
>
> He followed me a little sheepishly into the next room

14

the same time developing one or two minority proclivities peculiar to himself.

Nature or nurture? Or more probably some indefinable mixture of the two, evolving like some unique virus that in a billion-to-one chance survived a random series of circumstances to evolve into a messianic psychopath and penetrate the body politic of Europe at one particular moment in time and infect it with a lethal fever called Nazism – while proving inadequate and sometimes even useless at everything else, including sex and reproduction. 'A riddle wrapped in a mystery inside an enigma' is how his future mortal enemy, Winston Churchill, was to describe him, and there would be a number of decent, besotted German girls, and even one or two English ones, who would echo his description.

Much has been made, almost certainly with very good reason, of the fact that the young Adolf adored and worshipped his mother, probably the only human being he truly loved without qualification, while at the same time he loathed and feared his violent and drunken brute of a father. Thus there is a school of thought which interprets a passage in Hitler's autobiography and political testament, *Mein Kampf* (My Struggle), in which a young child witnesses at close hand a violent sexual encounter between his father and his mother – in effect father-mother rape – as (in psychologist's language) 'the primal scene trauma' which shaped his attitude to sex and sexual relations for ever after. The passage in question goes as follows:

> Let us imagine the following: In a basement apartment of two stuffy rooms live a worker's family . . . Among the five children there is a boy, let us say, of three. The smallness and overcrowding of the rooms do not create

17

favourable conditions. Quarrelling and nagging often arise because of this. When the parents fight almost daily, their brutality leaves nothing to the imagination . . . especially when the mutual differences express themselves in the form of brutal attacks on the part of the father towards the mother or to assaults due to drunkenness. The poor little boy, at the age of six, senses things which would make even a grown-up shudder. Morally infected, the young 'citizen' wanders off to elementary school.

What Hitler is describing here has been described as a recollection of the primal scene of abusive parental intercourse that he himself witnessed as a child. This interpretation was incorporated in the wartime American secret intelligence (OSS) report on the mind of Adolf Hitler and for a while was generally considered to be the origin of the pathological disturbance of Hitler's psyche that was the cause of both his sexual and his political perversions.

A later associate of his by the name of Ernst ('Putzi') Hanfstaengl wrote:

Psychologists could fill a whole text-book about Hitler, starting with his own description of himself as a 'Muttersöhnchen' – a mother's boy. Hitler claims this was a stage he grew out of, but many of them do not and neither did he. Germany and the world were yet to suffer from the fact that he had all the psychological faults of the type magnified to a daemonic degree. Uneasily aware that he was incapable of perpetuating himself as a father, he developed a substitute-obsession to make his name known – and feared – throughout the ages, whatever monstrous deeds such a mania involved. He became the modern counterpoint of Herostratus, who, desirous of acquiring eternal fame, if only by a great crime, burnt down the Temple of Diana at Ephesus.

But interpretations come and go and the central mystery – the infinitely complex inter-stellar galaxies of Hitler's endlessly explored but never quite mapped mind – remains an everlasting enigma.

There is no record of young Adolf even going out with a girl in his youth, and in the days of his early down-and-out manhood in pre-war Linz, Vienna and Munich, when he scratched a pittance as a failed art student, homeless vagrant and street drifter trying to peddle his own not very talented landscapes and townscapes, sleeping in doss houses and squalid backstreet rooms, it seemed he fared little better. As he was to admit later: 'I believe those that knew me took me for an eccentric.' Shy and inhibited, an introvert and a loner, a pale, thin, unshaven wreck of a young man, he simply lacked the confidence even to talk to a girl. In Linz, at the age of sixteen, he appears to have formed a distant and fixated calf love for a pretty young girl a year or two older than himself called Stefanie, whom he longingly gazed at from afar in the streets or the park. She was tall, slim and distinguished looking, and wore her blonde hair in a bun. Later it was claimed that her surname was Isac and that she was thus a Jewess (not true). Hitler himself lacked the courage to approach her, however, let alone speak to her, and the first she heard of his infatuation was a quarter of a century afterwards. Later he claimed to have sometimes been bold enough to pick up female streetwalkers in Vienna – usually Jewish ones. 'In those days,' he explained years later, by which time he had become a pathological anti-Semite well on his way towards becoming Führer and architect of the Holocaust, 'I felt that the whole sex business was an unclean act, best consummated with a member of an unclean race.' His one true love was his mother Klara, and when she died of cancer just before Christmas 1907, when Hitler was eighteen and had just failed his art exam and moved to Vienna, he was left bereft and alone in an emotional void.

Forming no meaningful relationship with any female, he instead acquired a lifelong horror of prostitutes and syphilis (for reasons that will become apparent), at length recoiling in horror at the prospect of sex with any of the wanton, painted cafe tarts and touting street hags who populated the urban maelstrom where he spent his lonely days and nights. August Kubizek, his bosom pal in Vienna in those days, recalled a typical encounter:

> Seeing a 'Room to Let' notice in the house in the Zollergasse, we rang the bell. 'Madam' appeared in the doorway, a real lady, wearing a silk dressing gown and very dainty slippers. The lady was visibly dismayed that it was I and not Adolf who wanted the room. While speaking she had become very animated and a sudden movement loosened the cord of her dressing gown. She at once readjusted the garment but the brief moment had been enough to show us that underneath she was wearing nothing but a diminutive pair of knickers. Adolf went as red as a turkey-cock, stood up, and took me by the arm saying: 'Come on, Gustl!' I don't really know how we got out of the house. All I

remember is that when we at last found ourselves in
the street, Adolf blurted out angrily: '*Potiphar's wife!*'

Many years later (a full eight years after the end of the Second
World War, in fact) Kubizek was to testify that it was not just
women, it was the whole sexual shooting match that Hitler
reviled, homosexuality included. 'It seemed to me quite natural,'
Kubizek related, 'that he should feel horror and disgust at this
[homosexuality] and other sexual aberrations in the capital and
that unlike most adolescents he did not indulge in frequent
masturbation – adhering, indeed, in all sexual matters to the rigid
code which he prescribed both for himself and for the future state.'

In Munich in the months before the outbreak of the First
World War Hitler's life seems to have grown even more monastic, his days spent entirely in painting pictures, his evenings
entirely in talking with his landlord and family about politics
and the looming war, with never so much as a hint or a whisper
of any woman around him at any time. 'What were God's
intentions,' his friend Kubizek felt compelled to ask himself,
'when he created this young man?' Heaven only knows.

Hitler served in the German Army in the First World War
with courage and distinction as an infantry corporal and bicycle
despatch rider on the Western Front, winning the Iron Cross
(both First and Second Class), and the Cross of Military Merit
(Third Class) and being wounded and gassed in turn. His prolonged front-line exposure to a war to the death – modern total
war – impacted on Hitler profoundly in various ways.

For a start, his perception of the shame and tragedy of
Germany's eventual total defeat was to be the start point of his
burgeoning resolve to help reverse the defeat and restore the
Fatherland to Glory and to Empire.

Then again, the unexpected fall-out of his experience of being caught in a British gas attack on the Western Front in October 1918, would turn his chaotic psyche into a single-minded realization that it was he who would be the chosen one to lead his defeated nation, indeed the entire Germanic race, to power and supremacy in the years to come. The gas attack that had triggered this process may well have cost the world dearly. Apparently blinded in the attack, Lance-Corporal Hitler was transferred back to a military reserve hospital at Pasewalk, 600 miles behind the lines, where he was cared for by a psychiatrist by the name of Dr Edmund Forster. Realizing that Hitler's blindness was more hysterical than actual, Forster set about a special form of psychiatric treatment that amounted to a kind of targeted form of medical deceit. He explained to Hitler that his blindness was actually physical (knowing that it was not) and that he ran the risk of it becoming permanent. Such a daunting handicap could only be overcome, he explained, 'by a man of destiny chosen by a higher power for some divine purpose'. Miracles, Forster went on, do happen to chosen people. 'For a person with exceptional strength of will-power there are no limits,' he told the languishing lance-corporal. 'Have absolute faith in yourself; then you will stop being blind.'

Later Hitler was to describe in his autobiographical political testament *Main Kampf* how he experienced 'a vision' while being treated for temporary blindness (in fact the vision was created by Dr Forster playing tricks with the lights). Hitler never looked back, and Dr Forster – along with some 40 million other human beings throughout Europe – would pay with his life for Hitler's seemingly divine resurrection.

'Hitler was an excellent soldier,' his commanding officer in the First World War, Fritz Wiedemann, was to testify to the

Nuremberg Tribunal at the end of the Second. 'A brave man, he was reliable, quiet and modest. But we could find no reason to promote him as he lacked the qualities to become a leader.' Now Dr Forster had let the genie out of the bottle and the world would never be the same again.

In other, more personal respects, however, Hitler remained the same as ever. His experience at the Front seemed only to have reinforced his built-in distaste for ordinary, casual, soldierly, 'bit-of-all-right-mate' sexual encounters, to the extent that his comrades dubbed him 'the monk' and a 'woman-hater'. In fact, he emerged from the war not only as a political messiah in the making but a sexual neurotic with his phobia about prostitutes and syphilis reinforced – and since syphilis could be caught from prostitutes and female prostitutes were indubitably women, his general view was that all women were dangerous and that straightforward sex with any of them was more dangerous still. But as time would show, it was all rather more complicated than that.

Hitler's wariness regarding women, his constant worry about having his name linked with a woman, was well known to those who were acquainted with him. Colleagues would remark at his desperate efforts to wriggle out of any close involvement with any female who was clearly available to him, as though fearful that when it came to bed he would be exposed as being sexually useless, or destroyed as being hopelessly trapped. Those women who did manage to inveigle or drag him to bed were later to confide that it did not always go according to plan. Hitler's close, almost exclusive association with special male friends in the early days – August Kubizek in pre-war Vienna, Ernst Schmidt in the war – led some associates who knew him then (and some historians who didn't) to assume that Hitler was

23

homosexual. But really the available evidence suggests otherwise. It was clear that he was normally attracted to normally attractive women – generally young, pretty, blonde, busty, healthy, lively, friendly, fun, extrovert, and not too challenging. And it would appear that he was also possessed, now and then, of an average to below-average level of male libido too.

The problem was – as it began to emerge in the early post-war years – that between the sex object (the woman) and the sex protagonist (himself) there was generally a failed connection, a blown fuse. In other words, when it came to it, and regardless of the strength or otherwise of the sexual desire, he could not perform – in short, he was impotent, or at least intermittently so. This is a fairly common problem of the human male from time to time, a bi-product possibly of a very large, over-complicated, highly sensitive and unusually self-conscious brain, particularly in periods of personal stress. For Hitler it was a deeply disturbing discovery, especially as he ascribed the failure to his having acquired syphilis, perhaps during one of his failed encounters before the war. His next step, therefore, was to find a cure, and that was why, a few weeks after leaving the army following the end of the war, he allegedly arrived at the door of a Munich-based specialist physician-cum-psychoanalyst, a mysterious Dr Kurt Krueger, who was believed to handle such problems – or so the book brought out in New York was later to claim.

Later too this Dr Krueger put on record his opinion that Hitler 'seemed terrified of love for fear it might destroy him'. The only cure available to Krueger was psycho-analysis – 'at best a guided, probing conversation', as its inventor, Sigmund Freud, allegedly told Krueger years before, but in Hitler's view 'a Jewish science invented by Israel as a means of bedevilling the rest of the world'. In any case it was to prove a long and inconclusive process that was to last for the next fifteen years, during which time Krueger seems to have garnered rather less information from Adolf Hitler about his sexual proclivities than any one of Hitler's woman friends did in five minutes. As late as January 1940 it seemed Hitler was still convinced that syphilis was the underlying cause of his problem, and it required a further series of tests to prove to him once and for all that he suffered from neither syphilis nor creeping paralysis.

'The asphyxiating perfume of modern eroticism'

It was evident, meanwhile, that Hitler, anxious to cut loose after the privations and deprivations of his pre-war and wartime years, was at times in deep despair over his apparent condition. Years later, when it was all over, Albert Speer, Hitler's friend, architect and armaments minister, was to tell his post-war interrogators that though Hitler was not a passionate man in his private life, he was sexually normal. This would remain to be seen.

The question of Hitler's sexuality – preferred partners, proclivities, libido, performance and the rest – was always a vexed and uncertain one, especially in his own lifetime, and speculation was rife (and grew rifer as Hitler himself rose speedily to power). The general consensus – the outsider view – was that there was nothing to hide and therefore nothing to see. Even one of America's most outstanding investigative journalists, John Gunther, was unable to penetrate the smokescreen obscuring Hitler's private life (or lack of it) and in his monumental pre-war report, *Inside Europe,* confidently declared at the time:

Hitler is totally uninterested in women from any personal sexual point of view. 'The life of our people must be free from the asphyxiating perfume of modern eroticism,' he wrote in *Mein Kampf.* His personal life embodies this concept to the fullest. He is not a woman-hater, but he avoids and evades women. His manners are those of the wary chevalier, given to hand-kissing – and nothing else. Many women are attracted to him sexually, but they have to give up the chase. It is quite possible that Hitler has never had anything to do with a woman in his life. Nor, as is so widely believed, is he homosexual. No evidence was discovered that Hitler had ever been intimate with anybody of any sex at any time. Most of those German writers and observers equipped to know think that Hitler is a virgin.

Magda Goebbels, wife of Dr Joseph Goebbels, Hitler's Nazi comrade in arms and future Minister of Propaganda, was particularly frustrated at her failure to find Hitler some suitable mate. She would arrange evening parties for him and invite pretty and distinguished women to meet him, but she was never able to arrange a match. She once confessed:

> My husband was most anxious to get Hitler interested in some nice girl - it would have done him good to be able to relax and pour out his troubles to a sympathetic woman. Alas, I was no good as a match-maker. I'd leave him alone with my most charming friends and he wouldn't respond. In some ways Hitler simply isn't human – he can't be reached or touched. My husband

was terribly disappointed when we couldn't get him to choose a confidante.

What Dr Goebbels and his Frau (who fancied Hitler herself) had in mind by 'some nice girl' was a suitably elegant and aristocratic lady, or even a film star of stunning éclat and acclaim, who could be seen and photographed arm in arm with the Führer to be, a consort of immense propaganda value who could enhance Hitler's public image in her role as vice-reine or empress to the nation's great leader. Outwardly at least, it seemed that Hitler over the years conformed to this ideal stereotype, and his name was romantically linked with various wealthy Munich society ladies, nearly all of them a generation older than he was. They included his rich patroness, Helen Bechstein, wife of the piano manufacturer, another rich patroness Gertrud von Seydlitz, whose family ran paper mills in Sweden, and the so-called 'Mother of the Nazi Revolution' Viktoria von Dirksen, as well as a headmaster's widow, a millionaire publisher's wife, a consul-general's wife, an ambassador's daughter, a German princess, an English milady, a Finnish beauty, and a retired nun (and fervent early Nazi).

'King of Munich'

Few, if any, of these mostly mature establishment ladies were in fact ever romantically involved with Hitler, most (but not all) admitting later that their feelings for the rising star of German politics were maternal rather than sexual. They treated him as a charming but slightly uncouth son with gauche but sometimes amusing social inadequacies (such as adding sugar to his wine to sweeten it) and remained content to do no more than stroke his hair and pat his head whenever it nestled (as it was sometimes inclined to) on their ample (but well-clothed) bosoms.

But Hitler was becoming well aware of his magnetic impact on women in general, and perhaps released from his anxieties and inhibitions in sexual matters as a result of his long, exploratory and cathartic sessions with his Munich psycho-analyst, Dr Krueger, it seems that as the 1920s progressed he was ready to embark on a new life as a born-again Lothario.

All this was rather remarkable, for to look at objectively Hitler was not a very prepossessing specimen of manhood, and not exactly endowed with the looks of Lothario at all. The secret wartime report on the Führer by America's secret intelligence organization, the OSS, presented a picture of a man who physically at least came nowhere near the image of the supreme sex idol of German womanhood, let alone the future Leader of the Third German Empire. The OSS report ran:

> In height he is a little below average. His hips are wide and his shoulders relatively narrow. His muscles are flabby, his legs short, thin, and spindly. He has a large torso and is hollow-chested . . . with his mouth full of brown, rotten teeth. From a physical point of view he could not pass the requirements of his own elite guard.

For a time in the early days he wore a pointed beard, and his dark-brown hair was parted down the middle and plastered down flat against his head with oil. His gait was hardly that of a political leader or military man. Rather, he minced along. 'It was a very lady-like walk,' ran one eyewitness statement in the OSS report. 'Dainty little steps. Every few steps he cocked his right shoulder nervously, his left leg snapping up as he did so. He also had a facial tic that made the corners of his lips curl up.' His dress was not much more attractive. In the early days he often wore a Bavarian costume consisting of leather shorts, white shirt and suspenders. On more formal occasions, before his Nazi uniform was designed, he would wear an ordinary blue suit.

Not surprisingly, some first-hand reports of close encounters with the man were far from adulatory – 'Was this provincial dandy, with his slick dark hair, his cutaway coat, his awkward gestures and glib tongue, the terrible rebel? He seemed for all the world like a travelling salesman for a clothing firm.'

An Englishwoman by the name of Dorothy Thompson reported: 'He is formless, almost faceless, a man whose framework seems cartilaginous, without bones. He is inconsequent and voluble, ill poised and insecure. He is the very prototype of the little man.'

Testifying as a witness in a law court in 1923, Professor Max von Gruber of the University of Munich, described Hitler as he was when he first set eyes on him at close hand:

> Face and head of inferior type, cross-breed, low receding forehead, ugly nose, broad cheekbones, little eyes, dark hair. Expression not of a man exercising authority in perfect self-command, but of raving excitement.

But even then, in the days when Hitler was still a no one at the foot of the political ladder to power, before he had perfected his self-presentation and mastered the power of oratory that could sway the masses, his piercing, bright-blue eyes had a phenomenally hypnotic power over those who were close enough to perceive them, with a depth and a glint that mesmerized and seduced anyone who stared into them. And it was the eyes, and the magnetism of his presence, that lured and hypnotized women who came close enough to sit with him or stand by him, in spite of his odd Charlie Chaplinesque appearance, his awful teeth, his bad breath, his rasping voice, his Austrian peasant dialect.

This might have been gratifying to Dr Goebbels and his Frau, but what they did not have in mind was that the newly liberated Hitler would start running off with teenage shopgirls and music students and getting up to all sorts of unbefitting antics with them – which is exactly what he did once he began to feel sufficiently confident in his own sexuality to cut loose in his dealings with them. Hitler himself remained unrepentant. Years later, when he was Führer and reminiscing at a luncheon in the Reich Chancellery in August 1942, he told the assembled guests frankly:

> My own particular tragedy is that, as Head of State, I
> always have the worthy ladies as my dinner partners!
> I'd far rather go on board the *Robert Ley* [a river cruise
> boat] and pick out some pretty little typist or sales-girl
> as my partner!

But here, now, in 1920s Munich, suddenly the world was full of them – young, busty, full legged, as dazzling as a prairie of sunflowers. Years later, holed up in his wintry and benighted military headquarters in the Wolf's Lair in East Prussia, where he was directing the war on the Eastern Front, he turned to reminiscing about his past life (as he often did when there was nothing better to do) and in particular the pageant of beautiful women that had crossed his past in times of yore:

> We were sitting in the Ratskeller in Bremen when a woman came in. It almost seemed as though Olympus itself had opened up! She was absolutely dazzling. Everyone stopped eating and all eyes were riveted on her. Then there was that other time in Brunswick. How I cursed myself afterwards! No one in my suite showed any more gumption than I did. A blond piece came tripping up to my car to give me a bouquet. It didn't enter anyone's head to ask the girl for her address so that I could send her a note of thanks. She was a wonderful girl, tall and fair! But there was such a crowd – and besides we were in a hurry. Once in the Bayerische Hof I was at a function that positively glittered with beautiful women and diamonds. Then in comes a woman so beautiful she puts all the rest into the shade – and she wore no jewellery! It was Frau Hanfstaengl. I once saw her and Mary Stuck together at Erna Hanfstaengl's place. What a picture! Three women, each more beautiful than the other!

Hitler belonged to that category of male who preferred the company of women to that of men. In the years before he assumed power he often asked his associates to find some female company for him as a change from what he called 'the bunch of louts' he was always surrounded by, and sometimes he would get his chauffeur, Emil Maurice, to drive around town in the evenings to find some. Women were enchanting to him and he in turn was charming and enchanting back – polite, attentive, respectful, old worldly, even admiring. Women could say things to him he would have men shot for, and do things in his presence (like smoke) that men – senior ministers included – would have been thrown out of the room for. He was forever kissing and patting their hands, bowing them first through doors, murmuring endearing Austrian diminutives at them, like *'Mein Prinzesschen'*, *'Meine kleine Gräfin'*, *'Tschapperl'*, or *'Flietscherl'* (my little princess, my little countess, my sweet little dumb cluck). This did not mean he had an unqualified admiration of the female sex, which he regarded as almost as dangerous as marriage itself, and he remained an extreme male chauvinist to his dying day, with a horror of female intellectuals almost as great as his horror of male ones (generals and politicians included). With women actresses, singers, dancers, artists, film stars, film makers, even pilots, he was on much more comfortable ground, but it was mostly with teenage girls around town that he felt confident enough – and lecherous enough – to embark on relationships of sexual intimacy.

According to British historian and psychologist Dr David Lewis, it seems possible that Heinrich Himmler, Head of the SS and Minister of the Interior in Hitler's future Nazi Government, may have kept a secret file known as the Führer File on the private life of Adolf Hitler, including intimate details of his sex life – a top-secret dossier he reckoned might prove useful in any future power struggle for the leadership of the Reich.

According to the alleged Führer File, a few parts of which Dr Lewis believes may have survived, Hitler embarked on an active, if unconventional, sex life in Munich as far back as 1919, when he met an eighteen-year-old Jewish girl by the name of Rosa Edelstein, with whom he remained on intimate terms until the summer of 1920. The following year Hitler began an affair with

nineteen-year-old Jenny Haug, who was the sister of his driver
and bodyguard, Ernst Haug, and who worked in a toy shop in a
Munich market. According to a document from the Führer File,
Hitler's love-making, which took place in his dreary little room
in a lodging house in Munich's Thierschstrasse, was not entirely
conventional. If he attempted normal sex he would frequently
suffer from erection problems or premature ejaculation, and on
the occasions when he did not his love-making could be quick
and rough. In due course he moved on to a different form of
sexual intimacy which was both alarming in its technique but
more or less satisfactory in its outcome.

Hitler's method was to persuade the naked and somewhat
nervous Jenny to lie face down on the bed while he lashed her
bare body (not very fiercely) with his ever to-hand dog-whip.
This made him sweat and tremble somewhat, but it also
succeeded in achieving an erection. All too often, however, this
erection proved too brief to be of use, and Hitler would then
move on to the second phase of love-making. He would lie
naked on the bed in place of Jenny and ask her to whip harder
and harder until he fell off the bed on to the floor and, seizing
her ankles, sobbed that he was not worthy of her, he was a louse
and a worm – at which point, at his request, she would kick him
and spit on him until, mirabile dictu, he had achieved a
satisfactory erection and they could make love in the normal
way.

The following year, 1922, according to the same File, Hitler
formed a similar relationship with a 25-year-old nun called
Sister Pia (Eleonora Bauer), a well-built woman and early Nazi
supporter, who thrashed him much more satisfactorily than
Jenny ever did and was especially exciting if she was wearing her
nun's habit at the time.

Such was Adolf Hitler's romantic reputation by this time that a local Munich newspaper dubbed him 'King of Munich – a lady-killer at whose feet the wealthiest and most beautiful women were said to prostrate themselves.' Six months later the 'King' – now the leader of a rapidly expanding new political party, the Nazi Party – found himself dethroned, languishing (up to a point) in a cell in the fortress-prison at Landsberg after receiving a two-year sentence following his ill-judged armed putsch or National Revolution of 8 November 1923. Sentenced to five years for attempting a coup d'etat against the Reich, he served only nine months before he was allowed to leave the prison on parole on 20 December 1924.

He was a public name now and imprisonment had reaffirmed his sense of his own inexorable destiny. But so long as he was on parole his movements were restricted and he was banned from public speaking. His reaction was to leave the constricting city for the freedom of the mountains, basing himself first in a sleepy little town in the Bavarian Alps called Berchtesgaden, and later in a mountain house called Haus Wachenfeld on the Obersalzberg not far away.

In a way that was utterly unforseeable, this move was to have a major impact on Hitler's love life, for it was here in the high hills, far from the hurly-burly of post-war German politics, that Adolf, by now in his late thirties, embarked upon his first serious love relationship, followed not that long after by his second. Not surprisingly, the first of these affairs was not with a Hitlerian version of Madame de Pompadour or Napoleon's Josephine, but with a pretty young girl of sixteen called Mimi who worked in her parents' shop in Berchtesgaden. And the second was with his ill-fated niece, Geli, who was not much older.

Mimi

Sixteen-year-old Maria Reiter (or Mimi, as she was affectionately known to her family), a local lass and convent educated, first set eyes on Hitler – not yet a household name in Germany, but on his way – in September 1926, just a fortnight after her mother had died. She was working as an assistant in her late mother's clothes shop on the ground floor of the Deutsches Haus Hotel in Berchtesgaden (which is where Hitler resided whenever he was in the town at that period) when her brother, who was with her, saw a familiar figure walking past. 'That is Hitler,' he told his sister, 'the politician who has been in prison.'

Maria went to the door of the shop and watched Hitler as he walked down the street. 'He was wearing light brown breeches,' she was to recall, 'a grey wind-jacket, brown high-boots, a light grey velour hat, and he carried a brown riding crop. Beside him trotted his Alsatian dog, Prinz.'

Two days later they met. Maria was taking her lunch break with her sister and their sheepdog Marko in the town park opposite the hotel when Hitler spotted them, crossed the road, bowed slightly and doffed his hat. They sat down on a bench, Hitler chatting away at the two of them, but all the time staring and smiling at Maria (who was unaware at that time that Hitler had been studying her through his bedroom window during her lunch breaks on the two previous days). At length he said to Anni, 'Tell me, who is this blonde bundle of happiness? Will you introduce me?' And so Maria was introduced to Hitler, who was then thirty-seven, and before long she received a personal invitation from him to attend a small political meeting (a Party reunion) at the Deutches Haus Hotel, where he would be giving a speech.

'He went on to the platform,' Maria remembered. 'I can see him now. I can see his lock of hair as it fell over his brow. His fist hammering on the desk. But all the time Hitler looked at me. I cannot tell you how uncomfortable I felt.'

After the speeches, Maria found herself alone with Hitler. Once again no one else seemed to exist for him. He moved his chair towards her and leaned forward. 'My mother had the same eyes as you,' he told her. 'She died when I was young – like you.' At this moment their hands brushed. 'I shall never forget it,' Maria recalled, 'though it was only a touch.' Then Hitler clasped her hands in his. For half an hour they talked alone together, till the landlord's daughter, seeing them together, interrupted. 'Herr Hitler,' she asked, point-blank. 'Why don't you marry?' Hitler looked up at her, then turned again towards Maria.

'Marry?' he said. 'I cannot marry. All I can do is to be with a woman I love. A woman I love with all my heart.'

'And as he spoke,' Maria recalled, 'his knee pressed against my thigh, and his right foot pressed on mine.'

Three days after their first meeting, Maria and Hitler met again for an evening stroll in silent Berchtesgaden. Thirty years later, in the different world of a post-war Germany, Maria was to recall the burgeoning of her affair with the future Führer of the Third Reich with all the mindset and language of a teenage country girl brought up on sentimental novels and the early Hollywood romances of all those years ago. When they returned to her sister Anni's flat, she remembered, Hitler asked her if she could play something on the piano. Maria began playing, and as she did so, Hitler gently put his hands on her shoulders and whispered in her ear.

'Will you let me kiss you?' he asked.

'No, Herr Hitler,' Maria replied as she continued to play. 'I cannot.'

Anni came into the room then, bringing a plate of sandwiches, and Maria went out to the kitchen to bring the coffee. Hitler followed her. He put his hands round her waist and pulled her to him.

'Why won't you let me kiss you?' he asked her. 'Don't I mean anything to you? Don't you want to do the same as I want to do?'

For Maria all this was far beyond anything she had experienced in her life. She had never been out with a man before, let alone been kissed by one.

'No, Herr Hitler,' she told him. 'I can't. Please!'

Hitler's face darkened. His voice was stern and fierce.

'Then we shall never see each other again!' he barked. '*Never!*'

And he stormed out of the room. As it happened, this was the second time that evening that Mimi had seen a different side to Hitler. Earlier, when they were strolling in the streets of the town with the dogs, Hitler's Alsatian dog, Prinz, had attacked her own Alsatian dog, Marko, and in a rage he had lashed them both with his riding crop. She remembered:

> His face was twisted with fury, as again and again he lashed out at them until Prinz reeled away from the blows. But in a frenzy Hitler still lashed at his dazed, bleeding dog. It was senseless but he couldn't seem to stop. I was horrified. I grabbed his arm and shouted: 'Stop it! Stop! You'll kill him!' And to my amazement he *did* stop – as soon as I touched his arm. He turned to me and whispered: 'I couldn't help it. I'm sorry.'

Next day Hitler was back, as tender and seemingly as gentle as ever, and that evening accompanied Maria on a walk to her mother's grave. Hitler spoke to her of his own mother and his love for her, of the poverty of his childhood, the uncomprehending brutality of his father, and of his plans to bring new glory to Germany.

'Fate has brought us together,' he told her. 'Will you please promise always to be by my side? My task is to rebuild Germany. Together we will see our Fatherland grow in greatness.'

What an odd man he is, she thought. But as he walked her home she was happy to let him put his arm round her waist. 'I was growing to like this strange man,' she recalled, 'beginning to feel a little sorry for him.' And when he asked her if she would like a ride in his big black Mercedes next day, she said yes.

There were four in the car for the outing – Hitler and his chauffeur Emil Maurice in the front, Maria and her sister Anni in the back. But up in the mountains three miles out of town they changed places and Hitler sat in the back with Maria. 'Then Hitler took my hands,' she was to remember. 'He smiled and said: "I shall hold your hands like this for ever." I let my eyes close. I felt his face against mine. I felt the warmth of his body against mine.'

After a few more miles Hitler stopped the car and went off for a stroll among the trees with his sixteen-year-old inamorata. Maria recalled: 'He stopped and held me against a tree, his hands upon my arms. "Just stay as you are," he said softly.'

Then he stepped back several paces and looked at her as the shafts of autumnal sunlight filtered through the branches.

'If only you could stay for the rest of your life as you are now,' he told her.

Then he walked quickly towards her and kissed her as she stood there against the tree. 'His lips pressed against mine,' Marie was to remember, 'as he kissed me passionately, his arms crushing me against his body. It was my first kiss.'

'My darling,' Hitler whispered to her. 'I am desperately in love with you. You are everything to me.'

He kissed her on the mouth again and again 'for a very long time'. He kissed her on her forehead and neck. 'He said he wanted to squeeze me until it hurt,' Maria was to recall. Then he began to talk about himself again, how his life was always in danger, how he always had to carry a gun with him because he had so many enemies.

When she had first met him she thought he was a rather strange, faintly elderly looking gentleman, and she did not like the look of him. 'I must say that this man with his tiny moustache was of no interest to me at all,' she was to recall of that first encounter. 'How awful that moustache is,' she told herself. 'If he kissed a woman it would tickle.' And his piercing eyes had made her ill at ease. Now all that had changed. 'I clasped his hands,' Mimi recalled, 'and thought I was beginning to understand this incredible man. I, too, was falling in love.'

Next day Hitler began a political tour of Germany and was away for several weeks. He asked Maria to write to him. She wrote two letters - 'I knew I was in love,' she commented – and received one in return, which arrived on 23 December 1926, her seventeenth birthday. She kept this letter for ever after. It read:

My dear child, You don't know what you have come to mean to me. I would so much love to have your sweet face in front of me so that I could tell you personally what your dear friend can only write.

December 23 is your birthday. Now I beg of you take my greeting which comes from the depth of my heart. From my present [two copies of his political biography, *Mein Kampf*] you should have seen how pleased I was that my sweet love is writing to me. You have no idea how happy a sweet little letter from you can make me. Out of it your lovely voice speaks to me. And then I am always taken by the desire for you as if it was for the first time. Are you also sometimes thinking of me?

You know, if I sometimes have troubles and sorrows, then I would like so much to be with you and to be able to look into your eyes in order to forget these things. Yes, child, you recall, don't you, what you mean to me and how much I love you. But read the books! Then you will be able to understand me.

Now again, my sincerest best wishes for your birthday and also for Christmas.

From your

Wolf

Wolf was Hitler's nom-de-plume. Aware that public knowledge of his relationship with a teenage girlfriend could dent his political reputation, he had agreed on this code name in his communications with her. But a few hours later the doorbell rang, and there, standing on the step, was the real Herr Hitler. 'Despite the deep snow he had come for a Christmas visit,' Maria was to recall. 'We held each other in our arms.'

It was there perhaps that the burgeoning affair might have ended. In the following year Hitler was increasingly preoccupied with politics and encounters with his beloved Mimi became correspondingly rare. Then in March 1927 Maria went off to Munich to take part in an ice-skating competition – and to her surprise and delight Hitler was there to watch her. Years later, after the war, in an interview with *Stern* magazine, she was to describe that evening:

Hitler shook my hand as enthusiastically as a little boy when a loudspeaker announcement was made that I had won through to the final, to be held at a later date.

'My dear,' he said, 'we must celebrate. Don't bother to change, pack your outdoor things in a suitcase and come and have a meal.'

Hitler, his driver, Emil Maurice, and I went to a nearby restaurant. Later, Hitler invited me to see where he lived in Munich's Thierschstrasse. The driver was dismissed at the door of the house – No. 41 – and Hitler took my hand as we walked up the stairs. He unlocked the door to his apartment and I followed him in.

'I expect you would like to change,' said Hitler, for I was still in my skating clothes. 'You may change here if you wish. I promise you I won't look.'

I hesitated. After all, I had never been alone with a man in his apartment before.

Then I said: 'Well, I will if you promise to turn round and not look until I tell you.'

Hitler pulled round a chair and sat facing the wall. Then, as he began to look at some papers, I started to undress.

Suddenly he said: 'May I look now?'

I answered quickly: 'No, I'm not ready!'

41

I pulled off my skating clothes and struggled into a blue evening dress. But I could not reach one button at the back and I had to ask Hitler for help.

He got up quickly from the chair and hurried across the room.

'Which button?' he asked.

'That one,' I said. 'The last one.'

Hitler fastened the button, standing behind me. Then he put his arms round me and pulled me back on my heels towards him.

'You are the most wonderful girl I have ever met,' he whispered, his breath warm on my neck. Then he swung me round and we were in each other's arms, kissing passionately. Hitler whispered: 'My beautiful Mimi, I love you so much.'

Hitler only had a cheap old narrow iron bed in his cramped little room but it was sufficient and they laid down and made love on that.

Many years later Maria was to remember that fateful night with affection, even nostalgia: 'We became true lovers – in every sense of the word.'

In April they met up again in Berchtesgaden and together roamed the mountains and made love in the hidden parts of the woods. It seemed Hitler had found a mate at last – hierarchically inappropriate, perhaps, but romantically true. But not long afterwards an anonymous whistleblower in Munich (in fact a female acquaintance of Hitler's who had met Maria) wrote a letter to Party Headquarters revealing the Leader's relationship with a teenage girl. Reacting with alarm, the Party chiefs insisted the relationship should be ended for the sake of the

Party. Hitler wrote to Maria to say he would be coming to Berchtesgaden to see her around two o'clock the next day. In fact, he went to see her sister's husband in his office in the town. He was going to have to part from Mimi, Hitler told him.

'Someone has done this to me and to the only girl I have ever loved,' Hitler explained. 'But I must put the Fatherland first. I do not want Mimi involved in the dirty business of politics. Will you please explain to her? It is more than I can bear to see her again, knowing that I must say goodbye.'

The message was passed on to Anni and she came to explain it all to Maria. 'Everyone has their first love,' she told Maria. 'Now we must forget it all.'

Many years later, Hitler's half-sister, Paula Wolf, who also survived the war, was to express her belief that in not marrying young Maria Reiter, the first woman he had ever truly loved, her brother made the biggest mistake in his life – a mistake for which the peoples of Europe, the Germans themselves included, were to pay a terrible price. 'I believe if he had married you,' Paula was to tell Maria years later, 'history might have been different.'

For Maria it was more than she could bear. She was to recall later:

> I resolved to end my life. I knotted a length of window
> cord round my neck, tied the other end to a door knob,
> and threw myself on the floor. I do not know how long
> I lay there, half strangled, but I was told later that I
> was found by my sister Anni. A doctor was called and
> later that night I regained consciousness.

Strangely, a surprisingly large proportion of Hitler's lady friends were to try and kill themselves – more than half a dozen in all. Some of them were successful, though it sometimes took up to two or three attempts before they finally achieved their goal. Maria Reiter was one of the lucky ones. But her failed suicide did not mean the end of the affair, nor did her marriage to an agreeable young Austrian of twenty-four by the name of Kurt Woldrich in Innsbruck three years later. For one thing, the marriage proved to be an unhappy one. For another, Hitler would not altogether forget her.

Geli and Uncle Alf

Hitler had first got to know the young Angela Raubal (known in the family as Geli for short) when she had accompanied her mother, who was Hitler's half-sister and also called Angela Raubal, to the country house Hitler had rented on the Obersalzberg, above Berchtesgaden, in 1927. Though this mountain house, Haus Wachenfeld, was a relatively simple place in those days – big living room downstairs, three bedrooms in the attic – it enjoyed a fabulous location and ample peace and quiet in which its new part-time occupant could complete the second part of his political biography, *Mein Kampf*. The idea was for his half-sister to look after the place as live-in housekeeper-cum-cook, but from the outset Hitler was smitten with his niece Geli, then only eighteen years of age, and pretty, straightforward and fun, and in due course his interest in the girl was to develop into a full-blown relationship – of a kind peculiar to him and him alone.

Later, in September 1929 – some two and a half years after Maria Reiter's failed suicide – Geli moved into Hitler's new nine-roomed luxury apartment (recently acquired and paid for out of Nazi funds) at 16 Prinzregentenplatz, in one of Munich's most fashionable squares, where a young married couple by the name of George and Anni Winter looked after the housekeeping for him. The move had been Hitler's idea. The mother (who was still running the Obersalzberg house) was looking for somewhere where her daughter could stay while she studied singing and acting in Munich. For Hitler's part he could do with some company in his new home, the most spacious abode he had ever had in his life, and he agreed to act as his niece's guardian. It was an arrangement of mutual convenience. And besides, Geli was now there at Hitler's side – indeed, in the bedroom next to his own.

Geli was now twenty-one, and a wholesome, buxom, exuberant, mischievous, flirtatious, uninhibited country girl of great natural charm. To many who met her she was beautiful and desirable, with brown hair, wonderful big blue eyes, and an engaging Viennese accent. She was not an entirely serious person and liked to have fun of any kind, but she was also religious and went to Mass every week. Before long Hitler – or 'Uncle Alf' as she called him – was taking her out, proudly displaying her to the Party faithful and his adoring admirers at his favourite Munich haunt, the Cafe Heck. He sometimes found himself in situations which for him would have previously been unimaginable, like accompanying her on shopping expeditions in department stores, or escorting her on swimming expeditions to a nearby lake, the Koenigsee – though Hitler hated the water and never swam himself (perhaps, it was whispered – by his old army comrades above all – because to be seen in a bathing costume might reveal the undeveloped nature of his private parts). There was gossip, naturally, but Hitler was not yet averse to cutting a dash and presenting a bohemian front. It seems that the uncle and his niece were hugely drawn to each other. 'He loved her,' Emil Maurice, Hitler's chauffeur (and friend) of that time, was to recall, 'but it was a strange affection that did not dare to show itself, for he was too proud to admit to the weakness of an infatuation.'

It seems that it was an even stranger affection than even Maurice thought. Ernst ('Putzi') Hanfstaengl – a well-to-do Munich-born Harvard graduate in his early forties with a German father and an American mother – was a good friend of Hitler in these early years and was later to become the Nazis' foreign press chief before breaking with Hitler and fleeing for his life, first to England and later to the USA. Hanfstaengl speculated at length about the probable nature of Hitler's physical relationship with Geli. He was to write:

> What particular combination of arguments her uncle used to bend her will, we shall never know. Whether he assumed that a young woman who was already no saint might be brought fairly easily to submit to his peculiar taste, or whether in fact she was the one woman in his life who went some way towards curing his impotence and half making a man out of him, again we shall never know with certainty. What is certain is that the services she was prepared to render had the effect of making him behave like a man in love. She went round very well dressed at his expense – or more probably, at the party's – and he hovered at her elbow with a moon-like calf look in his eyes in a very plausible imitation of adolescent infatuation.

Otto Strasser, Hitler's one-time Press Chief for the whole of Germany (and the brother of Gregor Strasser, the leader of the radical Left wing of the Nazi Party, who was liquidated in the Röhm Putsch of 1934), got rather nearer the truth when, very much against an enraged Adolf's orders, he took Geli out for what he called 'a very pleasant, high-spirited evening' in Munich in carnival time. On their way back to the apartment in Prinzregentenplatz, they went for a walk in the English Garden. Otto Strasser recalled:

> At the top of the Chinese Tower, Geli sat down on a bench and started weeping bitterly. In the end she told me that she really loved Hitler, but she couldn't bear it any longer. His jealousy wasn't the worst thing. He demanded things from her that were simply disgusting. She had never dreamed that such things could happen. When I asked her to tell me, she described things I had previously encountered in my reading of Krafft-Ebbing's *Psychopathia Sexualis* when I was a student.

In May 1943, Otto Strasser (who had fled abroad when he crossed swords with Hitler) was interviewed by intelligence officers from the OSS, the US Office of Strategic Studies, the forerunner of the CIA. In the secrecy of a hush-hush organization on the other side of the Atlantic, and far from the vengeance of the Führer, Strasser felt more free to enlarge on what Geli had told him that spring night more than ten years previously. He told the Americans:

> Hitler made her undress. He would lie down on the floor. Then she would have to squat over his face, where he could examine her at close range, and this made him

47

very excited. When the excitement reached its peak, he demanded that she urinate on him, and this gave him sexual pleasure. Geli said the whole performance was extremely disgusting to her and it gave her no gratification.'

This was proof, American OSS psychologists concluded in their 1943 Report, that Hitler was subject to an extreme form of sexual masochism.

Not everyone, it has to be said, accepts that Otto Strasser's testimony is necessarily true (or at any rate complete) or the OSS's conclusions necessarily right. Dr Fritz Redlich, Emeritus Professor of Psychiatry at the University of California, for example, considered 'the inconsistent statements of Otto Strasser to be political denunciation by a bitter enemy'. Strasser, it seems, had claimed that Heinrich Hoffmann's daughter had provided a similar service (known in the business as undinism) for Hitler. But the truth was, Geli Raubal was not the only young woman from whom Hitler had sought deviant sex. For any beauty, it seems, he could on occasion be the beast, and at times in his personal life as in his public life he could prove mad, bad and dangerous to know.

It is to revelatory insider material of this sort that Konrad Heiden, a respected Munich correspondent of the *Frankfurter Zeitung* and a future refugee from Nazi persecution, undoubtedly refers in his pre-war report on Hitler's intimate psychological processes – a report which best explains the kind of sexual behaviour to which Geli and others were subjected. There was documentary evidence, Heiden stated, currently in the hands of the Reich Treasurer of the Nazi Party, that threw a surprising light on Adolf Hitler's relations to women. Basically, this evidence placed it beyond doubt that Adolf was enslaved to the women he loved. Heiden wrote:

> The fact of Hitler's enslavement to women supplies the missing component which fits correctly into the total picture of Adolf Hitler's character. It is the secret contrast to his exaggerated, affected brutality in politics and business and towards friends and fellow workers – a contrast which is well known to authorities on sexual science.
>
> And now the peculiar nature of Hitler's relations with women becomes apparent. They are all obscure and mysterious; he gives himself, contrary to the reality, the air of a man without a private life. These relations, almost without exception, snap off suddenly at some place or other, and in many cases it is obvious that Hitler is not the forsaker but the forsaken. One of the women mentioned here, when questioned regarding her relations with Hitler, gave it to be understood that she had experienced a disappointment, which made her regard him as not altogether respectable.
>
> So the often expressed conjecture that Hitler's emotional life is not normal are correct. Only the conjecture has generally taken the wrong direction: Hitler is not homosexual or bi-sexual, he is merely subject to sexual enslavement.

'You'll never believe the things he makes me do'

For all that, Hitler was probably closer to Geli in an ordinary, casual, day-to-day way than anyone else he had ever met, laughing with her, cuddling with her, going out for drives with her, going to the opera with her, eating in restaurants with her, even listening to her, something he was never very good at with other human beings. 'I love her,' Hoffmann recalled Hitler telling him, 'but I don't believe in marriage. I make it my business to watch over her until such time as she finds a husband to her taste.'

And watch over her he did. Part uncle, part lover, part jealous, intolerant power freak, he would not let her go out by herself, or accept invitations to parties or dances. When Otto Strasser invited her to one of the famous Munich masked balls (the night he had the conversation with her in the English Garden), Hitler rang him in a rage and screamed, 'I learned you are going out with the young Geli this evening. I won't allow her to go out with a married man. I'm not going to have any of your filthy Berlin tricks in Munich!' When she went to her singing lessons – she had neither the talent nor the ambition but Hitler insisted she train to be a Wagnerian operatic heroine – she had to be accompanied by her mother or a Party henchman. Her mail was checked by Hitler's housekeeper, Frau Winter, and her movements were observed by the Party police. In short she could lead no life of her own – except, perhaps, by deception. When Hitler's chauffeur Emil Maurice caught Hitler in Geli's room (and what, one asks, was Maurice himself doing in Geli's room?) the enraged Hitler fell upon him with his riding whip and Maurice only escaped by jumping out of the window. As for Geli, she seems to have formed an irresistible fascination for her uncle and fallen into his magnetic thrall. 'Geli loved Hitler,' Frau Winter claimed later. 'She was always running after him. Naturally she wanted to become *"Gnädige Frau Hitler"*. He was highly eligible. But she flirted with everybody. She was not a serious girl.'

But she was serious enough to eventually become profoundly depressed by her state of near house arrest and her uncle's relent-lessly oppressive jealousy and sexually deviant regime. 'You'll never believe the things he makes me do,' she confided to a girlfriend. Hanfstaengl's first indication that there was some-thing wrong with the relationship came early in 1930 when he happened to meet the Party treasurer, Franz Xaver Schwarz, in the street. Schwarz was looking very down-in-the-mouth and invited Hanfstaengl to have a little talk over coffee in his flat in the shabbier part of Schwabing. Hanfstaengl was to relate later:

> His wife greeted me, gave us our coffee, retired to the kitchen again, and Schwarz poured out what was on his mind. He had just had to buy off somebody who had been trying to blackmail Hitler, but the worst part of the story was the reason for it. This man had somehow come into the possession of a folio of pornographic drawings Hitler had made. How he came by them I never heard. Perhaps he stole them from Hitler's car. They were depraved, intimate sketches of Geli Raubal, with every anatomical detail, the sort of thing only a perverted voyeur would commit to paper, much less oblige a woman to model for. Schwarz had bought them back. 'Heaven help us, man,' I said, 'why don't you tear the filth up?' 'No,' said Schwarz, 'Hitler wants them back. He wants me to keep them in the Braun Haus [Party Headquarters] safe.' So this is the man, I thought, who prates about cleaning up Germany, the dignity of conjugal life, *die deutsche Frau* and all that.

51

Then, on 18 September 1931, it all went wrong. The exact cause of what happened will never be known for sure and the reports of witnesses or would-be witnesses are confusing and contradictory. Hitler had set off that day on a trip to Nuremberg and Hamburg on Party business. According to a report in the socialist newspaper *Münchener Post* there had been recurrent disagreements recently between the uncle and his niece. 'The vivacious 22-year-old music student, Geli, wanted to go to Vienna, she wanted to become engaged. Hitler was strongly opposed to this. After a violent scene, Hitler left.'

Certainly it seems that prior to Hitler's departure on the afternoon of 18 September there had been a shouting match of unusual violence and duration, though what exactly it was about was not clear – it could have been Geli demanding more freedom, or permission to see someone, or go off to Vienna. Hitler's car was waiting and he eventually ran out of both time and patience. He ran down the stairs yelling at her in a fury, and when she went out on to the balcony overlooking the street, Hitler screamed up at her: 'For the last time, *no!*' Then the car drove off.

As they were driving out of Munich, Hitler turned to Hoffmann and said, 'I don't know why but I have a most uneasy feeling.' He hardly spoke at all throughout the rest of the drive to Nuremberg.

After he had gone, Geli helped Frau Winter tidy up his room. According to Frau Winter, it was then that Geli found a letter in the pocket of one of Hitler's jackets. It is very likely she already knew of its existence, for Frau Winter recalled another furious row between Geli and Hitler over a letter the previous month. After she had read the letter, Geli tore it into four pieces, then left the room – 'very flustered' – and went first into Hitler's room and then into her own room, locking the door behind her. Frau Winter saw nothing odd about this. Geli's was a beautiful room and she often spent a lot of time in it. Afterwards Frau Winter read the letter. As she recalled, the letter went like this:

Dear Herr Hitler

Thank you for the wonderful invitation to the theatre. It was a memorable evening. I am most grateful to you for your kindness. I am counting the hours until I may have the joy of another meeting.

Eva.

For some while Geli had suspected there was another woman in her lover's life, for though Hitler dedicated most evenings and nights to herself, she sensed there was a romantic flirtation going on elsewhere by day, at times. And indeed, up to a point, there was.

The Eva who had signed the letter was Eva Braun, whom Hitler had first met nearly two years previously, in October 1929, barely a month after Geli had moved into his Munich apartment. Eva was only seventeen years of age at the time and working as an assistant at the Munich shop and studio of Hitler's official photographer, Heinrich Hoffmann. Hitler – forty years of age and as yet only one of Germany's up-and-coming politicians – was attracted to the girl at once. And though Hitler's name rang no bells for Eva then, she was aware that she was in the company of a magnetic presence, an extraordinary charisma.

A good few months were to pass before Eva set eyes on Hitler again. His visits to Hoffmann's studio were few and far between. The fortunes of the Nazi Party were rising fast and Hitler was busy elsewhere. On the occasions he did visit Hoffmann's, however, he always asked for 'Fräulein Eva Braun'. As he explained to Hoffmann himself, 'She amuses me.' Whenever he did meet the young shopgirl he would treat her like a princess, bowing and kissing her hand and calling her 'my lovely siren from Hoffmann's'. One day he brought her her first flower, a yellow orchid, which she carefully preserved in her photo album. Another time he gave her a signed photo of himself in uniform. But that was all. To Hitler, Eva Braun was simply a pretty girl he doffed his cap to, one among many. To Eva Braun, Hitler was just an older man and a growing celebrity who from time to time paid her court and then went away – at least at first. But later Hoffmann's daughter, who was a friend of Eva, noticed a growing desire to please on Eva's part. 'When she was expecting a visit from Hitler,' she recalled, 'Eva would stuff her brassiere with handkerchiefs in order to give her breasts the fullness they lacked – this seemed to appeal to Hitler.'

It was not until the end of 1930 – more than a year after their first encounter in Hoffmann's photo studio – that Hitler began to take a more serious interest in Eva Braun. He would take her out to the opera or to dinner at his favourite Munich restaurant, the Osteria Bavaria. It was all very proper. Hitler's aide or a bodyguard or two were always present on these infrequent occasions, and the most Hitler would do was hold her hand or perhaps stroke it. They looked like father and daughter, and Eva was always brought home before midnight. These meetings were very sporadic, however, and relatively inconsequential. As Hitler was to warn the girl later, 'My bride is Germany.' His commitment, in other words, was the grand design, the pursuit of power, the transformation of the Fatherland. And in any case, he still had a live-in girlfriend in the form of his 22-year-old niece, Geli Raubal.

Though Geli Raubal and Eva Braun never set eyes on each other, the possibility that there was someone else in the offing made both of them anxious and insecure. And in Geli's case it may have led to her death.

It was not until the morning of 19 September 1931, following Geli's quarrel with Hitler the previous afternoon, that Frau Winter began to worry. First, Geli's door was still locked, and second, the pistol which Hitler kept on a shelf in his room was missing. When Frau Winter and her husband finally forced Geli's door open they were confronted with a tragical scene. Geli was lying face downwards on the floor in her blue nightdress, her nose against the floor, one arm stretched out towards the divan. Her nightdress was soaked in blood and a 6.35mm pistol lay on the divan. Geli Raubal had shot herself in the region of the heart, but very inaccurately, it turned out, so that the bullet missed the heart, pierced a lung, and ended up in the left side of her back just above the hip, so that the girl would in fact have died from slow suffocation over a period of hours. When she was finally found, she had been dead long enough for rigor mortis to have set in and her face was already dark blue. On the table was an unfinished letter, perfectly cheerful in tone which ended in mid flow: 'When I come to Vienna – I hope very soon – we'll drive together to Semmering.' But rather surprisingly there was no suicide note.

Frau Winter was careful to first phone Hitler's close Nazi deputy Rudolf Hess, and after that a doctor, and only finally the police. From Munich, Hess rang Hitler in Nuremberg. But Hitler had just left and a messenger boy was despatched in a taxi to give chase. Hess's message read: 'Your niece has just been found in her room, a pistol, yours, in her hand. Her condition is very critical . . . The police are here, in the foyer.'

By the time Hitler returned to Munich, in a state of near collapse, Geli's body was already lying in the mortuary chapel. There were many rumours, mostly to the effect that Geli had been murdered – by a jealous rival, by the SS, above all by Hitler himself, either because she was allegedly pregnant by him, or out of jealousy at her supposed affection for her Jewish singing teacher in Linz, by whom she was also allegedly pregnant. It was possible Hitler had earlier found her in the arms of his chauffeur, Emil Maurice, much to his towering wrath, and it was rumoured she had bestowed sexual favours on other members of his staff.

A public scandal involving the Nazi leader had to be hushed up at all costs. At any rate, the police, very possibly under pressure from the Nazis, chose not to pursue the matter, there was no inquest and only a perfunctory medical examination. The coroner's verdict, for what it was worth, was suicide.

Hitler was plunged in grief and mourning. Finding it intolerable to remain in the apartment where his beloved Geli had died, and unable to bear the prospect of the funeral, he holed up for a few days with Heinrich Hoffmann for company in the idyllic little house of an absentee associate by Lake Tegernsee. Hitler, recalled Hoffmann, was entirely inconsolable. He ate nothing, spoke seldom, hardly slept. All night long Hoffmann could hear him pacing up and down in his room upstairs, hour after hour throughout the long night. 'Geli's death had shaken my friend to the depths of his soul,' Hoffmann was to record. 'Had he a feeling of guilt? Was he torturing himself with remorseful self-reproach?' Next morning Hoffmann went up to the room but Hitler was virtually oblivious of his presence and took no notice of him. Hoffman noted:

With hands clasped behind his back, his eyes gazing

unseeing into the distance, he continued his eternal pacing. His face was grey with anguish and drawn with fatigue; a hairy stubble disfigured his face, dark shadows were blackly smeared beneath his sunken eyes, and his mouth was set in a bitter yet desolate line.

All through that second day, and through the night that followed and the day that followed that, Hitler paced up and down, up and down, the footsteps drumming and boring through Hoffmann's skull.

Meanwhile Geli's body had been shipped back post-haste to Vienna, and at her funeral Heinrich Himmler, head of the SS, stood in for Hitler, who was not well enough physically or mentally to attend, and was in any case banned from entering the country by the Austrian Government. Shortly afterwards, however, he was allowed into the country for twenty-four hours in order to visit the grave, and that very night set off, with Hoffmann for company, on a pilgrimage to the loved one's final resting place. They arrived in the early hours. All through the drive Hitler had not uttered a word. He did not utter a word when he set off on foot and alone to Geli's grave in the city's central cemetery. 'Here lies our beloved child Geli,' read the inscription on the tombstone. 'She was our ray of sunshine. Born 4 June 1908 – died 18 September 1931. The Raubal Family.'

Half an hour later Hitler came back to the car and gave orders to the chauffeur to drive to Obersalzberg. And then, for virtually the first time since the news of Geli's death, he began to talk. 'So,' he said. 'Now let the struggle begin – the struggle that will and must be crowned with success.'

Nearly a quarter of a century later, with Hitler ten years dead and a new Germany all around him, Hoffmann was to reflect on the epochal significance of those few days he had spent in Hitler's company. The death of Geli, he believed, was not simply a personal loss but a trigger for an historic catastrophe. Hitler was now seeking in the turmoil of his political advance 'an anodyne for the frightful pain in his heart'. Hoffmann wrote:

> If there were anyone he ardently desired to marry, it was his niece, Geli. His love for this beautiful and intelligent girl was as great as was the political urge that possessed him; and while she would not have hindered the vast work of internal regeneration which he most certainly accomplished, it is quite possible that in the ties of home and family, coupled with Geli's restraining influence, he would have lost the zest for those international adventures which brought him to his ruin.

Ernst Hanfstaengl went further years later:

> I am sure that the death of Geli Raubal marked a turning point in the development of Hitler's character. The relationship, whatever form it took in their intimacy, had provided him for the first and only time in his life with a release for his nervous energy which only too soon was to find its final expression in ruthlessness and savagery. With her death the way was clear for his final development into a demon ... His over-compensation for the inferiority of an impotent masturbator was the driving force for his lust for power.

And perhaps millions of other lives would have been spared, as well as hers. Perhaps. Meanwhile, the fiercely dissenting voices regarding Geli's death continued – though they, too, had a political axe to grind, and presented evidence that at best was unproven. According to Otto Strasser, his brother Gregor had revealed later that Hitler had shot Geli during a quarrel. Probably he had been in such a demented state, Gregor said, that he did not know what he was doing. As soon as he had killed the girl, he wanted to commit suicide, but Gregor restrained him and spent three days and nights with the man, who was acting like a lunatic. Rudolf Hess, too, lent a hand, at one point physically wrestling Hitler's gun from his hand when he tried to shoot himself.

'An inquest was opened in Munich,' Otto Strasser was to recall. 'The public prosecutor wished to charge Hitler with murder. But the Bavarian Minister of Justice, who was a Nazi and later became the Reich Justice Minister, stopped the case. It was announced that Geli had committed suicide.' Later a newsletter editor who had collected overwhelming evidence against Hitler was murdered, as was Gregor Strasser's lawyer, who also knew about the case, and eventually Gregor himself.

Was Otto Strasser right, was his brother Gregor telling the truth? The Strassers had their own corner to fight. They had given Hitler crucial help in the early days of his climb to power, but they had quarrelled with him and as a result been variously murdered or exiled on his orders. Clearly Otto had a grudge to settle and wished to damage Hitler in any way he could. And if it was indeed Hitler who had shot the girl, why had he, as a trained ex-infantry veteran of the First World War, made such a bad job of it?

It could be argued that it was far more likely that the person who fired the pistol was the victim herself, who knew nothing about guns and had never (as far as we know) ever fired a shot in her life. Though the fact that women almost never commit suicide by shooting themselves was put forward as another argument *against* Geli having taken her own life, only a few years later another young woman close to Adolf Hitler attempted to put an end to herself in exactly the same way, ending up, tragically, not as a corpse but a human vegetable.

But some years later, it was said, when Otto was living in exile in Paris shortly after the start of the Second World War, he received a letter from the priest who had conducted Geli's funeral service in Vienna all those years ago. The letter read:

> It was I who buried Geli Raubal. They pretended that she committed suicide; I should never have allowed a suicide to be buried in consecrated ground. From the fact that I gave her a Christian burial you can draw conclusions which I cannot communicate to you.

Who was lying and who was not? Frau Winter, right there in the firing line in Hitler's home, could easily have been coerced. But that did not necessarily mean she *did* lie. In fact, when she did first openly speak about Geli's death, the pressure was off her – the war was over, Hitler was dead, the Nazis were gone, and her interviewer was a genial fact-finding American by the name of Admiral Musmanno, a High Court Judge in uniform. There was no reason to withhold her version of the truth from him. Otto Strasser, betrayed, persecuted and exiled by Hitler (and both his brothers, loyal Nazi supporters in the early days, put to death by Hitler's henchmen) had every reason to lie – or alternatively to tell the truth. Was Hitler sufficiently homicidal a person in his private life to slaughter the love of his life? (Well – perhaps, if he had sufficient justification and rage.) Would the exhumation of Geli's body (now lying in a distant corner of the Catholic Cemetery in Vienna) and a proper autopsy solve this seventy-year-old riddle – or at least indicate whether she had been pregnant or not when she died?

The truth will never be known for sure. Probably suicide was the correct verdict. Geli had plenty of reasons for ending her life. Oppressed by her uncle lover, overwhelmed by his violent rages, under virtual house arrest, denied a life of her own, forced to participate in degrading sexual activities, at the same time aware he was seeing another woman – these were reasons enough for Geli being depressed and desperate enough to take her own life, especially after a bitter quarrel. But it was Hitler himself many years later who, in the most improbable and most apocalyptic circumstances, was to provide the most compelling evidence.

At his noon conference in his Wolf's Lair headquarters bunker in East Prussia on 1 February 1943, only hours after learning that the entire German army at Stalingrad had surrendered to the Russians – a catastrophe that inevitably spelled a total German collapse on the Eastern Front and ultimately final defeat in the war – Hitler railed at the fact that neither the German commander-in-chief nor any of the 180,000 men and twenty-three other generals under his command had chosen suicide rather than surrender and captivity as the hero's way out of this historic disaster. Suicide was brave, noble, honourable, in his view, and there were occasions when anything less was shameful. He recalled one suicide above all others, because he had been the reason for it, and though he never mentioned the name to the assembled generals in the Wolf's Lair, it was Geli he had in mind, as the surviving stenographic report at the time reveals:

> When you consider that a woman who has her pride go out of her, shuts herself in a room, and immediately shoots herself just because someone has made a few insulting remarks, then I can have no respect for a soldier who is too frightened to do the same thing . . . And there's this beautiful woman, a real beauty of the first rank, and she feels insulted by some words, nothing of importance, and she says 'Then I can go, I am not needed', and the man says '*Get out*!' So she goes away, writes a farewell letter, and then shoots herself . . . The heroism of so many tens of thousands of men, officers and generals is cancelled out by a man who has not the character to do in a moment what a weakling of a woman can do.

From this it would seem that Geli did indeed commit suicide, that it was the angry words of Hitler that drove her to do it, almost certainly in the final row at his Munich apartment before he left for Hamburg, and that she wrote a letter of explanation that was found with her body and spirited away before the police or the coroner could read it. It would also seem that in the years that followed, for all his preoccupation with the crushing burden of conquest and holocaust and total war, Hitler never got over the death of Geli, his one true and only beloved, and that in the very moment of his own and his nation's nemesis – the monumental and catastrophic defeat at Stalingrad, the beginning of the end – his mind turned above all to her memory, and his pride in her, and his loss of her, and his guilt at his part in that loss.

Far away on the other side of the world, some two years before the debacle at Stalingrad, the case history said to be written by Hitler's Munich-based consultant psycho-analyst, Dr Kurt Krueger, was published in New York. Krueger claimed he had conducted many confidential sessions with Hitler between 1919 and 1934, and though it seems he had been obliged to leave his notebooks behind when he was forced to flee Germany, he was able to remember most of his clinical consultations with Hitler, the write-ups of which he included in his book.

One of the most intense of these dealt with the death of Geli. This is how Hitler himself spoke of this matter in the privacy of his analyst's consulting room – his first session there for a very long time – shortly after Geli's demise. It begins not long after he had caught Geli in bed with his chauffeur. He had given her the scolding of his life. He actually even *spanked* her. Hitler recalled:

> That started the whole thing. I suddenly found myself swept by an emotional hurricane. Her crying ran through my blood. Her hands pinched my thighs, and her legs appeared to be kicking wildly in a deliberately lewd rhythm. For the first time in my life I was conscious of feeling a violent passion for someone of my own flesh and blood.

Shortly after that he paid his niece a return visit. He was in his nightgown (pyjamas came later, with Eva Braun). Hitler told Dr Krueger:

> I'll tell you. I approached her in the darkness of her room that night like a passionate lover. I clasped her

in my arms and kissed her eagerly on the lips. She reciprocated as if she had been waiting all of her young beautiful life. My bliss mounted to almost unbelievable heights. Then suddenly – when I needed the strength of my lust, mountainous waves of erotic emotion were swept away. Out of some strange fountain came a soft tenderness that cleansed my body of desire. I could only kiss her body tenderly, kiss it like a child, caress its nakedness in a holy act of love. Her flesh became too sacred to be possessed as a man possesses a woman. I felt a terrible profanation . . . I begged her – she refused . . . It was as if she were struggling to remain a harlot, while I wanted to resume the role of an angel . . . I wooed her in desperation that night. When she finally surrendered to my strange mood of love, the only way open to a man like me, it was because she had not the strength to continue the struggle. To her the surrender must have seemed abject, just as dreadful as the other thing would have seemed to me if I had been capable of it. And now I finally understand why she killed herself. She couldn't go on living with the memory of what had happened. Removing herself from life seemed to her the only exit. She felt degraded, because Geli thought I was some sort of god. I was right, wasn't I, Doctor? There was, really, no other way for me to live through that night?

'You were entirely right,' Dr Krueger concurred. 'It was either her life or yours, and the stronger element conquered. *You are not guilty.*'

'I am not guilty,' Hitler echoed. 'God knows I am not responsible.' And he was to tell the doctor, 'That girl was my niece. I loved her – and she loved me.'

So the good doctor recalled.

'Beyond good and evil'

At the time of Geli's suicide, Hitler himself had been shattered, it seems – on the verge of insanity. We have seen how he tried to kill himself and had to be restrained. Thenceforth he turned his back on his apartment and locked himself away elsewhere, refusing to see anyone. He lost all interest in politics and even considered pulling out of it altogether. It seems it was at this point that he finally gave up eating meat or any food cooked in animal fats, which he associated henceforth in his mind with carrion and ordure (though meat provides 20 per cent of the protein fuel for the brain, and his own concocted version of a vegetarian diet proved woefully inadequate).

For some years to come Hitler mourned for his lost darling, and whenever her name was mentioned – and only he was allowed to mention her name – tears would come to his eyes. He ordered Geli's room in his apartment to remain unchanged and for fresh flowers to be placed there every week. Her room in the house on the Obersalzberg remained exactly as it had always been, even when he had the house rebuilt and enlarged as the grand new residence he called the Berghof. Every Christmas Eve and anniversary of her death he went to her room to meditate and keep vigil for hours on end. Her photograph hung in his room in both Munich and Berlin, a bust of her was placed in the New Reich Chancellery in Berlin and a portrait of her was hung in the main drawing room at the Berghof. Until the very end of Hitler's life there were flowers in front of that painting every single day. And he always had a photo of Geli on his person, too, along with one of his mother. When, in 1938, he finally made a will, he bequeathed the contents of Geli's room to her mother.

It has been argued that the fallout from the death of Geli Raubal was infinitely more momentous for Hitler – and for that matter the world – than simply a tragic sense of loss. Since Geli was in effect his flesh and blood, almost a daughter, almost a wife, it could be said that she was closer to him than anyone else on earth. In bringing about her demise, therefore, he was guilty of the ultimate crime. The guilt was ineluctable; nothing could ever wash it away. From now on, therefore, Hitler was no longer bound by the normal obligations of morality. He could be as hard and ruthless and cruel as he chose. Mass murders, tortures, genocides, the ruination of nations, scorched earth – none of this meant anything to him any more. 'He had gone beyond good and evil,' British Intelligence officer Hugh Trevor-Roper declared, 'and entered a strange landscape where nothing was what it seemed and all the ordinary human values were reversed. Like Dostoevsky's Grand Inquisitor, he succumbed to "the dread spirit of death and destruction, and was free to bring about the death and destruction of everyone and everything he encountered".'

When Ernst ('Putzi') Hanfstaengl first met Adolf Hitler in the early Twenties, the future Führer of Nazi Germany was a minor provincial agitator, a frustrated ex-serviceman who 'looked like a suburban hairdresser on his day off or a waiter in a railway-station restaurant'. By 1933, when he was on the verge of seizing power, he had become a murderer, a power-hungry demonic monster – the result of a combination of circumstances, environment, ignorant or downright bad advisers, but above all, 'personal, intimate frustrations of the most abysmal sort'. It took even Hanfstaengl – an educated, balanced, above all perceptive observer of the human condition, a good few years to (as he put it) 'plumb the depths of Hitler's personal problem.' He was to explain, years later:

> The abounding nervous energy which found no normal release sought compensation in the subjection of his entourage, then of his country, then of Europe and would have imposed itself on the world if he had not been stopped. In the sexual no-man's land in which he lived, he only once found the woman who might have brought him relief.

Though the man was an orator of genius and a visionary of sorts, there was one thing missing in his existence – 'he had no normal sex life'. True, he formed some kind of infatuation with Hanfstaengl's wife, bringing her flowers and kissing her hands with adoration in his eyes (for she was probably the first good-looking woman of good family he had ever encountered) but as Hanfstaengl put it – 'somehow one never felt with him that the attraction was physical'. Something was wrong, Hanfstaengl reckoned. 'Here was this man with a volcanic store of energy, with no apparent outlet except his almost medium-like performances on a speaker's platform.'

Ernst Hanfstaengl was a shrewd observer of the eccentric and uniquely possessed man who was to become the Führer of the Third Reich and finally perish amid the ruins of the capital beside his bride of a few hours. But it took him some time to figure the man out. And when he finally did, the sexual profile was shrewd, and very probably true in part, but not necessarily complete. For in a psyche like Hitler's nothing was necessarily constant or permanently in place, and what might be true on one day or even during one decade was not bound to be so for ever. But Hanfstaengl's considered opinion of Adolf Hitler's sexuality, based on a number of years of close observation, was shrewd and at least in part very true. Years after it was all over – the friendship, the feud, his own escape into exile, the war, the defeat and ruination of Germany – Hanfstaengl delivered his final judgement. He declared;

> I felt Hitler was a case of a man who was neither fish, flesh nor fowl . . . Somehow the very rootlessness of his background, his very capacity for balancing out a situation, and his intuitive gift of always remaining above the petty jealousies of his supporters, were all a reflection of his sexual isolation. You could never pin him down, say that he was this thing or that thing, it was all floating, without roots, intangible and mediumistic . . . In the sexual half-light of his life he never found the physical release which similar unfortunates can somehow achieve. In his relations with women Hitler had to dramatise himself in his relations to the world as a whole. The barren hero, I suppose you could call him.

The cross that he had to bear in life was that he was not a normal man. His fundamental shyness when confronted by individuals, particularly women, to whom he knew he had nothing to offer, was compensated by this titanic urge to win the approval of the masses, who were the substitute for the female partner he never found. His reaction to an audience was the counterpart of sexual excitement. He became suffused like a cock's comb or the wattles of a turkey, and it was only in this condition that he became formidable and irresistible.

Elsewhere Hanfstaengl declared: 'If Hitler had succeeded in finding compensation in the humiliation of the few women he was able to consort with, he might never have swum into our ken.' In other words, if he had found a woman, and truly mated with her, all that later came to pass – the mass murders, the extermination camps, a war fought with horrific brutality from the English Channel to the Volga, 40 million dead and a Fatherland in utter ruin – may never have done so. If he had not had a drunken brute for a father, if he had not gone to the (for him) Sodom and Gomorrah of Vienna in his youth, if his adored Geli had stayed alive, if if if . . .

When it was all over, Hitler's alleged medic and psycho-analyst, Dr Kurt Krueger (possibly the nom-de-plume of Ernst Hanfstaengl himself) was to comment in remarkably similar terms:

> Hitler's failure to find a mate is at the core of his failure as a human being, and is the source of his demonic, destructive spirit. Like the primitive savage, he has a horror of looking into a mirror, for fear that his face must reflect his soul and cause his spirit to revolt. At his suggestion I removed a wall-mirror from my office, but he cannot rid himself of the psychological mirror in which his mind crumbles into madness.
>
> The Führer has not yet caught up with his tragic fate, but there are many women who have, and as a

consequence they have found themselves ground beneath the wheels of his evil destiny.

But there was one who outlived them all – and looked back with tenderness on the consummation of her love in her beloved Führer's arms – his Mimi, Maria Reiter.

'I was never as happy as during that night'

It would seem that Adolf Hitler – the imminent scourge and destroyer of Europe and one of the twentieth century's most monstrous demagogues – had been genuinely and inconsolably heartbroken over his beloved Geli's death. To soothe the wound, to fill the aching gap in his life, he looked elsewhere – for as Otto Strasser once explained, Hitler was notoriously an opportunist in love. He had not forgotten his once beloved Mimi, Maria Reiter, and in the autumn of 1931 he sent his Deputy, Rudolf Hess, to look for her and talk to her.

Hess found her one morning at the Hotel Berghof which she and her husband were running in Seefeld in the Austrian Tyrol. Herr Hitler still felt deeply for her, Hess explained. In fact, he was still in love with her. And he greatly regretted the overwhelming necessity that forced him to take the action he did. 'He has asked me to make sure that you are happy,' Hess went on. 'If there is anything he can do – if you still love him more than anyone else, please telephone him. You mean so much to him.' Hess wrote the phone number down for her. 'Germany is approaching its greatest hour. The greatest wish of our Leader is that you should be by his side.'

Next afternoon, the former teenager Fräulein Maria Reiter, now a maturer twenty-one year old by the name of Frau

Woldrich, walked out of the hotel and down into the town a mile away, and four hours later she was in Munich, where she telephoned the number Hess had given her. She recalled:

> My heart was beating because I was phoning my love, the man I now knew loved me. It seemed an age as the number rang. At last Hitler himself answered the phone. I found myself calling him the name he had asked me to use all those years ago.
>
> 'Wolf,' I said. 'It's Mimi.'
>
> Hitler did not reply for a moment. Then he said, 'My darling, I hope you will say what I am yearning to hear. That you love me still.'
>
> With tears in my eyes I whispered, 'I can't say that over the telephone.'
>
> You see, Hitler to me then was a gentle, sympathetic man trying to resurrect the ashes of his country. I was in love as I told him, 'Wolf, I am here, at the Central Station in Munich.'

Hitler told her to take a taxi straight to his apartment at 16 Prinzregentenplatz. He would be waiting for her.

Many years later, when she was poor and plain and scratching a pittance as a cleaner woman in modern post-war West Germany, she remembered still with longing and sadness her night of passion with the man who would be king – the king she did not yet know would become tyrant.

> At his flat I walked into his arms. Soon he was clasping me tightly. I felt his heart beating, his breath warm upon my neck. We walked towards his bedroom. Once

71

we had been sweethearts. That night we became true lovers in every sense of the word. It has been suggested that Hitler was incapable of making love. I know that was not true, even though I may have been the only woman he ever loved completely. He pressed me to his body and kissed me. It was well past midnight. I leaned back more and more on his sofa. Wolf grabbed me even more firmly. I let anything happen to me. I was never as happy as during that night.

When she was only sixteen, Hitler had crushed her in his arms and whispered: 'You mean everything to me. You must always love me.' She would never forget how he sobbed out his love. He told her of his unhappy childhood and his brutal father. 'Now,' she recalled, 'I tried to make him forget it all during that wonderful night with him in Munich. He talked to me as only a man can to the woman he really loves, and I know that I was *the only one*. To me he bared his heart and thoughts completely.'

The next day they had lunch at the Osteria Bavaria restaurant. Hitler, Maria noted, was 'like a little boy'. A dozen times he gazed into her eyes and murmured, 'Mimi, my beautiful Mimi, I love you so much.' He even spoke of marriage, albeit at some unspecified moment in the future when he had finally fulfilled what he called 'his mission' – the grand plan he believed Divine Providence had chosen him to carry out on behalf of Germany. In the meantime he installed her in her own flat in Munich, though he was always careful to keep his distance when they were seen together in public.

When Hitler became Chancellor of Germany and Führer of the Third Reich in 1933 he began to spend most of his time in Berlin and Maria saw less and less of him. And when her divorce finally came through, Hitler now ruled marriage out of court completely. She told him she was unwilling to remain simply his mistress. He replied that time might alter things. But it did not, and thenceforward she became troubled and unhappy and ultimately remote. In November 1936 she married again, this time to a young SS officer by the name of Georg Kubisch (later killed fighting the British at Dunkirk), and from that point forward she put Hitler out of her mind. She met him one last time in 1938 when he called at her Munich flat to enquire whether she was happy. He told her:

> You have meant – and still mean – more to me than any other woman. It is because of you I have built my mountain retreat at Berchtesgaden, where we first met. When I fell in love with you, I fell in love with Berchtesgaden. How beautiful are the mountains, and the snows there.

By now, of course, Eva Braun had been ensconced off and on at Berchtesgaden for several years.

PART 2

Valhalla Nights

Eva

Early in 1932, not long after Hitler's passionate re-encounter with Mimi Reiter following Geli's suicide, his friend and photographer, Heinrich Hoffmann, initiated a series of intimate little dinners for his grieving friend, to a few of which he invited Eva Braun. Little by little Eva began to replace the memory of Geli, and for that matter Mimi, in Hitler's affection, and in due course she received an invitation to tea in Hitler's private Munich sanctum at 16 Prinzregentenplatz. Later he began to buy her flowers, chocolates and jewellery, and step by step this curiously suited but as yet unimpassioned twosome drew closer.

At first it was merely another clandestine affair. She would come to Hitler's Munich apartment for the evening (but not for the night) whenever he asked her – which was increasingly seldom as his inexorable march to power grew ever more involving, for the Chancellorship was infinitely more desirable than any petit-bourgeois Bavarian blonde. So it began. It was not easy. Indeed, the integration of Eva into Hitler's life, from a discreet part-time mistress in Bavaria to 'First Lady' at the Führer's side in what was left of the Third Reich, was to take the rest of her life, beginning perhaps on New Year's Day 1933, when a small party which included Heinrich Hoffmann, Hess and his wife and other members of Hitler's circle all arrived at Hanfstaengl's house in Munich for coffee after attending a performance of Wagner's *Meistersinger* at the opera house. Among

them was a young woman by the name of Eva Braun. Hanfstaengl
was to record:

> It was not my first sight of Eva Braun. She was a pleasing-
> looking blonde, the slightly helpless type who appears to
> need protection, well built, with blue eyes and a modest,
> diffident manner. I had seen her working behind the coun-
> ter at Heinrich Hoffmann's shop some months earlier, and
> had certainly registered the fact. She was friendly and
> personable and eager to please. We had no sense that
> evening that she was there in any particular capacity, but
> rather as a friend of one of the girls to make up the party.

Hitler was in an unusually benign mood – almost the last
time, in fact, that Hanfstaengl was to see him in such a mood –
and all in all it was a very pleasant party. Hitler talked about the
old days, as he always did, and about the *Meistersinger*, the words
of which he knew by heart. And as he talked, Hanfstaengl could
not help thinking of a couple of lines which went:

> *Ein Glühwurm fand sein Weibchen nicht*
> *Das hat den Schaden angericht.'*

> (A glow-worm never did find his mate,
> and that was the cause of the problem.)

'Hitler never did find his mate,' Hanfstaengl was to conclude,
'and Eva Braun was no answer to the problem.'

But that was a judgement that turned out to be not quite
correct – though Hanfstaengl, soon to be hounded out of
Germany and flee for his life, would have no way of knowing.

Eva

Eva Braun had no interest in politics or national or world affairs and there was little in her upbringing that could have foretold the extraordinary role she was to play in future history. Born in Munich on 6 February 1912, with doting and respected lower middle-class parents to care for her – her father was a schoolteacher, stern but adoring – and two chummy sisters to romp with, Eva had an idyllic, comfortable, untroubled childhood, acquiring early on a passion for physical expression in the form of dancing, swimming, skating and skiing. Extrovert, fun-loving, pretty and bright, her passions were movies and musicals, novelettes and clothes, and she proved too frivolous to apply herself at lessons (though in her school tests she got mostly credits), and when she began to take an interest in boys her parents sent her to a convent school run by English nuns, which she loathed.

The convent's surviving medical reports confirm that Eva was a virgin during her time there, which in itself is not surprising, and even less surprising when, years later, her mother revealed that her daughter had suffered from an unusual condition – her vagina, she said, had been 'narrowly built' – a condition which was successfully remedied in her mid-adolescence by a Professor Scholten, a Munich gynaecologist of note, by means of pioneer surgery followed by lengthy specialist medical attention. It is an ironic coincidence that a little while after Adolf Hitler had sought medical help to sort out his psycho-sexual problem and patch up his potency, the future woman of his life was to seek medical help to address her physical-sexual problem and sort out her potentiality. And in the case of both, the experts seemed eventually to have effected a cure.

What on earth did a pretty blonde bourgeois teenager like Eva Braun, a straightforward, wholesome girl, and still a virgin, see in the odd-looking fellow she had first described as the 'elderly gentleman'? Today it is not possible for us to judge this for ourselves – all we have to go on are ageing images on paper or celluloid, the archive photos and the old newsreels projected at the wrong frames per second; we can only view the shadow many times removed, not experience the impact of the substance. And it is overwhelmingly evident that in its day the substance, the living Hitler – his presence, charisma, magnetism, in short his sex appeal – was truly monumental indeed.

'Like sitting next to the sun'

Absolute power, it has been said, corrupts absolutely. In Adolf Hitler's case it could also be said that it seduced universally. Hitler's impact on women was as devastating among the female public of Germany en masse as amongst those individuals who found themselves in his immediate presence. It was the money devoted by wealthy and adoring women that in large measure funded the burgeoning Nazi Party in its early days (though not exclusively – another sponsor was Henry Ford); and it was the votes of the women of Germany that contributed substantially to bringing Hitler to power in the 1932 national election. In many ways the enthusiasm of the women of Germany, or many of them, closely resembled the sexual hysteria that greeted the rock stars of later generations – Elvis Presley, for example, or Mick Jagger. Hans Baur, Hitler's personal pilot, reckoned that whenever he discussed Hitler with women they were either 'enthusiastic, fanatical or hysterical'. Maria Reiter had noticed it straightaway when Hitler took her to an opera in a Munich theatre. As they took their seats the entire audience responded to Hitler's presence – especially the women. 'I watched jealously,' she was to relate later, 'as beautiful women in the audience curtsied to the man who was soon to be the Führer of Germany. I could see the adoration in the eyes of the women as they looked at him. And I told myself: "He is the man I love."'

Hugo Jaeger, Hitler's official colour photographer, recalled a similar, even more hysterical occasion:

> We were in a hall, thousands and thousands of people, and something monstrous happened. There was a mass suggestion at work, a fluid in the air, and everybody, men as well as women, abruptly began to tremble and weep and howl, and all the while Hitler sat up there without saying a word, without stirring, just staring at them.

Not for nothing did Hitler compare his mass audiences with women and call them his 'only bride'. One historian was tempted to describe Hitler's meetings as having a peculiarly 'obscene, copulatory character' climaxing in 'unblocked oratorical orgasms' – 'like sex murders' as one German writer put it. Often the stewards at these meetings had to hose down the floors because so many of the women had apparently wet themselves in their excitement at seeing and hearing Hitler.

It wasn't just in the auditoriums, it was out in the streets, anywhere. Hitler's chauffeur reported that teenage girls would throw themselves under Hitler's car in the hope that the Führer himself would rescue them and give them succour. Girls from the Nazi BDM (the German Girls' League) would arrive at Hitler's house in Berchtesgaden virtually naked under their uniforms and offer themselves to the Führer. Others would bare their breasts in his presence. Groups of women, crowds of them even, would react collectively like a single woman utterly in thrall to a revered male sex god or some tribal paramount chief accustomed to the right of *jus primae noctis*.

All this was true even in such sanctums of metropolitan respectableness at the Kaiserhof Hotel in Berlin, where during the pre-war years Hitler was accustomed to take tea to the strains of a palm court orchestra in the airy lounge. Whenever Hitler took his place at table a crowd of pretty ladies would gather to stare at him. For a large tip the waiters would try and arrange for a particularly enamoured lady to be seated at a table near to Hitler's, and the boldest or most enthralled would even venture up to his table to present flowers to him or place their hand on his. Not surprisingly, Hitler did not think the Kaiserhof was a suitable place to bring Eva Braun for tea. Meanwhile the love letters addressed to the Führer, c/o the Reich Chancellery, Berlin, poured in, both now and into the future. An unhappily married lady in Spandau named Emmie Mayer probably spoke for them all. At night she slept with his photo clasped to her breast, never stirring so that he could rest with her undisturbed. By day she would bombard him with missives of adoration and desire.

'My dearest beloved, my only, Adolf,' she would address him, 'my best beloved of my heart, king of my soul.' And she spoke for them all – teenage Fräulein and matronly Frau, shopgirl and baroness – when she poured out her heart in love letter after love letter:

> You are my thoughts by day as by night, you are my
> only love, I live only for you, you are my homeland, I
> want to come home to you, you are my life, my light,
> my heart and soul belong only to you, oh everything is

yours. Love, my heart is so filled that my mouth over-
flows.

And again:

Oh, my Adolf, what have you done now! You have
lighted everything inside me, my body is a single
glowing star. Only you have lit the flame, it still burns
now, oh how it burns. Oh Adolf, my Adolf, beloved,
come – take what is yours, take everything, everything
there, and the flame will glow, glow, glow for you . . .
Your eternally loving Emmie.

Hitler received many such letters from women of all ages and
ranks in society, and the barmiest of them were stored in a
voluminous set of files in his private office under the generic
heading of CRACKERS! And still the erotic gifts and cushions
embroidered with the words *'Ich liebe Sie'* (I love you) poured in,
and women continued to cry out 'Heil Hitler' during childbirth,
orgasm and surgery.

To be actually in Hitler's presence face to face was an even more
extraordinary experience, whether one was a female or a male, or
for that matter a child or a general, a servant or a visiting prime
minister. Hitler had a magnetic presence, a hypnotic power that
is almost impossible to define or analyse without having
experienced it. As one of his most devoted admirers, a high-born
English milady, once said, 'Being with Hitler was like sitting next
to the sun.' When Eva's sister met him for the first time, she
reported afterwards, 'I felt myself melt in his presence.' In short,
Adolf Hitler possessed total sexual charisma. But how come? He
wasn't handsome, he wasn't youthful, he was sometimes peculiarly

dressed. If it was the power of his carefully rehearsed, almost theatrical oratory that overwhelmed the crowds, it was his targeted charm which seduced those close to him in private, particularly if they were women. With women he was unfailingly gallant, deferential, courteous in an almost old-fashioned way. To any and every woman he gave his all. He kissed their hands at every opportunity, his normally gruff voice melted to a soft, intimate, mellifluous warmth. Every woman felt uniquely special after encountering Adolf Hitler. Every woman experienced a feeling of intense delight. And many women felt the upwelling of an intense erotic desire. Eva Braun was therefore not alone in feeling honoured and flattered and enthralled by Adolf Hitler – though she was to prove unique in never letting him go.

'This copulation business'

Just when exactly Hitler and Eva Braun became lovers no one knows, but it was probably about five months after Geli's death. Both of them were habitually reticent about private matters and witnesses were few. One person who did speak up was Anni Winter, Hitler's live-in housekeeper, who was not her greatest fan. 'Eva Braun was often at the apartment when Hitler was in Munich,' she was to report. 'She was always running after him, insisting on being alone with him. She was a most demanding woman.' To her closest friend, Herta Schneider, Eva herself dropped a few hints. Looking through her photograph album one day, she pointed out to Herta a snapshot of Hitler shaking her hand at Hoffmann's, with her handwritten caption under-neath: 'If people only realized *how well* he knows me!' A much later photo, taken after Hitler had become Führer, showed

Adolf Hitler – signed photo dedicated to Gretl Braun, Eva's sister

Signed photo of Hitler's wife-to-be Eva Braun

Signed photo of Geli Raubal, Hitler's half-niece and mistress

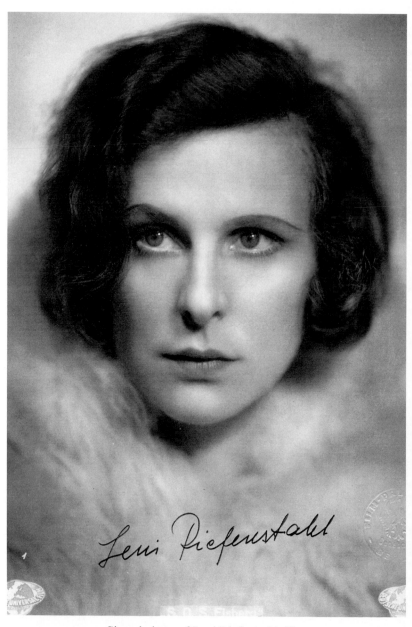

Signed photo of Leni Riefenstahl, film
director and admired friend of Hitler

Signed photo of Jenny Jugo, an actress much admired by the Führer

The Berghof before and after its destruction

Hitler at tea with his tragic British admirer, Unity Mitford

Signed photo of Renate Müller, film actress and Hitler's one-time lover

Mussolini and Chamberlain sitting on the big red plush sofa in Hitler's Munich apartment. 'If only Chamberlain knew the history of that sofa,' quipped Eva with a nudge and a wink. For it was on this sofa rather than in his bedroom that most of Hitler's sexual encounters (such as they were) took place.

There has been much speculation whether Eva Braun and Adolf Hitler were really lovers in any ordinary physical sense. According to Speer, the sexual relationship between Eva and Hitler in the past had been 'perfectly normal'. But Speer did not inspect the sheets. The wife of Hitler's administrator at the Berghof *did* inspect the sheets – *and* Eva's and Adolf's dirty linen – and so did all the chambermaids, and at no time could any of them ever detect the slightest indication of any trace of a normal male-female sexual union between the two. On the other hand, given the role of the plush red sofa in Hitler's Munich flat, the bedroom sheets were not necessarily the right place to be looking for evidence – always assuming that sheets are the infallible or only reliable evidence of sexual congress anyway. And Eva's maid at the Berghof went a long way towards proving that Hiltler and Eva did indeed make love when she later testified that whenever Hilter came to the Berghof, Eva would take pills that suppressed her menstrual cycle (a form of contraception).

The matter was warranted of sufficient importance for America's wartime secret intelligence organization, the OSS (Office of Strategic Services), to pen a file on the sex life of Adolf and Eva, carefully recording every crumb of first-hand evidence gleaned via a handful of Hitler's former associates, as follows:

> Eva Braun is frequently a guest at Berchtesgaden and
> in Berlin. Oechsner was told that after one of her visits
> in Berchtesgaden, some of her underwear was found in

Hitler's bedroom. Wiedemann, according to Hohenlohe, says that she has sometimes spent the entire night in Hitler's bedroom. It is reported that Eva moved into the Chancellery … and it is said that Hitler intends to marry her when the war is over. Beyond that we know nothing about the affair.

Professor Redlich's summing up of this subject is cautious:

One might gain the impression that Hitler was sexually normal and happy. He certainly talked a good game. Yet some data indicates sexual unhappiness. A severe perversion is very unlikely. Hitler was not an overt homosexual. His syphilophobia in all likelihood was associated with disturbances of potency. This statement, however, is nothing more than what clinicians call a guesstimate. In summary, Hitler was most likely sexually impaired, but our knowledge about his sexuality is not secure.

'And besides, she's over thirty'

It is true that Hitler's relationship with Eva Braun did not have the urgency, the drive, the intimacy, the all-involving concern of his relationship with Geli. Hitler had been closely focused on all aspects of Geli – from her private parts (which he mooned over) to her progress as a trainee opera singer (which he willed on her). There is no apparent evidence to suggest that anything about Eva Braun excited a comparable passionate involvement – neither her body, her personality, her interests, her conversation ('and besides,' he was to advise his psycho-analyst some years later, 'she's over thirty.') Hitler did not care a hoot how many times she swung up and down on the parallel bars or went up and down the ski slopes. He did not care a fig how many dresses she put on each day or how one differed from the other. Her happy prattle went over his head, she was far removed (as Geli was) from his increasingly total preoccupation with politics and power. But he did find her amenable, discreet, appropriate, above all relaxing (perhaps her most valuable quality to him in a life that became excruciatingly demanding by the day). And she looked well beside him. If he was going to have a mistress in his Munich flat, his Alpine headquarters, his Berlin Chancellery, she fitted the bill, and she knew how to deport herself, at any rate far more than a raver and a tearaway like Geli (who inappropriately was a blood relative anyway).

So though Hitler at this time did not love Eva as intently and erotically as he had Geli or even Mimi, he was happy to have her around and be seen around with her, at least in private company. Eva Braun clearly loved him, and admired him, and was happy to be with him. He was her man. And for a loner like Hitler, who seems never to have had more than two or three friends in his life, who indeed had no other private life, no ambition for family, for domesticity, this was worth its weight in cuddles and prattles – even though it allowed little or no scope (as far as we can tell) for his favourite forms of masochistic sexual psychology or deviant proclivities.

In an interview a long time after the end of the war, Hitler's personal secretary in the war years, Traudl Junge, who knew both Hitler and Eva Braun, was to comment:

> Eva Braun was a comfort to him. But he didn't *depend* on women. He was so obsessed with this vision – to be

the leader of the German nation – that he felt like a prophet. So women didn't play the first role in his life. This was the reason he didn't marry earlier, indeed until the day of his death. In any case, he didn't have a very strong feeling for sex. Even with Eva Braun it was just a warm sort of feeling he had for her. She was one of the few people who had his absolute trust. Her fidelity was what was important to him. Not anything else. He adored her for that.

If Geli was the love of Hitler's life, Hitler was the love of Eva's. Why? She never explained. In part it was for all the usual reasons that various women adored the man and even died for the love of him. As Traudl Junge was to put it:

He was an exciting man to meet, though not especially attractive in his appearance. But he had a radiance. His eyes were very interesting. And he had a sort of charm – and there *is* a fascination about extraordinary people, independent of themselves. He had an old-fashioned opinion of a woman's place. He thought it was his right to possess any women he wanted. But he was very charming. As a man to woman, that is. He had a nice way of flirting ... With Eva Braun, for instance, he was very tender and friendly and fatherly to her. And he admired beauty and he admired the female sex. But I think it was not erotic. He liked to flirt, but I think he was a bit afraid of the consequences. I think he never let it go too far. He was very against being touched. He would not even let his doctor examine him. But he often put his hand on people's brows. And with women he liked to stroke their skin. I cannot imagine him being very passionate. Never full of passion. He would never kiss anyone . . . He would tolerate any weakness but he would never accept women as equals. They could not be his partners in anything. But so far as I can say my feeling is that Hitler was not a pervert. He was not a very potent man. And this is the reason why he had a very primitive relationship with women.

But from Eva Braun's point of view there must undoubtedly have been another dimension. Hitler was Eva's first love and her only love. There was no one else. In her eyes he represented her destiny, and as he rose in status and grandeur, so her aspirations – as the king's consort, so to speak, the uncrowned, albeit un-known Empress of Germany – rose with him, even though she was for much of the time only a closet consort, his secret partner or common-law wife. And that destiny she would loyally and lovingly follow, even unto death.

Adolf Hitler was not an easy or straightforward choice as a young woman's first serious boyfriend. He was not only a lot older than Eva Braun, but more intelligent, more knowledge-able (in his random and eccentric way), more articulate, more streetwise, infinitely less scrupulous and a lot less nice. While Eva's world view was myopic, Hitler's was panoramic. While Hitler sought to change continents, Eva was content to change dresses, and did so frequently. While Eva Braun was a kind of sweet and bourgeois gangster's moll, the man who was the choice of her life and the only lover in her life was a political genius of breathtaking scope and infinite wickedness who would bring down a continent in ruins. What was greatly to Eva's credit, however, was her ability to placate, subdue, and pleasure

89

– at least within the domain of a lounge or boudoir – the dauntingly complex, hauntingly random, monstrously violent personality of her beloved, the intricacies and contradictions of which the world is still trying to puzzle out today.

Probably Eva Braun was never aware that the lover in whose arms she lay under the stars of the Berchtesgaden summer night, whose tie she lovingly straightened and whose hand caressed hers, was a monster whose barbarities against his fellow human beings and toll of mass slaughter far outweighed those of Genghis Khan and other tyrants of a bygone age, and were only exceeded by those rival twentieth-century despots, Joseph Stalin and Mao Tse Tung, who had the advantage of bigger populations to ravage. Intellectually Hitler was well equipped and his IQ was undoubtedly high, with a broad reach of arcane and chaotically unrelated knowledge, and a phenomenal memory. But he lacked even a basic higher education, so his mind, untrammelled by systemic knowledge or conventional lines of thought, was free to rove wherever his chaotic emotional impulses drove it, which was usually to extremes – hence the political revolutionary and the criminal barbarian of his maturer years, inured to mass slaughter by his experiences on the Western Front in the First World War and his concept of 'Necessity Supreme'.

Emotionally, Hitler was chaos. In part, probably, this was due to the behavioural system he was born with, in part to the negative impact of his brutal, drunken, loveless father – an impact his lifelong affection for the memory of his loving but helpless mother could not assuage.

Many latter-day psychologists and psycho-analysts, not to mention wartime secret Intelligence specialists (mostly American), have attempted to delve into the mind of Adolf

Hitler since the pioneer efforts of the mysterious and elusive Dr Krueger, interpreting such evidence as has come to hand according to whatever school of psycho-analytic thought they favoured most (generally Freudian). But even his closest friends, who unlike the psychologists of the future were close to the man in the past, remained baffled by the paradoxes of his personality. Many years later Albert Speer was to comment that he was 'cruel, unjust, unapproachable, cold, capricious, self-pitying, and vulgar'. But he added, 'He was also the exact opposite of almost all these things.'

Of special and fundamental interest has always been the possibility, or probability, or even certainty, of a cause and effect relationship between Hitler's private life and public career, or more exactly between his chaotic sexual make-up and his wickedly demonic and universally destructive political mindset. But though his political drive has been well understood and charted, his sexual make-up has remained a labyrinthine enigma, to which both those who had known the man (in so far as it was possible to know him) and those who have studied him from afar (from the vantage of another continent or another era or both) have bequeathed a variety of labels, many of them speculative, some rather closer to home.

The labels that can be attached to Hitler from the psychiatric repertoire are many and include one or several of the following in various combinations: schizophrenic, megalomaniac, egomaniac, hypochondriac, paranoid, hysteric, depressive, bacteriophobe, syphilophobe, and more, including (in the sexual arena) homosexual (probably not), impotent (almost certainly sometimes), sado-masochistic (undoubtedly sometimes), coprophilic, monorchic, celibate and all or some or none of these and other things.

But interpretations come and go and the central mystery – the infinitely complex inter-stellar galaxies of Hitler's endlessly explored but never quite mapped mind – remains an everlasting enigma. Indeed, in recent times the Freudian interpretations and all the rest of the paraphernalia of psycho-analysis have been replaced in part by a somewhat less guilt-ridden and doom-laden image of a Hitler who (shock horror) fancied pretty young women, was at ease in their company, and even liked to see the more private bits of one or two of them if they allowed him. Historian-biographer John Lukaks, for example, has argued that Hitler's sexuality and sexual appetite (like Churchill's) played 'a less than decisive part' in his life. 'In my considered view,' he argued, 'his relations with women were fairly normal.' If anything he was undersexed, not because of deformity or dysfunction but because of a temperamental lack of interest (and, it should be added, increasing lack of time and opportunity). Furthermore, Lukaks ventured, evidence of abnormal sexuality was 'rare, inauthentic and difficult to judge'. That, it must be said, remains to be seen.

At the end of the day, only one thing was certain: in love, as in politics and power, Hitler was indubitably (but virtually unfathomably), a psychopath – tender and violent, loving and loathsome, attractive and repulsive, life giving and death dealing, hypnotically magnetic but dangerous to know.

He had charm when required, courage, self-confidence, insight, a kind of eccentric (and often misanthropic) wisdom. He was also cruel, ruthless, dissembling, lying, wicked in anything and everything. Perhaps the characteristic that most struck those who knew him well – or even hardly at all – was his propensity for violent mood swings and hysterical, almost catatonic rages, when his face could change colour – from bleached to puce and back again in seconds – and his whole body turn rigid in a kind of living rigor mortis. But behind and above all this – defying virtually all explanation – was his extraordinary and wicked and catastrophic genius for power, both the vision of it and the achieving of it, seemingly cosmic in extent and randomly molecular in structure, all from a standing start of zero, like a human big bang.

'Laughable cosmic bacterium'

But it was perhaps Hitler's eccentricity in matters big and small that struck most people at a casual day-to-day level. These were the eccentricities of a random and utterly undisciplined spirit who had somehow slipped through the interstices of conventional life, and they were many and varied. His pet hates (some with good reason) included smoking, alcohol, microbes, moonlight, tortoises, baby chickens, meat, prostitutes, venereal disease, radios, boats, swimming costumes, hunting, horses, cats, American and British jazz and dance music (which he described as 'negro perversions'), American and British political newspaper cartoonists (especially Low of the *Daily Express*), dentists, anaesthetists, sick people, criticism (except from Eva Braun), other people's jokes (except Eva Braun's), and other people whistling (though he liked whistling himself, especially the Walt Disney song 'Who's Afraid of the Big Bad Wolf'). Hitler's deepest, darkest hate – the hate that perhaps explains all that he was and all that he stood for and all that he did – was for the human species itself. He was later to describe the human species as nothing but 'a laughable cosmic bacterium' ('*eine lächerliche Weltraumbakterie*') – an epithet that underlined his fundamental contempt for all human life and human suffering, whether it was the Jews, the Slavs, or for that matter the German people themselves.

By contrast, Hitler's pet likes included first and foremost pretty young women, then little children (for up to a minute or two), little animals (including mice but not rats), wolves, (hence his nom de plume of Herr Wolf), drives in his Mercedes (especially at night), hill walking, map reading, star watching, star signs, fortune telling, devouring cream buns all day, listening to the music of Richard Wagner, Johann Strauss and Franz Lehar, talking the night through, reading books about German history and the pioneer heroes of the British Empire, watching home-made striptease porn movies now and then (including one allegedly featuring a short-term girlfriend of the time in various intimate and revelatory postures), watching real-life horror news film (inmates of the pre-war Buchenwald and Dachau concentration camps undergoing torture, for example), horoscopes, the colour red (his lucky colour – hence the background hue of the Nazi flag), and his enormous collection of little cage birds in the vast lounge at the Berghof (the room with the gigantic panoramic window). If one of the birds died, so it was said, it would be buried with honour in a special little plot outside, complete with it's own little headstone.

Nothing, perhaps, could be quite as eccentric as Hitler's daily programme and way of life at the Berghof or the Berlin Chancellery. For a man preoccupied every day with the burden of the affairs of state he got up incredibly late – never before ten and sometimes past eleven in the morning. He would take a light breakfast – a glass of orange juice or milk, a slice or two of rye bread and butter (he would eat up to half a pound of butter during the day) then potter about, settling to no coherent job of work – at least at the Berghof in the early days – before it was time for lunch. Normally this would be around midday, but later, as the political and military affairs of the Third Reich grew apace, there would be staff conferences at midday and lunch might not be served till as late as four o'clock in the afternoon. Though it was served on the finest china and eaten with the finest silver cutlery, the food was often almost inedible – at least to Hitler's guests – and with political discussion banned during mealtime the conversation was generally banal and innocuous, especially if the wives of some of the Nazi elite were present, for Hitler found most of them ponderous and dull (hardly surprising, for like almost everyone else they were in awe of Hitler's god-like status). Hitler himself was not a total vegetarian – he loathed meat, but would eat fish and sometimes a Bavarian dish called *Leberknödel* (liver dumplings) – though generally he confined himself to dishes like noodles with tomatoes and *Hoppelpoppel* (fried potatoes with egg), one of his favourites. In general he ate little of anything but would drink up to sixteen cups of black coffee a day.

It was a paradox that, given the magnetic awe he inspired in both mass audiences and face-to-face encounters, Hitler could, on closer and more prolonged acquaintance, prove dull, boring and conventional. 'Every day at the same hour,' ran a wartime US Counter Intelligence Corps profile by way of example, 'he would go with the same dog to the same corner of the same field and pick up the same piece of wood and throw it in the same direction.' For his secretaries and aides – though not usually, it seems, for Eva Braun – there were times when life with Adolf could be a prolonged and excruciating agony of boredom. Never was this more so than after the main six-course evening meal, on those occasions when Hitler chose not to get down to the official paperwork of the day. Sometimes a movie would be shown (Mickey Mouse cartoons were a great treat), or records of German music played on the gramophone, but more often all those present would be treated to one of Hitler's endless monologues about his past life and present prejudices, and since he suffered dreadfully from insomnia, these monologues, sometimes repeats of previous monologues, would drone on into the early hours of the next day until sleep eventually overwhelmed him and allowed his numb and captive audience to head for their bedrooms — and their cigarettes and schnapps flasks. As Magda Goebbels once complained to a foreign dignitary after one such session: 'He can be Führer as much as he likes, but he always repeats himself and bores his guests.'

Part of Hitler's problem was that, though he was rarely alone, in the sense that there were always other human beings near and around him, he remained isolated from meaningful human contact, for his egocentricity and his almost infantile emotional disposition made it virtually impossible for him to relate, let alone bond, with another human being in any ordinary normal social sense. Though he was a tremendous talker, and could hold forth for hours, he was only an intermittent listener, and could enter into conversation with another person only with difficulty. As Gregor Strasser, a close political ally in the early days of the struggle but later murdered on Hitler's orders, had once tried to explain:

> Hitler is suspicious and vain. He is ignorant of the world. He works without knowledge of man, even without the ability to judge people. He lives without any inner contact with others. He is only genius and

body. He does not smoke, he eats only greens, he does
not touch a woman. Where can one start to explain
other people to him?

Possibly there were one or two exceptions. His mother was
probably one, though she died when he was still only eighteen.
His former architect and future armaments minister, Albert
Speer, who was still only in his late twenties when the recon-
struction of the Berghof under his aegis was begun, was very
possibly another – though even he could not be described as a
close friend (he was to say at his post-war trial in Nuremberg,
'If Hitler had ever had any friends, I would have counted as a
friend'). And then there were the women, who offered and
occasionally provided, the human social (and sometimes personal) contact Hitler so obviously lacked.

'Me, the mistress of the greatest man in Germany'

By the summer of 1932 Eva Braun was fatally hooked. Hitler,
on the other hand, was increasingly preoccupied with matters of
infinitely greater moment and urgency – the national elections,
the Nazi seizure of power, his own elevation to absolute rule as
Chancellor and then Führer of a Third Reich. Compared with
what was now at stake in the political arena, his relationship
with a twenty-year-old shop assistant called Eva was a matter of
relatively trivial concern. He no longer found time to come
down to Munich and his communications with her became less
and less frequent. It was also apparent to Eva that from time to
time Hitler chased after other women, and since she had become

obsessed with the idea that Hitler might eventually marry her, even though he had no intention of ever taking a wife, she lived in constant fear of being discarded.

Eventually the long absences, the sense of loss, the unending loneliness proved unbearable. On 1 November 1932, all of twenty years of age and alone in her parents' flat, Eva wrote Hitler a farewell note and then, borrowing her father's 6.35mm pistol, shot herself, just like Geli.

Like Geli, Eva missed, and instead of putting a bullet in her heart, she lodged it in her neck. But unlike Geli, she was found before she had bled to death. It was her sister Ilse who found her. 'My sister was lying on the right side of the bed, but she had regained consciousness,' she recalled. 'There was blood everywhere – on the sheets, on the pink cushion, on the floor in little pools. The bullet had lodged just near the neck artery, and the doctor had no difficulty in extracting it.'

In a way, perhaps, this was a defining moment. Hitler, aghast and laden with flowers, hurried to Eva's bedside in a private clinic. For his part, he was moved that a pretty young woman – a model of discretion and selflessness – was prepared to die for her love of him. For her part, she was happy that the man she loved had taken time off from the crescendo of politics to come and hold her hand.

Three months later Hitler became Chancellor of Germany (and later Führer and Supreme Commander), and less than a week after assuming power he splashed out on jewellery for his special lady on the occasion of her twenty-first birthday. Shortly afterwards he invited her to spend the night with him at his Munich apartment – the first time he had asked such a thing of her in his life. And so began her gradual rise from girlfriend to a politician to mistress of the Head of State.

At first Hitler's inner council – Goebbels, Bormann and the rest – deeply disapproved when they first heard of her. An ordinary shop girl was not what they had in mind as consort to the Führer of the Greater German Empire. But she persisted – and so, in his way, did Hitler. For the first time she was invited to visit Hitler's Alpine refuge, Haus Wachenfeld (later reconstructed as the Führer's famous Berghof), at Obersalzberg, overlooking Berchtesgaden in Bavaria. But still contact was sporadic, still she was an unofficial state secret, still she worked as a shop assistant and lived at her parents' home.

The problem was that Hitler did not want the public or the Party – above all, German womanhood – to know about the secret woman in his life. He wished to present himself as their undivided leader, a single Führer at their single-minded service, devoid of any other human ties or frailties. 'In politics,' he once said, 'feminine support is essential – the men follow automatically.' And when asked if he ever planned to marry, he would reply, 'I am already married – my wife is Germany.'

So still Eva Braun remained the clandestine mistress of her increasingly preoccupied lover, for ever unheard of by the nation at large, never even seen except by a handful of confidants and attendants at Hitler's court – above all still mostly alone.

'It's hell to be twenty-two and in love with a man twice your age,' Eva told a waiter in a Munich restaurant who happened to be her confidant, 'and not know if he's in love with you or not.' It was, she wrote around this time, 'a backstreet existence'. Hitler gave her no money, no home, above all no passion. Like the majority of women in Germany at that time, Eva thought Hitler was the greatest man on the planet. But his neglect of her for long periods of time hurt her deeply, especially when he failed to turn up on her twenty-third birthday.

She wrote in her diary on 6 February 1935:

> If only I had a little dog, then I wouldn't be quite so alone. I did so want a basset puppy, and still no sign of one. Perhaps next year, or even later, it will go better with somebody approaching spinsterhood. This evening I am going to dine with Herta. What else can a very simple woman of twenty-three do? And so my birthday will end with guzzling and boozing.

Even when Hitler did visit her it was an up-and-down experience. Five days after her birthday, Hitler came to Munich and went to see her. 'He was here just now,' she wrote in her diary, 'but no dog and no cupboards full of dresses. He didn't even ask me whether I had a birthday wish. So now I bought myself some jewellery. I hope he likes it. If not, he can buy me something himself.'

A week later, Hitler came again and told her he was thinking of taking her away from Hoffmanns' shop and buying her a little house of her own. 'Dear God, please let this come true and let it happen in the near future,' she wrote. 'I am so infinitely happy that he loves me so and pray that it will always be like this.' But it wasn't and by March she was suffering again. He had come to Munich early in the month and she spent 'two marvellously beautiful hours with him' before going off to the annual Nocturnal Ball. He had promised to meet up with her again the next day, but when he failed to show up she phoned the Osteria Bavaria and left a message for him, only to learn he had flown off in a plane, and when he got back he left again, this time by train, and the distraught Eva arrived at the station just in time to see the rear lights of the last coach receding into the darkness.

'I'm racking my brains to discover why he left without saying goodbye to me,' she wrote. 'The Hoffmanns have invited me to *The Venetian Night* but I shan't go. I'm too sad for that.'

A week later she was more lonely and more desperate still. She wrote in her diary:

> I want only one thing, to fall very ill and to hear nothing of him for at least a week. Why has nothing arrived for me, why do I have to bear all this? Oh, if only I had never met him. Now I'm buying sleeping tablets again. Why doesn't the devil carry me off? Hell must be infinitely preferable to this. I waited for three hours outside the Carlton Hotel and I had to watch him buy flowers for Anny Ondra [an actress married to the former world boxing champion, Max Schmeling] and invite them to dinner . . . I am desperate. He is only using me for a very definite purpose. It can't be otherwise. When he says he loves me, he thinks it is only for the time being. The same with his promises, which he never keeps. Why doesn't he have done with me instead of tormenting me?

In practice, if she went out with him to dinner in company in Munich, she could not even sit next to him or exchange a single word with him, as she recorded on 1 April 1935, the day after a dinner given by Hitler at Munich's grandest hotel, the Vierjahreszeiten:

> I had to sit beside him for three hours without being able to say a single word to him. As a farewell gesture, he gave me an envelope with some money inside, as he

already had done once before. How lovely it would
have been if he had also written a line of greeting or a
kind word. But he never thinks of such things.

'Things are tough,' she wrote in her diary on 29 April 1935.
'Very much so in every respect. Love does not seem to be on his
programme at present.'

Sometimes she would have to stand in the crowds in the street
or stare with her nose pressed to a restaurant window to catch a
glimpse of her first and only true love.

By the time of the Party Rally at Nuremberg in 1935, Ernst
Hanfstaengl, Hitler's old supporter from the early days, was
almost persona non grata with the Führer and his henchmen and
before long would be forced to flee abroad in fear of his life.
Before that it was another neglected old Party stalwart who
brought him up to date on the Eva Braun situation, for his
second wife had gone to school with Eva and still saw a lot of
her. Of this conversation Hanfstaengl recalled:

> It was clear that Eva was no more than a piece of
> domestic decoration in the dream world in which
> Hitler now lived. She could hardly leave Munich with-
> out Hitler's or Bormann's permission and one day
> appeared in tears to complain of her serf-like existence.
> 'I am nothing but a prisoner,' she blubbered, and then
> volunteered the telling information: '*Als Mann habe ich
> von ihm nichts*' – 'Above all I have nothing from him as
> a man.'

It could only get worse. On 10 May she heard that she had
been superseded.

Herr Hoffmann lovingly and tactlessly informs me that he [Hitler] has found a replacement for me. She is known as the Walkure [Valkyrie] and looks the part. Including her legs. But these are the dimensions he prefers . . . I find it monstrous of him not to have informed me. What happens to me must be a matter of indifference to him. I shall wait until 8 June, in other words a quarter of a year since our last meeting, and then demand an explanation. Let nobody say I'm not patient.

The weather is magnificent and I, the mistress of the greatest man in Germany and in the whole world, sit here waiting while the sun mocks me through the windowpanes.'

More than a fortnight passed and still there was no word. On 28 May Eva wrote:

I have just sent him a decisive letter. If I don't receive a reply before ten o'clock tonight, I'll simply take twenty-five tablets and fall asleep very gently.

I'm afraid there's something else behind it all. I've done absolutely nothing wrong. Absolutely nothing. Perhaps another woman, not the Walkure girl, that would be really rather unlikely, but there are so many others.

What other reasons could there be? I can't think of any.

Later that day she made her last diary entry:

Oh God. I'm afraid there won't be a reply today. If only

103

somebody would help me. Everything is so horribly bleak.

Dear God, help me, please make it possible that I speak to him today. Tomorrow will be too late. I have decided on thirty-five pills. This time I must be dead certain.

If only he got somebody to telephone me.

But Eva's second suicide attempt was no more successful than her first. Perhaps it was not meant to be, for she only took twenty of the pills. In any case, her sister found her before it was too late, gave her first aid and called a doctor. But her failed death was to bring about a changed life.

'Casual enchantments'

Eva had been right, of course, to suspect that Hitler's three-month neglect of her was not just due to the pressures of state, which were colossal, but his interest in other women, which was unceasing. And she had been perfectly right in assuming the woman she called the Walkure had something to do with her lover's long absence – and indeed also (as she had jotted in her diary) 'perhaps another woman, not the Walkure'. There were indeed (as she noted again) 'so many others'. So many others, both now and later – so many that even historians find it hard to sort them out. In this respect, it must be said, Adolf Hitler, with an eye for a curvaceous figure, pretty face and glamorous persona, seems no different from the majority of normal and sexually mature male human beings throughout time and the planet.

Evidently the lonely, insecure, down-at-heel, Austrian ex-corporal with the goatee beard who had presented himself at Dr Krueger's surgery one summer evening in 1919 and complained of impotence (though he had hardly been near a woman in his life) had come a long way in the last fifteen years or so, not just in matters of power, wealth and historic import but in affairs of the heart and groin as well. Though clearly most of these mainly young ladies with whom his name was briefly associated from time to time were ephemera who passed by in the night (or more usually the day) – brief encounters, casual enchantments, twinkles in eyes, promises of what might have been – some had a more solid basis in mutual lust and admiration, and even earned the approval of the Nazi court establishment (Dr and Frau Goebbels et al.) as potentially worthy and prestigious future candidates for the left hand of the almighty Führer.

Among the casual enchantments of past, present and future, the roll of honour includes the names of sisters of friends (like Erna Hanfstaengl), sisters of employees (like Jenny Haug, whose brother was Hitler's one-time chauffeur) and local ladies like Ada Klein (an attractive young Munich cabaret dancer who did her best to seduce him) and Suzi Liptauer (who tried to kill herself in a Munich hotel room, but unlike some of Hitler's other ladies, did not succeed). There were film stars Brigitte Helm and Olga Tschechowa (and Pola Negri too, so rumour would have it), along with singers Maria Müller and Margaret Slezak (daughter of a rival to Caruso), cabaret dancer Lola Epp, and actresses Jenny Jugo and Marika Roekk, and the Russian film star (and possibly Soviet spy) Olga Chekhova, as well as the Argentinean singer and film star Imperio Argentina, whom Hitler was said to have adored (though the feeling was not mutual), Hilda Krahl, Henny Porten and Paula Wessely.

Then there was the ravishing blonde Inge Ley, a soprano by profession, but married to Hitler's coarse and drunken Labour Minister ('he treats me outrageously,' she once complained, 'he'll end up killing me one day'). Inge always excited Hitler's admiration, but like some of the others eventually managed to kill herself – she jumped out of a window in Berlin following another petty quarrel with her brutish husband – though not before writing Hitler a letter that left him visibly depressed. Jenny Jugo makes a spectacular appearance a little later, while Margaret Slezak, for her part, is more typical of the numerous sirens that passed in the night.

Ernst Hanfstaengl well recalled the night Hitler met her, though it is doubtful if Fräulein Slezak did for long. Dr Goebbels and his wife, Hanfstaengl was to record, were tireless in their efforts to find Hitler a female companion. One such offering was the vivacious and blonde Slezak, then around twenty-seven or twenty-eight years of age, and endowed with a lovely voice in her own right. One evening at their large flat in the Reichkanzlerplatz in Berlin's west end, the Goebbels tried to arrange a little get-together. Ernst Hanfstaengl was there and was asked if he could play a few appropriate melodies on the piano to induce a suitably romantic mood. 'I felt rather like the man must feel who plays incidental music in a brothel,' Hanfstaengl was to recall. 'However, I thought this was all in a good cause and if only we could keep him interested, who knew what might come of it.'

The music seemed to do the trick. Hitler and the lovely Gretl retired into the darkened drawing room next door. Assuming they were fondling each other, Hanfstaengl kept his foot off the loud pedal, hoping fervently that this was the start of a beautiful friendship. Eventually, about one in the morning, it was time for everyone to leave.

'I must take the young lady home,' said Hitler.

If she brings you round to some sort of normalcy, Hansfstaengl thought, she will be doing us all a service. And when he got back to the hotel (the Kaiserhof) it seemed as if the evening, and perhaps even the music, had done the trick. Hitler's boots, Hanfstaengl observed, were the only missing ones outside the door in the corridor.

> 'Well, well,' I thought, 'this is really an auspicious beginning.' I believe, in fact, that he returned quite late, but there was no clue to be obtained from his behaviour next morning as to what had happened. Gretl Slezak continued to be seen around and I got to know her very well. One day she was in a confidential mood and I asked her what had been going on. She just looked up at the ceiling and shrugged. It was all I needed to know.

Leni Riefenstahl, the talented young film director and Nazi propagandist, was another of the Goebbels' introductions. She, Hitler and Ernst Hanfstaengl all went to dinner at their Berlin apartment one evening, then went on to Leni's own studio flat afterwards. 'There was a piano there,' Hanfstaengl recalled wryly, 'so that got rid of me.' While he played, the Goebbels lent on the piano, chatting away, leaving Hitler on his own with Leni, a very vital and attractive woman, as well as a rising star in the film world. Hitler, isolated from the main group and all alone with a sexy young woman, clearly went into panic mode. While Leni danced around to the music from the piano – 'a real summer sale of feminine advance,' noted the pianist – Hitler hid himself away by studying the titles of the books in the book-cases. Hanfstaengl caught Dr Goebbels' eyes as if to say 'If the

Riefenstahl can't manage this one no one can and we might as well leave.' So they made their excuses and made their departure, leaving Hitler alone with a beautiful young woman dancing her advances all around him. 'But again it was an organized disappointment,' Hanfstaengl was to record. 'The Riefenstahl and I travelled on a plane together a day or two later and once more all I got was that hopeless shrug.'

But she had left her mark and for a while Hitler was besotted with her (and she with him), until he was bowled over by the glittering figure of the seventeen-year-old, blue-eyed Baroness Sigi von Laffert, who so dazzled the Führer that she was even introduced into Berlin society and graced the Berghof tea parties. 'She had a delightful bosom,' the Italian Ambassador of the time was pleased to recall, 'long legs, and the smallest mouth in the world, with never a trace of lipstick. She wore her ash-blonde hair in braids, coiled round her head like a crown.' Once, when Sigi fell ill, Hitler sent her twenty-four red roses as a token of his affection. Later, just before the war, in an attempt to keep her in the family, so to speak, he tried to marry her off to Ambassador Walter Hewel (of the Foreign Ministry), and when that failed, he tried to marry Eva's sister to him instead. Matchmaking was one of his hobbies, one of the lesser sinecures of power that went with the job. But not all Hitler's more casual affairs with singers and actresses and so forth were happy, either in practice or in outcome. Renate Müller was a case in point.

Renate Müller was a young film star with Ufa, Germany's leading movie company, when she first met Hitler on location in Denmark in 1932. 'It was really funny,' she was to say of that first encounter, 'he just sat there, not moving at all, looking at me all the time, and then he would take my hand in his and look some more. He talked all the time – just nonsense.' Not long afterwards, Hitler invited Renate to a party at the Chancellery in Berlin. He ignored her throughout the reception, then afterwards took her on a tour of the Chancellery, showing her everything, even his black silk socks in a drawer. Then suddenly, Renate had no idea why, he leapt to his feet and stood to rigid attention with his arm stiffly raised in the Nazi salute. 'I can keep it up for hours at a time,' he told her. 'I always laugh because Göring has so much trouble doing it.'

But the more Renate Müller got to know Hitler in a more personal way, the less inclined she was to spend time with him, and eventually she became desperate to escape from him. In 1936 she confided why to a film director of her acquaintance.

Hitler, she explained, was not sexually normal in his lovemaking with her. For example, after they had both taken off their clothes, he would throw himself on the floor, screaming that he was nothing, that he deserved only to be kicked, and would writhe on the floor, then roll towards her, begging for chastisement. In the beginning she recoiled, then, using her hands and fingers in explicit sign language, she would explain that she was here for more conventional sexual congress. But it was no good, so she let fly a kick at the most powerful man in Germany, then kicked him again, tentatively at first, then as hard as she could manage, and the harder she kicked, the more excited he became, squirming and writhing and screaming on the floor, and when he came it was with a howl like a wounded fox.

So it went on, and in return for her services Hitler would buy her a diamond bracelet and a riding horse and endless bouquets of flowers, until she had had enough and asked his leave to go to London for a holiday. That was to spell the end of her. In England she was watched by plain-clothes German agents. It was reported that she had been seeing her former lover in London, a German

Jew. Because it was against the new Race Laws to consort with a Jew, she was blacklisted by the German movie industry, which was in Nazi hands. In her despair she began to resort to drugs, became a morphine addict, and was eventually taken to a sanatorium. She tried to see Hitler to clear her name, but he wanted nothing to do with her. Shortly afterwards she happened to see a car drive up to the entrance of the sanatorium and four SS men get out. She wasted no time then. She opened the window of her upstairs room and hurled herself to her death on the pavement below. She was thirty when she died in 1937. Officially it was stated that she had died 'of epilepsy'.

'Class, clout, brain – and even beauty'

So much for the young, the pretty and the ephemeral, who distracted Hitler's attention from the most devoted woman in his life and from the no less serious matter of ruling the Fatherland and planning total war. After them came the heavyweights, the serious opposition, women of class, clout, brain and even beauty. Not all in this category fell for Hitler, far from it indeed, as this first-hand account of the experience of Elisabetta Cerruti, wife of the Italian Ambassador to Germany, vividly recounts. This highly placed lady met Hitler several times at various formal occasions after he had become Chancellor and found him 'repellent, hideous, menacing and dangerous'. When she was in his presence she did not feel inclined to smile. In fact he made her shiver. She recalled her encounter with him at one state function:

When dinner was announced he offered me his arm. As I touched his arm, curiously enough, I received a strong electric shock. I was already so keyed up with excitement it unnerved me a little and although I'm a sceptic and don't believe in the supernatural, I became convinced that he possessed some mystic, magnetic power that he could exercise at will. The shock was so strong I looked up in astonishment. He stood there as pale and calm as ever. Somewhat shaken, I walked in with him to the dining hall.

Dining beside one of the most powerful and certainly most controversial rulers in the world was a strange experience for this high-born lady and she decided that her peasant-born host was not so much coarse as common.

He held his fork and knife in his clenched fists as simple people do, although he knew enough not to eat from his knife. The latter was of little use to him in any case since he never touched the meat. His eyes were large and fine, though the expression in them was always troubled; his skin was clear and of a healthy colour; his speaking voice was soft and warm. The worst feature of his face was his abominably shaped nose. His hands had no character, being white and lifeless. They did not seem to be natural attributes of his physical being but, rather, weapons for the natural gestures that accompanied his conversation.

There were two others in this class and clout category, and as it happens both were English, a fact from which Hitler (who admired the English, mainly because they still ruled a third of the world) took comfort – for it proved, he said (not altogether inaccurately) that the English were really Germans in disguise and therefore (not at all accurately) the natural allies of Germany in any future conflict. It took 3 September 1939 for him to revise this view, at which point one of his English ladies (following a well-established precedent as far as Hitler's women were concerned) felt the time had come to shoot herself.

The first of these Englishwomen was Winifred Wagner, the Hastings-born daughter-in-law of Hitler's favourite and most inspirational composer, Richard Wagner, to whose transcendental operas he owed much of the soul and ceremony of his Nazi movement. Hitler had first met her in Bayreuth back in 1923 when he began to attend the annual Bayreuth Festival in celebration of her father-in-law's music, one of the great inspirations in Hitler's life. From his earliest days Hitler had revered Wagner's music. On one occasion he had admitted that a literally hysterical excitement had overcome him when he recognized his own psychological kinship with Wagner. 'Whoever wants to understand Nazi Germany must first get to know Wagner,' he would say later. It was Wagner's epic opera cycle of the 'Ring' that had given Germany and especially the Third Reich so much of its primitive mythos, vividly recalling the world of German antiquity, with its fighting gods and heroes, its blood feuds and tribal codes, its sense of destiny and the nobility of death.

It was not just the themes and symbolism of Wagner's operas that so moved him – it was the music as well. Hitler's one time friend and supporter in the early days, Ernst Hanfstaengl, was among other things an accomplished pianist who played the classics with a romantic, ringing, orchestral style that Hitler adored. Hanfstaengl used to play for him on many occasions. It was soon clear that Hitler's appreciation of the great composers was limited. He had no time for Bach or Mozart, and not a lot more for Schumann and Chopin to start with – there were not enough soaring climaxes to fire his own turbulent nature. Eventually he always came back to Wagner. His knowledge and appreciation of Wagner's music was genuine and heartfelt and it was not just the music but the message and the meaning of it that fired him. And before long Hanfstaengl realised it was more even than that. The structure of Wagner's music, in particular the *Meistersinger* prelude, was the blueprint for Hitler's own oratory, it underpinned his own emotional impact on the crowds that roared their support at his mass rallies, especially the women in those crowds – and those mass rallies were the foundation of his political power.

'The whole interweaving of leitmotifs,' Hanfstaengl was to note later, 'of embellishments, of counter-point and musical contrast and argument, were exactly mirrored in the pattern of his speeches, which were symphonic in construction and ended in a great climax, like the blare of Wagner's trombones.' The first two-thirds of Hitler's speeches were in march time, Hanfstaengl noted, growing increasingly quicker and leading up to the last third which was primarily rhapsodic. Hanfstaengl went on:

> There was a curious tinge to the finale. It was gradually being borne in on me that Hitler was a narcissus type for whom the crowd represented the satisfaction of some depletion urge, and to me this made the phenom-enon of his oratory more intelligible. The last eight to ten minutes of a speech resembled an orgasm of words.

And not just of words. It was the women in the crowds who reacted most emotionally to these speeches, and to some of them the impact of Hitler's performance was quite literally orgasmic.

It was not just the musical structure of his speeches, either, it was the elaborate range of gestures that went with them, which were as varied and flexible as his arguments. 'It had something of the quality of a really great orchestral conductor,' Hanfstaengl noted, 'who instead of just hammering out the downward beat, suggests the existence of hidden rhythms and meaning with the upward flick of his baton.'

For years Hitler had made a pilgrimage to the annual Wagner festival in Bayreuth – 'one of the blessed seasons of my existence' – and had become a close friend of the Wagner family, notably Wagner's son and English-born daughter-in-law Winifred Wagner, with whom he had enjoyed a close and intense friendship for a number of years. But Hitler was not simply inspired by Wagner's operas, he borrowed from them too. The Nazi salutation 'Heil!' meaning 'Hail!' was borrowed from Wagner and recycled in such all-too-familiar expressions as 'Heil Hitler!' and 'Zieg Heil!' ('Hail victory!'). Above all it was Wagner's massive stage sets which inspired the colossal style of public ceremonial in the Third Reich – the music, the flags, the uniforms, the banners, the serried ranks in their tens of thousands, the sheer theatricality.

Winifred Wagner was herself a supporter of the Nazis and before long Hitler became a guest at the Wagner house in Bayreuth. When Winifred's husband died in 1930, Hitler became a more frequent visitor, and by 1932 the two were very close – which is remarkable, given that he was also seeing Geli and Eva and Mimi at that time. As women go Winifred was not quite Hitler's type in romantic terms – too old, too big, too matriarchal – but the Party hierarchy were delighted at the budding relationship, for it seemed a perfect match: the man born to be king and the woman bearing one of the greatest names in the land, a match that would add an aura of legitimacy and glory to the excitement of revolutionary power. To those who saw them together they looked like a couple – 'Winni and Wolf', as they were popularly known – and they seemed to complement each other and treat each other as equals.

In a hitherto secret statement made to American military counter intelligence (CIC) shortly after the end of the war in Europe, Winifred Wagner was quite clear (and unapologetic) about her early relationship with Adolf Hitler. 'My relations to Adolf Hitler,' she declared, 'depended on personal esteem and friendship and were chiefly founded on a veneration for the genius of Richard Wagner. Political matters were hardly ever discussed between us.' Personal matters likewise – or so it would seem.

At Christmas and New Year and on their birthdays they exchanged written greetings. To Adolf, Winifred was always 'Meine verehrte und liebe Wini' – My esteemed and beloved Wini!' His letters were respectful, admiring, confiding and close (though not intimate). Early in the New Year of 1933, for example, when he was on the brink of supreme power, he wrote from the Nazi Party headquarters in Munich:

'My adored and much loved Wini!

For weeks I have been stuck in hard and difficult work. Worry after worry . . .

But I believe that the time is surely coming when I can give proof of my thankful attachment to you in deeds rather than words. Unfortunately there are always new mountains to climb – the endless struggle against hate, envy and stupidity. They are the same causes for concern, worries and cares . . .

Once again my thanks and truest greetings, good fortune and blessings.

Your AH Wolf'

The rest, as they might say, would be history.

Winifred was not at first opposed to the idea of marriage with the man she called 'Wolf' and her children called 'uncle'. But nothing concrete ever transpired. Marriage was never on Hitler's agenda and before long it was not on Winifred's either. Eventually the reason became known to a handful of confidants. Winifred Wagner breathed word that in matters of sex Hitler was unconventional. He could be soft and gentle one minute and 'like a beast' the next. Hitler was beyond her control, she believed, and she was afraid. As for Hitler, though he never seems to have contemplated marriage to Winifred, he stayed on good terms with her and continued to visit Bayreuth every summer for the Festival, latterly accompanied by another close friend by the name of Eva Braun. And years later, after the war, Winifred gave her honest (if politically incorrect) view of the man. 'He was a good friend,' she recalled, 'someone you'd like to have as a guest. To us he was not the Führer, just a fascinating and talented person.' And she added, 'If Hitler came through the door today I'd be just as happy to see him as I was then.'

The second Englishwoman to be involved with Hitler – and perhaps the most serious rival to Eva among these English challengers – was the woman she had correctly identified as the Walkure, 'who looks the part, including the legs'. Her name was the Honourable Unity Valkyrie Freeman Mitford, one of six daughters of Baron Redesdale, a retired general and peer of the realm, who hated all foreigners, especially the 'Huns'. Although they were all members of the English Establishment they could hardly all be described as conventional. True, one daughter married a diplomat, another an Oxford don, and a third the son of a duke, but Diana (the eldest), after divorcing the multi-millionaire head of the Guinness family, became a Fascist and then married Sir Oswald Moseley (the leader of the British Union of Fascists), Jessica became a Communist, and Unity (who knew Churchill and had been presented to the King) became a Nazi and decamped to Hitler's Germany (much to the disgust of her family and many of her fellow-countrymen).

As Eva Braun knew full well to her cost, it took Unity no time at all to track down Adolf Hitler to his favourite restaurant, the Osteria Bavaria in Munich, and it was there during Eva's troubled spring of 1935 that the Führer first met his 'Walkure'. Golden haired, satin complexioned and blue eyed, long legged, narrow hipped and flat chested, six feet tall and twenty-one years of age, she was more the Führer's type than Mrs Wagner could ever be, and his attention was soon drawn to the fixed and dreamy stare she unblinkingly beamed at him day after day from the next table in the Osteria. Eventually she was invited to join his party and make herself known. Hitler was intrigued. This was not your average provincial Fräulein. This was an English milady with a mind of her own, a Nazi sympathizer with pro-German sentiments, and pretty and intelligent with it. As for Unity, she was in thrall to the man and wrote home to her sister on 30 December 1935:

You've no idea how sweet the Führer was yesterday. I love him more and more each time, though it doesn't seem possible to love him any more than I always did . . . Heil Hitler!

Albert Speer, who met her at the Osteria at this time, was to recall:

She was highly in love with Hitler, we could see it easily, her face brightened up, her eyes gleaming, staring at Hitler. Hero-worship. Absolutely phenomenal. And possibly Hitler liked to be admired by a young woman, she was quite attractive – even if nothing happened he was excited by the possibility of a love affair with her. Towards an attractive woman he behaved as a seventeen-year-old would . . . She was never bored and never boring. Her features were those of a woman with some intelligence, thinking in her own way, not the Eva Braun type who had no serious interests.

As for Hitler, he was beside himself with enthusiasm at this paragon who had seemingly fallen to earth so fortuitously in the vicinity of the Osteria Bavaria. 'Only English girls have such complexions,' he mooned. 'It must be the English rain, the walks in the English rain that produce this skin.' From now on she was his 'Lady Mitford' (not a correct title), and she would prove the most serious rival in Eva Braun's quest for the heart and soul, let alone the body, of her beloved of a lifetime, Adolf Hitler.

Before long Unity would be seen everywhere at the Führer's side, a privilege Eva Braun could only aspire to. Unity was not only with him in Munich but in Berlin too, as Bella Fromm, a socialite and columnist for a German newspaper, duly recorded:

September 16, 1937:

I got the usual news of the Nuremberg Party Congress. Unity Mitford, in her usual ecstasy, dogged Hitler's heels, as last year and the year before, the party badge tossing stormily on her heaving sweater.

Unity is heartily unpopular with most Nazis. Ribbentrop dislikes her. Hess is jealous and suspicious. But Hitler seems to like her, and that's all anyone needs around here. Evi Braun, former assistant to Hitler's 'court photographer', Heinrich Hoffmann, has given Unity some rather bitter moments. She is terrified that Evi might make headway into the sanctified heart of Adolf.

Unity did not just make it to Berlin, but to Berchtesgaden also – and before that Bayreuth. And it was in Bayreuth, at the home of the other close lady of his life, Winifred Wagner, the English-born daughter-in-law of the immortal Richard, that the absolute truth about Hitler's love life was finally – though only very many years later – revealed.

For several years in the 1930s, Unity Mitford had been attending the annual Bayreuth Festival, a public programme of Richard Wagner's operas, wholly organized by his daughter-in-law, Winifred. Hitler also attended the Festival, usually as Winifred's guest in the Wagner home, Haus Wahnfried, latterly in the company of Eva Braun. At the 1936 Festival the three coincided. Aware that it might make for a happier week if Eva and Unity were kept apart as far as possible, Unity was accommodated in the main house, and Eva and Hitler in the guest annex.

As it happened, on the sixth night of the Festival, Hitler and Unity decided to take a walk through the gardens of the Haus Wahnfried. It was a lovely, balmy, moonlit night and the two of them eventually found themselves approaching the annex veranda. It was there that Winifred Wagner's French maid, Monita Garnier, came across them. According to testimony she provided in 1970, when she was tracked down to the small hotel in London where she was now living, they were on the couch. The maid had heard a few strange rumours about Hitler's sex life, and his difficulty in having normal sexual relations with a woman, but from what she could see going on in front of her these rumours would seem to be wide of the mark. As she stood there wondering what to do, she heard footsteps approaching and to her dismay saw Eva Braun walking towards the veranda. Suddenly Eva stopped dead in her tracks, staring intently at the couple for a whole minute, before turning on her heels and disappearing into the darkness. In view of the potential rumpus that might descend upon the Haus Wahnfried, the Bayreuth Festival and the Third Reich, Monita immediately reported all the circumstances to her employer, who replied: 'We won't mention this to anyone, will we?'

The Mountain Palace

Eva, too, kept the peace. She was playing a long, painful, sometimes hopeless game, and it would take a world war to resolve it to her ultimate advantage. Meanwhile, following Eva's second suicide attempt, Hitler had begun to go through a sea change in his attitude to her. A second suicide attempt was truly a *cri de cœur*, an emphatic indicator that something was fundamentally wrong, above all a blinding realization on Hitler's part that here was a human being who loved him dearly and that if she went he would miss her profoundly.

His first act of contrition was to find her somewhere more fitting to live: first an apartment of her own in the quiet Bogenhausen district, a nice part of town not far from his own home, and then in the following spring of 1936 a modest but pleasant little two-storey villa at 12 Wasserburgerstrasse in the same area on the edge of Munich, into which Eva moved, along with her dogs and her sister Gretl. It was not exactly a love nest, more a gilded cage, for Hitler rarely visited the place and certainly never stayed the night. But Eva, overjoyed to be free of the claustrophobic and disapproving atmosphere of the parental home, loved the place and called it my 'my dear little Braunhaus'. Here she lived happily incognito, with her own Mercedes, a salary of 450 marks a month for life, a phone, a television set (one of the first in Germany) and unusually for peacetime (but perhaps not unexpectedly, knowing who her friend was) her own bunker, designed by Hitler himself, complete with air pump, electricity generator, armoured door, medical supplies, emergency exit, radio, telephone and provisions galore.

Hitler's second move was to raise Eva's status. This was a gradual process, but though she was never seen in Munich society, she did, over a period of time, move up from ex-shop girl and 'pretty woman' to the gracious lady who eventually was to preside over Hitler's own private social circle. Now and then she was even invited to stay at Haus Wachenfeld, Hitler's large Alpine chalet at Obersalzberg, which he had first rented and then purchased out of the royalties from his political testament *Mein Kampf*, part of which had been written there. His half-sister, Angela Raubal – the dead Geli's mother – was the housekeeper of the place, and she took a strong dislike to Eva Braun when she came to stay, feeling that through her Hitler had betrayed her daughter's memory. *'Die Blöde Kuh'* is what she called Eva behind her back – the bloody cow – 'the disgraceful blonde' who ran after the Chancellor and was worse than a common streetwalker. But when, early in 1936, Hitler decided to convert his modest chalet into a mountain palace fit for a Führer, he dismissed his half-sister and bit by bit installed his girlfriend as his unofficial consort in his imposing new residence, now called the Berghof. From now until the final days of Hitler's reign, this is where she would spend some two-thirds of the rest of her life.

In the opinion of Albert Speer, the young architect whom Hitler enlisted to help transform the modest mountain chalet called Haus Wachenfeld into the grandiose Berghof, or Mountain Palace, Eva Braun was essentially a simple woman with petit-bourgeois tastes. 'She had no interest in politics and never attempted to influence Adolf Hitler,' he recalled. A sports lover and a good skier, she often went off with Speer and his wife on ski trips in the surrounding mountains, once for a whole week to Zurs, where she danced with great passion into the early hours with young army officers. She was, Speer noted, 'rather small and delicate of build' – not at all Hitler's type, for he preferred tall, full-figured women. 'Out of sympathy for her predicament,' Speer was to recall, 'I soon began to feel a liking for this unhappy woman, who was so deeply attached to Hitler.' But in his way Hitler was attached to her too, at least he saw his long-term future as involving her. Sometimes at table he would talk about when he retired from politics he would go and live in Linz. 'Aside from Fräulein Braun, I'll take no one with me,' he would say. 'Fräulein Braun and my dog. I'll be lonely. For why should anyone voluntarily stay with me for any length of time?' Later, however, as affairs of state and deteriorating health took over, he foresaw a different future and once told Eva Braun, 'I'll soon have to give you your freedom. Why should you be tied to an old man?' But in general he seldom revealed his feelings. 'If he did so,' Speer noted, 'he instantly locked them away again.'

Even towards Eva Braun he was never completely relaxed and human, and though she never used for personal ends the power which lay within her grasp, Hitler always banished her to her room when ministers and generals turned up – though if she went out skiing and was late for tea Hitler would get worried and keep looking at his watch, desperately hoping she hadn't had an accident.

The Berghof was designed by Speer to Hitler's specifications to serve as both the official out-of-town residence and conference centre of the head of state, and the private out-of-town home of that same head of state and of his consort and guests. As such it was constructed on a scale of great grandeur out of materials of great value and furnished with immense opulence – all regardless of cost. The drawing room had a magnificent fireplace of green faience; the vast lounge had a gigantic window ('the biggest moveable window in the world,' Hitler claimed) looking out over a vast sweep of the Alps; the dining room had a round table big enough to seat twenty-four guests in armchairs round it; the gothic-style great hall (where movies on occasion could be shown) was draped with priceless tapestries, and a huge corridor on the first floor, as impressive as the great hall downstairs, but silent as a tomb, had doors that led to the private apartments of Hitler and Eva Braun. Eva's room had walls hung with silk, a portrait of Hitler on one wall and a naked woman (whom some thought might have been Eva herself) on the wall opposite. Hitler's room was simple, almost spartan, with only a camp bed to sleep on, but a magnificent balcony from which to watch the stars at night. Joining the two bedrooms was a huge bathroom with a resplendent marble bath, and further down the corridor Hitler's spacious studio.

In support of this palatial complex were the support areas — the Chancellery offices, the quarters for aides, secretaries and other staff, the extensive modern kitchen and pantries, the medical and dental surgeries, the store rooms and underground passages. Though it was a supremely comfortable place in terms of facilities, it was less so in terms of atmosphere — at least to some of those who lived and worked there. Traudl Junge, for example, a young woman some eight years younger than Eva Braun who was one of Hitler's most trusted secretaries, never quite felt at ease there. 'The place had a strange, indefinable quality,' she was to admit later, 'that put you on your guard and filled you with odd apprehensions.'

The grandeur and remoteness of the Mountain Palace — the very awesomeness of its reputation as the Führer's alternative centre of absolute power outside Berlin — led to much speculation on the part of the local populace, and many rumours and wild fantasies about both the place and its chief denizen, Adolf Hitler. Some of these fantasies (along with a number of valuable insights) were collated in a book published in London in 1939 under the title *I Was Hitler's Maid* by a certain Pauline Kohler, one of the housemaids at the Berghof — or so the book claimed — who was later supposed to have fled Germany, first to France and then Brazil. The authors were unable to trace a Pauline Kohler who had worked at the Berghof, but the author of *I was Hitler's Maid* appears to have had access not only to the rumours and the gossip — the below-stairs kitchen-table gossip and speculation about the kind of things a servant around the place might see that the Generals and Ministers might not — but also a more intimate and insightful picture of the Führer that would normally be beyond the range of a junior housemaid at all. So in her intriguing and often amusing 1939 account of Berghof life – written, it was claimed, in exile – she was to slip effortlessly from the uniquely insightful to the sometimes apparently fantastical without a step in between.

For example, she might claim that Hitler's vast lounge – the room with the gigantic windows, 'the biggest in Germany' – also housed Hitler's aviary of rare birds, as well as three parrots that would repeat ad infinitum 'I am the Führer! I am the Führer!'

'One day I counted them,' she was to write. 'There are seventy-eight – all chattering and screaming at the same time. The only time I saw Hitler display any normal kindness and humanity was towards these birds. He always fed them himself. The death of one of them brought tears to his eyes. Its little corpse was buried in a small plot of ground with a tiny headstone of bronze placed on the grave.'

More than that, right at the top of the Berghof, or so Fräulein Kohler claimed, there was a suite of rooms like a cross between a penthouse and an observatory where Hitler's astrologer, Karl Ossietz – 'a slim, dark man of thirty-five, the Rasputin of Germany, perhaps the most important man in the Third Reich outside Hitler himself' – foretold the future from his study of the stars and the planets. (Eva Braun's sister, Ilse, confirmed Hitler's obsession with astrology, once observing him during an evening at the Berghof when he poured molten lead into a basin of cold water and endeavoured to interpret his future by the shapes the lead formed.)

Additionally, Kohler related – and this could well be true – Hitler had three doubles who were indistinguishable from the Führer at a distance of twenty yards – one at Berchtesgaden (who worked under the code-name of 'Little Willy' and was a great ping-pong player), and two others in Munich and Berlin (and indeed a Hitler look-alike was found by the Red Army in a dustbin at the Reichschancellery with a bullet in his head following the fall of Berlin in 1945).

Above all, Kohler was to relate, Berghof life was remarkable for its sexually fetid atmosphere:

> I suppose the virtual imprisonment of the staff at Berchtesgaden had the effect of creating a desire for the opposite sex, as real imprisonment does. One reason I was glad to leave Berchtesgaden was to escape from the feverish morbidity of its atmosphere – largely caused by these strange love-affairs. They cast over it the atmosphere of an expensive brothel. There was nothing clean and natural about it. A fog of unclean sex hung over the place. [To be accurate, she was talking about the complex as a whole, SS and staff quarters included, and not just Hitler's residency.]

By way of example, Pauline Kohler – putting one and two together and making four – recalled a memorable blue film that was shown at the Berghof – memorable not least because the lead part was played by another girlfriend of the Führer by the name of Jenny Jugo. A small, very pretty brunette who hailed from a poor peasant family in Bavaria, Jenny Jugo was now a rising star in Berlin. For a few months of 1937 she was also one of Hitler's temporary inamorata, and in that short time – according to wildly speculative and exaggerated gossip – he spent a fortune on the girl, including a diamond bracelet, a mink coat, a villa in a village near Wiesbaden, two motor-cars, three horses and one four-seater plane, as well as the usual perfume, flowers, lingerie and other luxuries. According to Pauline Kohler, she was living proof that the Führer could be normally sexed at times. 'All the tales that say Hitler is impotent are lies,' she was to relate. 'He is not strongly sexed, and his fondness for women is often only platonic. But I once heard him say to Göring, "I know what women are for just as well as you do, Hermann."'

Sexy and curvaceous, Jenny was also wilful and mischievous, it seems – she once served Göring a rubber sausage on his plate, or so Kohler claims – and if Hitler was in a bad mood she would refuse to come down to meals at the Berghof. But she was also extremely obliging, in a rather outré kind of way. In a room at the Berghof, so it was claimed later, a studio with a small stage was fitted up at one end. On this stage Jenny used to perform. Her performance was filmed and then later projected on Hitler's private screen in the downstairs bowling alley at the Berghof (to which, as Hitler's secretary Traudl Junge was to confirm, members of the Berghof staff could also be invited). At Christmas after the staff dinner a select few were taken into the cinema room to watch one of these short films starring Jenny. It turned out to be a strip-tease act, though Hitler claimed it was art. According to Pauline Kohler the action proceeded as follows:

> Fräulein Jugo entered a luxuriously appointed bedroom. She was wearing a tweed suit. She yawned and stretched her arms high above her head, then slowly took off her jacket and dropped it over the back of a chair. Then her skirt dropped to her ankles. The men in the audience sat forward in their chairs. This was getting interesting. Her blouse came off next. Taut

stockings were drawn high above her knees, leaving an inch or two of gleaming white flesh before her thighs disappeared into short, skin-tight panties. Her ripe young breasts strained within the confines of an open network brassiere.

With her back to the camera she stooped and took off her shoes and stockings. Her brassiere slipped to the floor and with a good deal of seductive pantomime her panties followed. She turned round and faced the camera completely naked.

Then, for ten minutes before getting into bed, she did various exercises. I am sorry I cannot describe them. They threw a terrible light on the perversity of Hitler's sexual desires, and on the mind of the woman willing to enact such obscenities.

Ernst Hanfstaengl and other erstwhile associates of Hitler have confirmed that Hitler greatly enjoyed watching lewd and pornographic movies in his private theatre, some of which were made by his personal photographer, Heinrich Hoffmann, for his pleasure. But in this instance it was Pauline Kohler's opinion that Hitler showed the Jenny Jugo film to them so as to display the charms of the woman he had conquered and thereby publicly proclaim his own virility. But Jenny Jugo was not destined to last. Why the affair ended was not clear, at least to the Berghof maid, but unusually there was no tragedy involved, Jenny simply packed her bags and left for her more usual routine as a movie starlet in Berlin.

'An Austrian psychologist who happened to be a good Nazi visited Berchtesgaden,' Pauline Kohler was to recall. 'He could not help studying the Führer as a patient. I know what his verdict was, for he told a Munich doctor who afterwards attended me.' According to Pauline Kohler, these were his words:

> The Führer is a great man, but that is not to say that he is sane. I admire his work for Germany, but I still have my beliefs as a doctor. If I were speaking of him as a patient, I should say he was an ego-maniac with a split personality. One side of his is brutal. The other is weak and sentimental. When this side predominates he needs the company of women. They flatter his ego, reassure him about his virility, and bolster up his pride. That, I am certain, is the only reason the Führer has affairs with women – not because he is really in love with them, but because he is madly in love with himself.

A profound insight indeed for a junior country maid barely out of her teens to concoct. In fact it sounds more like the mysterious Dr Krueger, the alleged author of *I Was Hitler's Doctor*, another puzzling memoir that was published in America only two years after the no less puzzling *I Was Hitler's Maid*. So who did write the book? One supposition – reasonable but almost impossible to prove – is that the true author was none other than Hitler's English-speaking and half-American former associate, press chief and subsequent opponent, Ernst Hanfstaengl.

I Was Hitler's Maid was published in London in 1939, by which time Hanfstaengl had fled Nazi Germany and emigrated to London, where he lived in a small flat in Kensington until the day after Britain declared war on Germany, at which point he was interned as an enemy alien in a bathing-hut on a draughty stretch of the coast at Seaton-on-the-Sea. Thence he was in due course transported across to North America and eventually appointed to a post as one of Roosevelt's political and psychological warfare advisors in the war against Hitler's Germany.

'A young cock and a hen'

The Berghof itself was only part of the Nazi establishment at Obersalzberg. Göring, Speer, Ribbentrop, Bormann and Goebbels also had homes here or hereabouts, and there was luxury accommodation for visiting heads of state such as the British Prime Minister, Neville Chamberlain, and the Italian Duce, Mussolini, along with a hotel for other visitors (including eventually Eva Braun's friends), spacious barracks for Hitler's SS honour guard, and eventually an extensive underground air-raid bunker complex, which Hitler could reach by lift straight from his bedroom. In short, the Obersalzberg served as an alternative state capital of the Third Reich, sealed off from the world at large, with the Berghof as its Alpine Chancellery.

At first there was never any public hint of a special relationship or any overt physical affection between Eva and Hitler at this rural Chancellery. She was never invited to formal or state occasions, when she had to take her meals alone in her room. Even during informal gatherings at the Berghof, Eva remained Hitler's secret mistress and was required always to address her lover as 'Mein Führer', while she herself was always just plain 'Fräulein Braun'. At Hitler's birthday reception she was introduced simply as 'a loyal employee of the Führer' or 'the Führer's private secretary' or 'the housekeeper of the Berghof'. She was a taboo subject. As her cousin Gertraud Weisker was to recall: 'She was just an appendage who had to be tolerated. She was neither a lady of the house nor a housekeeper. But she never grumbled. She just accepted it like everything else.'

But gradually Hitler's own attitude and manner towards her in private and on informal social occasions began to change completely. Expensive jewellery, clothes and other luxuries were lavished on Eva by her exalted but increasingly pre-occupied lover. A young housemaid at the Berghof by the name of Antonia Sternig estimated that Eva owned around 500 dresses, a considerable number of fur coats and shoes, and 'generally the best of everything'. She also had two other chambermaids, one of whom, Liesl Ostertag, was her Special Chambermaid and used to accompany her on her visits to Berlin, while another was exclusively responsible for feeding her two little black dogs, Negus and Stassy. It helped Eva's rising status that her best friend, Herta Schneider, married a certain General Schneider, and before long both were visiting the Berghof as Eva's and Adolf's honoured guests. Before long, too, the SS honour guards were required to present arms to Eva, and in turn the Führer himself became totally charming towards her.

'The way Eva and the Führer are carrying on is sickening,' Hermann Fegelein, the dashing SS officer who would one day become her brother-in-law, was to complain later after having tea with them at the Berghof. 'They act as if they were a young cock and a hen.' Hitler was always very affectionate towards her now if they were in a small, informal gathering. He would pat her hand and call her 'my *Patscherl,* my pet, my honey-bun'. He was always urging her to eat this or that. 'Now my *Patscherl,*' he would say, 'eat this little morsel, it's good for you.' Sometimes he also called her '*Schnaksi*' (an Austrian term of endearment) or increasingly 'Effie'.

The staff at the Berghof, aware of her elevation in status, began to refer to her as '*Die Chefin*' – the female equivalent of '*Der Chef*', the Boss. Not all of them liked her. Mainly it was women who didn't.

'I made it my business to study this woman,' Fräulein Kohler was to relate, 'as for a considerable time we all thought she was to be the Führer's wife. Anyhow, here is what she is like:

> She is about five feet four inches tall. Her lips are full and red. She is plump, with a well-developed figure. Her voice is soft, but she has a slight impediment in her speech. It is something between a slight lisp and a stammer. She sometimes sounds as if she is a foreigner speaking German with a slight accent.
>
> I saw a good deal of her. I did not like her. She is a permanency at Berchtesgaden. She does what she likes, goes where she likes, says what she likes – un-questioned. And that is about all I know.

The men saw her differently. Several of the young SS officers at the Obersalzberg were reported to have become obsessed with her, and one – a certain Sigmund Breuer, who had known her since the days she worked in Hoffmann's photographic studio in Munich – is alleged to have jumped to his death from the Kehlstein when Eva rejected him.

Though Hitler saw other women from time to time, in-creasingly he came to recognize that Eva was his woman, the one he came home to, relaxed with, billed and cooed with, listened to Wagner and 'Who's Afraid of the Big Bad Wolf' on the gramophone with, laughed with, slept with (or, more often, near), and became human with, in so far as that was possible.

Though Eva Braun was aware of Hitler's interest in other women and often deeply distressed by it, it seemed her new and unique position at the Berghof was never seriously threatened now. Little by little Hitler was becoming dependent on her – at least in that tiny enclave of his life that could be called his private life. At first she was simply someone to switch off with. She was considerate, attentive, unchallenging, and crucially – by and large – human in all the normal ways. She was a fresh, simple, generally cheerful, usually unproblematic girl, warm hearted, rather empty headed – definitely not an intellectual (though neither stupid nor uneducated) – she did not overstep the mark; she did not trouble Hitler with thoughts or doubts; she left politics to others, did not bother herself (or him) with concerns about matters of state; she liked to chatter on about things that interested her – clothes, jewellery, film stars, popular music – and it all passed over his head like a balm. 'She keeps my mind off other things,' Hitler once told a former housekeeper, 'which is a rest for me sometimes.'

Her physical presence was a comfort to him, her devotion and trust a constant reassurance in an unsure world. She was the perfect opposite that complemented the other partner. She was the perfect partner in every respect but one – she did not look like or sound like or think like or behave like an appropriate future wife and lady, and grande dame of the almighty Führer of the Third Reich. 'I am the mistress of the greatest man in Germany and the world,' she would exclaim. But she was no Frau Göring, living in her viceregal palace at Karinhall; she was no Frau Goebbels with a mind of her own; she was not even a

Frau Bormann, bearing babies year in year out for the sake of the Fatherland. As things stood, she was just a mistress, and a mistress, it seemed, she would remain.

Hitler's secretary, Traudl Junge, recalled:

> Eva Braun was a woman who enjoyed life, loved to love, loved to laugh, loved beautiful things. I can really say she loved life. She was not the standardised National Socialist woman. She was only Hitler's follower because of his personality and only interested in him as a man.

Traudl Junge vividly recalled how Eva was the first time she met her at the Berghof – very well groomed, with tinted blonde hair and tastefully made-up face, very well dressed, with Nile-green wool dress, close fitting and low cut with two gold clips that accented the cleavage of her breasts. She was very possessed, Traudl noticed, had a striking openness and naturalness, a very pretty face, a wonderful figure, and a graceful walk that made her leopard-fur fringed skirt swish. Hitler very respectfully addressed her as *'gnädiges Fräulein'* but liked to complain that her pet dogs were 'hand-lickers' and teasingly remonstrate with her about her figure. 'When I first met her,' he would say, 'she was nice and plump like a good German girl should be. But now she is slim and skinny!'

For Hitler, Eva Braun was his refuge from all the burdens of absolute rule – from solitude, treachery, boredom, nightmare, himself, above all the sheer weight of the pressures of state. For Eva Braun, Hitler was her refuge from obscurity, ordinariness, impecuniousness, meaninglessness, nothingness, life without a desirable goal or future. He gave her life, she gave him peace, and a chance to be happy now and then, even human in any normal sense – and yes, in their different ways, they both gave each other love. Previously Hitler had never envisaged marriage with Eva. 'I will never marry her,' he told his adjutant, Julius Schaub. 'I haven't got the time. I am always away and cannot behave to a wife as a married man should. But I am very fond of her.'

But in time all this changed. For both of them a future paradise was not palaces and parades and glittering banquets but a quiet, private sort of life together in a pleasant house in Hitler's provincial home town of Linz, far from the devious and secretive politics of ministers and the pomp and circumstance of rule. 'Eva and I will be married,' Hitler used to muse about his autumnal years, 'and we will live in a beautiful house in Linz, and I promise you, there won't be a single uniform there, nothing to remind one of the war.'

At first Eva had been overwhelmed by the sudden prestige and glamour of it all, but as her status rose and Hitler's inner circle began to show more respect, her self-confidence soared to a point where she could talk to the Führer on equal terms – or even banter with him, as in this table talk repartee at the Berghof:

EVA (to Hitler): Sit up straight! You're stooping like an old man!

HITLER (defensively): I've got some heavy keys in my pocket – and then don't forget I'm lugging a whole sackful of worries about with me . . . Like this we're better matched, Tschapperl. You put on high heels to make yourself taller, while I stoop to make myself smaller, and that way we go well together.

EVA (indignantly): I'm not small. I'm one metre sixty-three, like Napoleon.

HITLER (impressed): Why Napoleon? You know how tall he was? How do you know?

EVA: Every educated person knows that. I learned it at the convent.

Exit Hitler to fetch an encyclopaedia.

Or again:

HITLER: he starts whistling 'The Donkey Serenade'

EVA: That's wrong!

HITLER: It's not.

EVA: It is.

To settle the argument, Eva puts a record of 'The Donkey Serenade' on the gramophone.

EVA: You see – you're wrong!

HITLER: You witch – it's the composer that's wrong!

Everyone laughs except Hitler. There was not another human being left alive in the kingdom of the Third Reich who could get away with that sort of thing except Eva Braun.

In the beginning, when she first moved in to the Berghof as a permanent resident in 1936, Eva had been allowed to sit on Hitler's left when he threw a private lunch, but was required to eat alone in her room whenever there was a big reception or formal dinner. She was also obliged to live by Hitler's own stringent rules: no smoking, no dancing, no sunbathing. But gradually her position of anonymity was relaxed. Before long they were travelling together to other cities in Germany, where she was given money (enough to buy a different dress for every meal of every day of the year) and allowed to go dancing while Hitler looked benignly on. Eventually she even went abroad with Hitler, on a State visit to Italy, where she was judged the loveliest of all the women in the Nazi entourage, given salutes normally reserved for the highest dignitaries, shopped like a maniac and danced the nights through. Her parents, too – including her father, who was almost foolhardily opposed to Hitler and all he stood for, his relationship with his daughter included, and was for ever the one man in the world Hitler dared not confront or overrule – were made welcome on visits to the Berghof. 'But she was deeply in love with Hitler,' her mother was to recall years later.

By the summer of 1938 it was evident that there was now only one woman in Hitler's life, for in May he wrote out his will, in which he provided Eva Braun with a small monthly allowance for the rest of her life in the event of his death. At the same time, having established her right of abode in his Alpine headquarters at Berchtesgaden, he took steps to provide her with accommodation in the old part of the New Reich Chancellery, still under construction in Berlin, though it was not till early in 1939 that she was finally able to move in.

Eva's apartment had once been the bedroom of Hitler's predecessor, President Hindenburg, and boasted a huge fireplace, a portrait of Bismarck, and a big window permanently covered with heavy curtains, as though hiding a State secret from public curiosity. But though the 27-year-old Munich woman was now installed close to the heart of power in the Third Reich – her bedroom was actually next to Hitler's – her true position remained carefully concealed and she was even more isolated than at the Obersalzberg. Officially she was classified as a secretary. She could only reach her apartment via the servants' entrance and a rear staircase, had to take her meals in her room, and was almost never seen in Hitler's presence in the grand official part of the New Chancellery building. Nor was she ever invited to the glittering receptions and the grand balls of the high season in Berlin. If she complained, Hitler would tell her, 'Effie, you are not made for such society life – you're like a flower, and the outside world is a dung heap.' To anyone within earshot, Hitler included, Eva would complain loud and long, *'Ich bin Fräulein Kein Privatleben.'* (I am Miss-No-Private-Life.) She was out of luck too, it seemed, when during one of her early insinuations into public life at the Berlin Chancellery she came a cropper, as her special assistant, Liesl Ostertag, was to relate to a friend:

> It was one of Eva's visits to the Berlin Chancellery. She entered through the private door which leads into a great hall with highly polished parquet flooring. This hall ends in a large door leading to Hitler's private apartments. On either side of the door, facing it, stand two burly bodyguards in immaculate uniform. They stand rigidly to attention for three-hour shifts, and are more like statues than men.
>
> Eva, proud at having lunch with Germany's supreme ruler, walked across the hall, head held high. A little too high, for just as she was approaching the open door flanked by the bodyguards, her heel

slipped on the polished floor. She flung her hands out and managed to grab the trouser-seat of the right-hand guard. For a second he remained motionless, but as Eva's feet slid from under her and her clutch on him tightened they both crashed on the floor together. A second later Hitler appeared in the doorway just in time to see the flurry of Eva's legs as she struggled to scramble to her feet with her skirt almost up to her hips, while the guard found himself with his nose buried in her neck.

By way of compensation for her ambiguous situation at the Führer's court, Eva went shopping in Berlin on a grand scale, driven from one expensive store to another in a big Mercedes chauffeured by a classic blond Aryan SS man. The wives of the Nazi bigwigs in Berlin were a dull lot on the whole and Eva was like a movie star in their midst. Her shoes came from Italy, her underwear from Paris, her sports clothes from Vienna, her dresses from the best costumiers in Berlin. The bills, which were considerable, went straight to Party Secretary Martin Bormann, though sometimes, so it was said, Hitler settled them with cash out of his own pocket.

By the outbreak of war, Eva was not only the mistress of Berchtesgaden in her own right but an honoured guest in the Chancellery in Berlin at the very heart of the Third Reich, which in time was to stretch from the English Channel almost to the very gates of Moscow. She was no longer a mere girl but had become a mature woman of poise and stature, elegant and charming and self-assured, outclassing all other women at the Berghof, and beautiful enough to pose in the nude for one of the Third Reich's most acclaimed sculptors,

Arno Becker – very possibly the statue that was later put on public exhibition under the title 'Ammut' (Grace) at the House of German Art in Munich. Hitler's secretary, Traudl Junge, recalled:

> She was not a model from the pages of a fashion magazine and still less the personification of Nazi womanhood exalted in the Nuremberg parades. Her elegance was not a reflection of opulence but rather of good taste and discretion. She tinted her naturally fair hair to make it more golden, and she made herself up heavily, especially in our eyes, for we didn't even use lipstick then – it was considered unwomanly, un-Germanic. Her makeup was cleverly applied, though, and heightened her beauty. She moved gracefully – what a contrast to the other ladies of the hierarchy, who were elephantine in their gait! She must have stacks of dresses and shoes. I never saw her wear the same outfit twice.

In addition to collecting shoes – fashionable high-heeled shoes, which Hitler hated – Eva collected gloves, of which she had a fantastic number. Her more intimate clothing included the following preferences: silk petticoats with matching silk brassieres and panties (flower pattern for choice) – she loathed woollen, cotton or lace underwear – silk suspender belts (never corsets), and silk nightgowns, preferably short.

Eva's favourite perfume, it seems, was Worth's 'Air Bleu', she took a bath twice daily, had her hair done once a day ('She was a perfectionist,' her wave-setter, who was married to Hitler's barber, recalled, 'but her tips seemed to me rather meagre'), and (unusually for a German woman of her time) regularly shaved off any superfluous hair. As for her jewellery, which she adored, her collection was vast and included rings, bracelets, brooches, necklaces, pendants, earrings and watches, of gold and diamond and silver and emerald and ruby and sapphire and beryl – the list was endless.

By comparison with Eva, the bourgeois girl turned princess manquée, Hitler, a peasant boy turned ruler of Europe, was much more modest in both dress and private habits. He wore woollen underwear in the winter and a nightshirt at night. He only had one bath a day and had his hair cut at midnight. He always dressed himself and hated any minion touching him, not even his tailor, who had to measure his uniforms by guesswork. His one luxury in this area of his life was to change his shirt when he felt like it, which was often. His long list of class-one hates included alcohol, boats, radios, meat, smoking, and hunting, and in addition he had an extensive repertoire of class-two dislikes, including horses, cats, tortoises and baby chicks. On the other hand he had a passion for his Alsatian dogs – Bella, Muck and above all Blondi – and both he and Eva loved children. But while Hitler's favourite popular tune was 'The Donkey Serenade', Eva's was 'Tea for Two'. So it goes.

This, then, was the couple (of a kind) who stood at the heart (or near it) of the most brutal, murderous and perverted regime in the history of Europe and the world.

'A very avant-garde kind of position'

By the summer of 1940, with France overrun and the Battle of Britain about to begin, Eva Braun was supreme among the women at Hitler's court. Her own father, too, had undergone a sea change and emerged as a born-again Nazi and Hitler supporter. With paternal disapproval removed, Eva was free to invite her parents and sisters to stay at the Berghof, while Hitler himself, as relations with his lady became more tender and conjugal, would increasingly address her with colloquial endearments, such as *'Tschapperl'*, meaning 'little thing' or 'luvvy ducky', and also use the German singular for 'you' – *'du'* meaning 'thou' – as well as more cuddly variants of her first name, such as 'Effie' and 'Veverl' or 'Feferl'. But in spite of such intimacies Hitler was always strictly formal and 'gallant' in his physical behaviour towards his lady in public. He might stroke her hand in company, or kiss her hand with slightly ceremonious gentlemanliness when she came downstairs in the morning. If he happened to need to knock at her door – ignoring the fact that he had direct and private access to her room from his own, at least at the Berghof – he would always discreetly enquire, 'Fräulein Effie, are you dressed and fit to be seen?'

The overriding question – then even more than now – had to do with the sexual nature of their relationship. Did they sleep together (literally), and if they did, then did they have sex together, and if they did, was this within what might be called the normal bounds of male-female sex? Hitler never ever spoke about such matters, and Eva, born of a polite bourgeois family and convent educated, was generally very tight-lipped on the subject, even with her sisters or her mother.

Given the rumours and some of the known facts concerning Hitler's earlier relationships with various women, from Geli Raubal to Renate Müller, there were many – the vast majority of them outsiders with little insight or knowledge – who speculated that the answers to one or all of these question was probably 'no'. There were others, too, in Hitler's inner court, whose instinct told them that whatever this relationship might be – a love match, maybe, a meeting of souls of a kind – it was not an overtly sexual one. Heinrich Hoffmann, who had known them both from the day they first met, was adamant: 'I believe Hitler's relationship with Eva Braun was strictly platonic.' Pauline Kohler, the alleged maid at the Berghof with a keen ear for household gossip, believed the relationship only became platonic later. Allegedly Eva herself once confided to her hairdresser that she and Hitler had never had sex, but though the hairdresser later claimed she had repeated this under oath to a Munich attorney, the attorney subsequently (after the war) denied he had ever heard such a thing.

It seems likely that there was sex between the two, but no less undoubtedly, increasingly less of it, for Hitler was not young, he was not fit, and – given he had a totalitarian state and eventually a continent-wide war to run – he did not have much time and was increasingly away. But the fact remains that from about February 1932, for better or worse, Eva Braun was Hitler's only permanent mistress, and though he might dally elsewhere from time to time (or want to and try to) she was the only woman he always came home to, for the rest of both their lives.

There remained, moreover, a tiny band of intimates who were privileged enough to be privy to the probable truth, or at least as well informed as anyone was ever going to be. Ten of these intimates – Hitler's personal valet, his adjutants, his doctor, his favourite secretary, his finest commando leader, his best friend, Eva's best friend and a woman close to the couple who has chosen to remain anonymous, as well as Eva herself – have all averred in their different ways that the relationship between the

Führer of the Third Reich and his young girl friend was 'normal'.

The valet was Heinz Linge, who had access to Hitler's bedroom and was free to prowl around the Führer's private sanctum. After the war he confirmed that as far as he could tell the relationship was normal. One morning, he recalled, he inadvertently entered Hitler's bedroom in his Chancellery apartment without knocking and was astounded to observe Eva and Adolf in bed together in what he obscurely but suggestively described as 'a very avant-garde kind of position'.

On another occasion, Hitler's personal adjutant, Julius Schaub, reporting for duty ahead of time, happened to notice a rather touching sight – Hitler's big boots and Eva's dainty shoes side by side outside the Führer's bedroom door, waiting for the morning shoeshine. Likewise his SS and Luftwaffe adjutants, Otto Günsche and Nicolaus von Below, years later indicated to historian David Irving that though the sexual relationship between the two was infrequent, it was normal, both of them confirming they had specific reasons for this belief, though tact constrained what they were prepared to divulge.

Another definitive piece of evidence came from Hitler's personal physician, Dr Morell, who in 1945, after the war was over, stated in a letter to the United States Commission which was investigating him that Hitler absolutely certainly had sexual intercourse with Eva Braun. Morell also confided to one of his patients, Dr Paul Karl Schmidt, that while on domiciliary visits to the Führer he was often asked by Eva Braun to prescribe drugs that could increase Hitler's libido.

The favourite secretary was Traudl Junge, who had a close and intimate knowledge of both of the partners in question, and never questioned the normalcy of it. It was tacitly understood by everyone, she recalled, that Eva Braun was the 'mistress of the Berghof.'

The commando leader was Otto Skorzeny, who was to win worldwide fame in the war for his rescue of the Italian dictator Mussolini from the Italian partisans, and who in an interview with an American investigator after the war recalled a conversation he had had with Eva Braun in which she admitted that he was not always conventional in his love-making. 'Sometimes he doesn't even take his boots off,' she told Skorzeny, 'and sometimes we don't get into the bed. We stretch out on the floor. On the floor he is very erotic.'

The friend was Hitler's architect and later Armaments Minister, Albert Speer, who stated that when he first met the couple way back before the modest Haus Wachenfeld was converted into the palatial Berghof, he had no reason to believe that the relationship was other than 'perfectly normal'. He explained:

> She was pleasant and fresh-faced rather than beautiful and had a modest air. There was nothing about her to suggest that she was a ruler's mistress: Eva Braun . . . I could only wonder at the way Hitler and Eva Braun avoided anything that might suggest an intimate relationship – only to go upstairs to the bedrooms together late at night.

For in those early years only Hitler and Eva Braun, plus a secretary and an adjutant, stayed in Hitler's small house – the rest had to put up in the local hostelry. 'It has always remained incomprehensible to me,' Speer was to ponder later, 'why this needless, forced practice of keeping their distance was continued even in this inner circle whose members could not help being aware of the truth.' For in those early years, Eva Braun kept her distance from every one of Hitler's intimates. Later, when Speer got to know her better, he realized that her reserved manner, which made her seem haughty, was actually embarrassment – 'she was well aware of her dubious position in Hitler's court.'

Eva's bosom friend, Herta Schneider, also confirmed in the 1980s that sex between Eva and Hitler was infrequent but normal. As for the 'anonymous woman' – this was very probably Eva's maid, Liesl Ostertag. She was captured at the end of the war and interrogated for thirteen months by US military intelligence in Spandau and Landsberg prisons, only disclosing what she knew more than twenty years after the war in a letter to Nerin Gun, an Italian-born German journalist and ex-inmate of Dachau concentration camp, who was then investigating the life and times of Hitler's lady on his own account. He was to record:

> According to this intimate source, sexual relations between Hitler and Eva Braun were perfectly normal. True, they were not of Latin intensity, but they could be defined as natural compared to those of any German couple. It must be borne in mind that Hitler was approaching fifty, that he was often away, and therefore separated from Eva for a large part of the time, that he worked at night and often returned to his rooms exhausted after councils of war or important governmental decisions. Theirs was no honeymoon situation. Eva was a submissive and loving woman, but she did not have a flaming sexual temperament. The ladies of the Braun family give the impression of being very

sober and reserved in this respect. When Eva confided to her friends, she spoke constantly of the anxiety that her lover's absence caused her, her desire to see him, of her worries and jealousies, but rarely of any sexual deprivation or expectation.

Liesl Ostertag was probably the same Berghof maid who went on record to say that she was convinced Eva and Hitler had sex because she took pills to repress her menstrual cycle whenever Hitler came to the Berghof – a form of contraception that provides a convincing if recondite piece of evidence about the couple's sex life.

But perhaps Eva's own brief reference to the subject in her diary for March 1935 is the most concrete private evidence. 'I wish I had never seen him,' she wrote. 'I am desperate. *He is only using me for a very definite purpose.* When he says he loves me he takes it about as seriously as his promises, which he never keeps.' What that 'definite purpose' was she does not say. In ordinary parlance – and Eva was a fairly ordinary young woman when it came to expressing herself – the phrase is a polite euphemism for sex. If so, it remains her only recorded reference to the subject in connection with Adolf Hitler.

Summing up, Dr Werner Maser, Professor at the Munich Institute for Politics and one of Hitler's biographers, was to state categorically in 1973: 'Hitler's sexuality was absolutely normal.'

But though Eva longed to have children, according to her close friend Herta Schneider, there was never any sign that she had ever become pregnant or had late periods, an abortion or a miscarriage. As for Hitler he would reiterate again and again, 'My bride is Germany', and 'I am married to the women of

Germany.' And as the years went by he would tell Eva: 'We'll only get married after the war. Until then I don't want any children, no clandestine or illegitimate births. In time of war I belong exclusively to my people.'

By the time Germany was on the brink of war, Eva Braun, 27, spinster, was truly the First Lady of the Third Reich, at least in the eyes of Hitler's inner circle, and so firmly ensconced in the Führer's home at the Berghof that Göring thought it ought to be renamed the Braunhof. And by now, inevitably perhaps, she had thrown off her political detachment, and though she never joined the Nazi Party, she did begin to involve herself more in day-to-day affairs, more especially feminine issues, on one occasion even persuading Hitler to overturn Himmler's decision to have all ladies' hairdressers closed down for the duration.

'My own life is of no account now'

On 1 September 1939, German forces invaded Poland. Two days later, to Hitler's utter astonishment and dismay, Britain declared war on Germany in support of Poland. It might have crossed the Führer's mind that he could one day lose the very war he had started less than forty-eight hours previously, for now he was confronted with the military strategist's classic nightmare, a war on two fronts – and behind Britain loomed the might of Britain's past possession and present ally, the United States of America.

The outbreak of the Second World War did not fundamentally change the nature of Eva's relationship with Hitler – at least for a while. As Adolf's war spread in every direction and before long was being fought on four fronts (east, west, north and south) and four dimensions (land, sea, air and underwater), Eva and her mother Fanny continued to spend their holidays at Portofino in sunny Italy, where Eva was free to break Hitler's rules and drink and smoke her head off, party and dance all night with anyone she fancied, wear her way through thirty-seven pairs of shoes and return to the Fatherland laden with all the usual impedimenta of clothes and jewellery. In this new atmosphere of tenderness and forbearing, war or no war, Eva's position became more secure. In the early period of the war he spent more time at the Berghof than ever before, and when he was away at his field command post at the front (which Eva was not allowed to visit) he would phone his young lady every day; he even allowed her to watch American movies, including her favourite, *Gone with the Wind*, which were *streng verboten* throughout the rest of the Reich.

Above all there were no longer any other women in Hitler's life. It was the war itself, which had seen to that. An hour after her homeland declared war on the land of her adoption, Unity Mitford had delivered a large sealed envelope to the Gauleiter of Munich, Adolf Wagner. The contents of the letter were such that the Gauleiter felt obliged to telephone them through to Hitler's command headquarters himself. The letter read:

> I am torn between my loyalty to you, my Führer, and
> my duty as a British subject. Our two nations have
> thrown themselves into the abyss, one will drag the
> other with it . . . My own life is of no account now.

Highly alarmed, for by now he had grown accustomed to the suicidal tendencies of his women friends, Hitler ordered the Gauleiter to find Miss Mitford at once. But she could not be found. It was not until the afternoon of the following day that the police were informed by a Munich clinic that an unidentified young woman with no papers had been brought in with two gunshot wounds to the head, having been found alone on a bench in the town's large central park, the Englischer Garten. One of the bullets was still lodged in the woman's head and her whole nervous system was totally paralysed.

But Unity's misfortune was to prove Hitler's good fortune, for the bullet that would eventually end her life would save Hitler's. When Hitler visited her in the clinic on 8 September, Unity was unable to recognize him. Profoundly dismayed by the turn of events, Hitler stayed longer than planned at the clinic. He ordered an immediate operation, but the surgeon believed it might kill her, and by the time Hitler left he was nervous and ill at ease. 'Hoffmann,' he mumbled to his photographer who was with him, 'I seem to bring only misfortune to my women.' He was due to give a speech at a Party rally in the Munich Bürgerbräukeller that evening, but he felt so anxious that he left the rally earlier than planned. Eight minutes after he had gone, a dynamite bomb planted by would-be anti-Nazi assassins and intended to kill him blew up in the hall, killing eight of those present and wounding sixty.

For months Unity Mitford lay in a coma, saying nothing, recognizing nobody, until slowly, in the spring of 1940, she showed signs of recovery. On 16 April 1940 she was finally put aboard the Munich-Zurich express on the first leg of her return journey to her home country, her departure supervised by Eva Braun. Then she was gone. It would be eight bleak, lonely, crippled and incontinent years before the world heard of her again – in the form of a brief announcement of her death (in a cottage hospital in Oban, Scotland) in *The Times* of 20 May

1948. Her death certificate stated her cause of death as: 'Purulent Meningitis, Cerebral abscess, Old Gun-shot Wound.' She was thirty-four.

The Damsel and the Demon King

The years 1939 to 1942 were years of victories for Germany, and while millions died in battle and in the camps, Eva and Adolf, the damsel and the demon king, continued to live and laugh and even love in abodes fit for a king and queen in Hitler's Alpine Berghof and his Reich Chancellery quarters in Berlin. Eva was now Adolf's one and only, if often far-away, consort. With the loss of the catastrophic Battle of Stalingrad in February 1943, however, the tide of war turned against Hitler. The strain of running a modern war on such a colossal scale now began to drain him of his physical and mental resources. Based for long periods in the Wolf's Lair, his Eastern Front command bunker in East Prussia, he began to withdraw into himself, walking alone, eating alone, lost in silence, rarely conversing with colleagues except about trivia, seldom sleeping for more than two hours at a stretch. 'One of these days,' he remarked to a colleague, 'I'll only have two friends left – Fräulein Braun and my dog.'

By now, too, it seems Hitler's sexual potency – always at best an intermittently unreliable commodity in his personal life – was in a state of steep decline, and to remedy this Hitler consulted his personal physician, a dubious quack, formerly a specialist in venereal disease, by the name of Dr Theodor Morell. To try and deal with the Führer's sexual inadequacy – greatly intensified by the total stress of supreme command in total war – the bad doctor prescribed a potency drug called Orchikrin, a medical compound derived from the seminal vesicles and prostates of young bulls and widely judged to be useless. In any case, the Führer was relentlessly falling prey to a plethora of maladies that were to turn his body into a disintegrating shambles.

In spite of this, by April 1943, Hitler's valet, Heinz Linge, attending the Führer at his Wolf's Lair command centre in East Prussia, noticed a significant shift in his attitude to Eva Braun. Linge now found himself listening to long perorations in praise of Eva – the finest and most caring woman he had ever known, Hitler declared, since he took office. He spoke openly for the first time about the bond between them, praising her loyalty and generosity, her total trust and discretion. Every other morning he asked Linge to put through a call to the Berghof so that he could speak to Eva Braun, and when Linge offered to leave the room, Hitler told him, 'I have nothing that needs to be said to Eva now that you or even the world can't hear.'

Later in 1943, when Hitler was back at the Berghof, his young secretary, Traudl Junge, was fascinated to note the dynamics of his relationship with Eva Braun and the sense of equality between these two very unequal people. For by now, though she was as yet unknown to the public at large, within the heady confines of Hitler's mountain headquarters she was a woman to be acknowledged and respected.

The occasion was a typical Berghof luncheon following a long and very serious military conference in the Great Hall. Until a few minutes previously Hitler had been absorbed in all the heavy concerns of a military briefing but now he was as relaxed as any ordinary genial host. When Eva had appeared, accompanied by the yapping of her two black Scotch terriers, Hitler went up to her and kissed her hand. Traudl was surprised by the ease with which the two of them teased each other, as though enjoying complete equality in a perfectly balanced relationship – or so it seemed. Hitler teased Eva about her dogs. They were, he said, nothing but a couple of dusting brushes. To which she retorted that his Alsatian, Blondi, wasn't a dog at all, it was a calf. Eva could be as forthright as she liked, even scold the Führer, though only about matters of little moment. Traudl heard her have a go at persuading Hitler to see a movie at the Berghof for a change – he seldom saw them now that the war preoccupied most of his time and much of his mind.

'You see,' she exhorted him, 'you can have it screened in the hall so easily, and this film is art too, it's not light, it's a very serious film. I mean, you listen to gramophone records, and I'm sure the German people would have no objection if the Führer saw a movie for once. In fact I'm sure the people would like your colleagues to go to the movies more instead of driving around in big, important-looking cars getting drunk.'

Hitler would put up with this sort of thing from his lady with barely repressed good humour but later gleefully get his own back.

'Do you know what lipstick is made of?' he asked, noticing the red imprint of lipstick on Eva's napkin.

Eva retorted that hers was French lipstick, made of nothing but the finest ingredients.

Hitler gave the assembled lunch guests a pitying smile.

'If only you knew,' he said, 'that in Paris, of all places, lipsticks are made of the fat skimmed off sewage, I'm sure no woman would paint her lips any more.'

Eva's figure had changed since she first met him. Then she was full, even a little buxom, but these days she was slim and *à la mode*. Perhaps it was this that made Hitler exclaim, not entirely in teasing mood:

> 'I don't know what's supposed to be so beautiful about women looking as thin as boys. It's just because they're differently built that we love them after all. Things used to be quite different in the old days. In my time it was still a pleasure to go to the ballet because you saw lovely, well-rounded curves, but now you just get bones and ribs hopping about on stage. Since I've been Führer I don't have to pay for it any more. I get free tickets.

Hitler hated change in these sort of matters – especially where Eva was concerned. Take her clothes, for instance. She was a very good dresser but never wore the same dress twice, and never even wore the same outfit at dinner as she had at lunch or in the tea-house near the Berghof. 'She usually preferred dark colours,' Traudl Junge observed, 'and liked to wear black best of all. Hitler's favourite dress was a heavy black silk one with a wide bell-shaped skirt, very close-fitting at the waist, sleeveless, with just two broad straight shoulder straps in old rose, and two roses of the same colour in the deep square neckline. A short bolero jacket with long, close-fitting sleeves was part of this ensemble.' To Hitler's chagrin this dress too enjoyed only a very short life.

'I don't know why you women have to keep changing your clothes,' he complained. 'When I think a dress is particularly pretty then I'd like to see its owner wearing it all the time. She ought to have all her dresses made of the same material and to the same pattern. But no sooner have I got used to something pretty, and I'm feeling I haven't seen enough of it yet, than along comes something new.'

It was the same with Eva's hair. She was always changing the style, and even the colour. One day she piled it all up on top of her head. Hitler was horrified.

'You're totally strange, quite changed,' he told her. 'You're an entirely different woman.'

In the summer of 1943 Hitler and his entourage moved back to the Wolf's Lair in East Prussia. By now the place was beginning to look like a burgeoning pioneer settlement in the outback. Albert Speer had an estate there, Hermann Göring had a kind of palace, Hitler's medic, Dr Morell, reviled by all except his patient, even had a bath of his own, though he was so fat and gross he was unable to get out of it without assistance. But though this outpost in the woods on the Eastern Front was well established and well provided, to Traudl and most of the others who worked there it was like a kind of moon base, cut off from real life – and even more so when, with British and American planes now bombing at will all over Germany, the Wolf's Lair bunkers were reinforced and the whole place ringed with barbed wire and land mines that dreadfully disfigured the forest.

Hitler's long-established personal routine remained unchanged, however. As before, his meals were taken with the young women of his entourage, Traudl included, and when his new dietician, Frau von Exner, joined them, the total of young women who lunched and dined with him every day rose to five. To these generally bright and attractive companions at the war front Hitler was unfailingly courteous, attentive and flattering. And he never stopped talking – about his past, about his beliefs, about his likes and dislikes, about anything that came into his head that wasn't about the war, the Russians, the generals, and the whole unendingly burdensome weight of Führership.

Often the conversation would turn to marriage and on one occasion he talked about his former associate, Ernst Hanfstaengl, who eventually had to flee for his life from Nazi persecution and unknown to Hitler was now working in the USA as special intelligence advisor to President Roosevelt. 'Hanfstaengl had such a beautiful wife,' he told his table companions, 'and he was unfaithful to her with another woman who wasn't pretty at all.'

Apparently, commented Traudl, he could not understand that a woman's beauty alone was not a sufficient basis for a successful marriage. Yet often, Traudl Junge noted, he would talk about his special friend in seemingly faraway Bavaria – Eva Braun – and it was clear that it was not just her beauty that attracted him, but her human qualities as well, and that there was an element of admiration, of concern, of companionship, even perhaps true love in his feelings towards her. Traudl was to record:

> He often took his chance to talk about Eva. He phoned her every day, and if there were reports of an air raid in Munich he would pace up and down restlessly like a caged lion, waiting to get in touch with Eva Braun by phone. Usually his fears were groundless. The 'little Braun house' was damaged only once, when several buildings near it burned right down. He was always talking about Eva's courage. 'She won't go down into the air-raid shelter, although I keep asking her to, and one of these days that little place of hers will collapse like a house of cards. And she won't move to my apartment, where she'd be absolutely safe. I've finally persuaded her to have a little air-raid shelter built in her house, but then she takes in the whole neighbourhood and goes up on the roof herself to see if any

incendiary bombs have fallen. She's very proud. I've known her for over ten years, and when she first started to work for Hoffmann she had to scrape and save. But it was years before she would let me so much as pay a taxi fare for her, and she slept on a bench in the office for days on end so that I could reach her by phone, because she didn't have a telephone at home. It was only a few years ago that I got her to accept her little house in Bogenhausen.'

In the light of all this, Traudl felt bound to ask Hitler a fairly obvious, but rather blunt and not unbrave, question.

'My Führer,' she said, 'why haven't you married her?'

To which Hitler replied, ' I wouldn't make a good father, and I think it would be irresponsible to start a family when I can't devote enough time to my wife. And anyway I don't want children of my own. I think the children of men of genius usually have a very hard time of it. People expect them to be just like their famous progenitor, and won't forgive them for being average. And in fact most of them are feeble-minded.'

To give her her due, Traudl Junge was rather disappointed by this revelation of private megalomania. And later he was to go further and proudly state, 'I am an instrument of fate, and must tread the path which a higher Providence has set me.'

As for Eva Braun, she saw less and less of her loved one as the situation at the front grew ever more desperate and time-consuming, and what she did see of him made her more and more concerned. Hitler looked ill and seemed to be prematurely ageing – grey, bent, drained of energy. By Christmas 1943 he was a cause for serious concern. In some considerable measure his physical deterioration was caused by his personal physician,

Theodor Morell, whose daily dose of his own medical concoctions, which included large percentages of strychnine and other harmful drugs, were clearly causing his patient more harm than good. But to a large degree it was also the superhuman pressures of the war that bowed him down.

Hitler spent part of the summer of 1944 at the Obersalzberg, lovingly tended by his Eva, who brought him back nearer to a semblance of sanity and health. But in mid-July, little more than a month after the Allied armies' D-Day landings in France and the opening of a Second Front in the West, the rapidly deteriorating situation on the Eastern Front, where Stalin's summer offensive had brought Russian forces within a whisker of the German borders in the East, forced him to return to his command headquarters at the Wolf's Lair in East Prussia. Weary and in despair, his gaunt face like the face of a man who could hardly bear to be alive, he told his shocked valet, Heinz Linge:

> When we leave the Berghof this time, it will be with a heavy heart. Fräulein Eva has done everything possible to persuade me to stay. You and I know I can't stay here now, surrounded by enemies, beset by petty treasons. On two fronts, the generals are calling out for more: more tanks, more aircraft, more fuel, more men. I must go where this war takes me; accept whatever destiny has in store for me. I have explained the situation to the Fräulein and thank providence that she, at least, understands.

But it was a blow inflicted by his own side that finally turned Hitler into the human wreck he now was. This was the Bomb

Plot of 20 July 1944, a narrowly failed assassination attempt on Hitler's life plotted by a group of disaffected senior army officers.

In the heart of the Wolf's Lair in East Prussia that morning, Hitler's secretary, Traudl Junge was an on-the-spot witness of that morning of unthinkable trauma. She was to record:

> I can still feel the oppressive, sultry heat of that day. It made the air quiver slightly. All was noonday peace. All the secretaries were in their rooms. Then, suddenly, a terrible bang broke through the quiet. It was unexpected and alarming, but we often heard bangs near by when deer stepped on landmines, or some kind of weapon was being tried out. I was writing a letter and didn't let the bang disturb me. But then I heard someone outside shouting for a doctor in urgent, agitated tones. I ran out. My colleagues came rushing out of the other rooms with pale, frightened faces. Outside we saw two orderlies coming from the Führer bunker with distraught expressions, looking for the doctor. 'A bomb has exploded, it was probably in the Führer bunker,' they stammered. We stood there like sheep in a thunderstorm, paralysed by terror. 'What will become of us if Hitler's dead?' Frau Schoeder suddenly asked in the oppressive silence. The spell was broken. We scattered wildly in different directions.

It was curiosity that lured them to the Führer Bunker. Fräulein Junge almost laughed at the sight of Hitler. He was standing in the little ante-room surrounded by several of his adjutants and servants. His hair had been set on fire by the blast and was now standing on end so that he looked like a hedgehog. Tiny wood splinters from the blown-up map table were sticking in his skin. His black trousers were hanging in strips from his belt, almost like a raffia skirt, and his bottom had turned completely purple from the impact of the blast. His right arm was bruised and he had stuck his right hand between the buttons of his tunic. His eardrums had been shattered, rendering him temporarily deaf and impairing his sense of balance. He greeted the new arrivals with his left arm, and in spite of everything still managed a smile.

'Well, ladies,' he gasped. 'Everything turned out right again. Yet more proof that Fate has chosen me for my mission, or I wouldn't be alive now.'

They would like to have learned more details, but Linge looked at his watch and said, 'My Führer, I think you'll have to change your trousers. The Duce will be arriving in an hour's time.'

Hitler looked down at his rags. 'You may be right,' he said.

He left the group and went to his room, his stance more upright and erect than Traudl had seen it for a long time.

Though three others had died, Hitler emerged from the bomb blast with just a damaged arm, burst eardrum, singed hair, torn trousers and the conviction that he had been saved by fate to lead his nation to final victory. Eva was hysterical when she heard the news, and when she finally got through by phone to her man at his command post in East Prussia, and he reassured her he was safe, she said to him, 'I love you, may God protect you!' She was leaping about, eyewitnesses noted, dancing for joy, shedding tears of relief. That day she wrote to Hitler on her blue notepaper with the monogram EB in a four-leaf clover in one corner:

My love,

I am beside myself. Desperate, miserable, unhappy. I am half dead now that I know you are in danger. Come back as soon as possible. I feel slightly crazy. You know, I've always said so, that I shan't go on living if anything happens to you. From the time of our first meeting, I promised to follow you everywhere, even to death. You know that my whole life is loving you.

Your Eva

Hitler, too, had written a letter, badly typed and full of errors, from the Eastern Front:

'My dear Tschapperl,

I'm fine, don't worry, just a trifle tired perhaps. I hope to come back soon and so be able to rest, putting myself in your hands. I greatly need tranquillity, but my duty to the German people comes before all else. Don't forget that the dangers I run are nothing compared to those of our soldiers at the front. Thank you for your proofs of affection . . . I've sent you the uniform I was wearing that ill-fated day. It is proof that Providence protects me and that we no longer need fear our enemies.

With wholehearted affection

AH

Inevitably the assassination attempt was the main subject of every conversation for a long time to come. Not surprisingly,

Hitler was now in even worse shape than he had been before. The explosion had not only burst one eardrum but damaged the other, and he was suffering from recurring headaches. He hardly went out into the fresh air at all now, had no appetite and ate next to nothing. He had experienced trembling in his right leg before the assassination attempt, but now it had moved to his left hand, so that he felt bound to keep it behind his back where no one could see it. He was often silent now, and looked old and tired and listless, and his daily intake of medication and injections was prodigious. Finally he took to his bed. Hitler in bed! This was something no one present had ever observed before, certainly not Traudl Junge.

The little room in the bunker was very shabbily furnished, just like a soldier's cubicle. In addition Hitler had a huge wooden crate in the room, which was meant for Blondi and her family, so there was really very little room. He lay in bed in the kind of plain white nightshirt that only the Wehrmacht could design. He hadn't buttoned up the sleeves because they chafed him, so we could see the white skin of his arms. Bright white! We could understand why he didn't like wearing shorts! It was a desperate feeling to see the man who could have ended all this misery with a single stroke of his pen lying almost apathetically in bed, staring into space with tired eyes, while all hell was let loose around him. It seemed to me as if his body had suddenly understood the pointlessness of all the efforts made by his mind and his strong will and had gone on strike. It had just lain down and said, 'I don't want any more.'

Though the Führer was to rally, this was truly the beginning of his end, medically speaking. And the news up top, where the Russians were advancing into East Prussia and bearing down on the Wolf's Lair with uncanny speed, spelled the beginning of the end of his military and political might. Yet even now, in the immediate wake of the assassination attempt, the extreme polarities of his emotional make-up were in evidence, and the monster who destroyed millions was still capable of a glimmer of genuine human tenderness and compassion, especially where a simpatico young woman was concerned. Not long before he took to his sick bed in the bunker, and just after Traudl Junge had learned of the death of her husband of less than a year in the fighting at the front, Hitler had called for her to offer her his sympathy. Traudl recalled:

> Hitler came towards me without a word. He took both my hands and said: "Oh, child, I'm so sorry. Your husband was a splendid fellow." His voice was very soft and sad. I almost felt sorrier for Hitler than for myself, because it's so difficult to express sympathy. "You must stay with me, and don't worry, I'll always be there to help you!" Suddenly everyone wanted to help me, and I felt like running away.

'My place is with *him!*'

On 11 October 1944 the Red Army crossed the German frontier into East Prussia. Hitler had no option but to pull out of his headquarters at the Wolf's Lair and away from the advance of the Soviet forces, and one morning in November finally abandoned the Eastern Front altogether to return to Berlin and the last battle. He and his entourage departed by special train, travelling by day so that they would arrive in the capital in the darkness of night and thus keep Hitler's return a secret from the populace. But Hitler did not wish to be seen by day either, nor did he wish to look out on scenes of the Fatherland on the verge of imminent ruin and defeat. So the windows of the Führer's carriage were kept darkened and his compartment lit only by electric light.

Traudl Junge recalled:

> Lunch in his saloon car was very gloomy! I never saw Hitler so depressed and distracted as he was that day. His voice hardly rose above a loud whisper; his eyes were lowered to his plate or stared absently at some point on the white tablecloth. An oppressive atmosphere weighed down on the cramped, rocking cage in which we were gathered together, and an eerie feeling came over all of us.

It was hardly surprising that Hitler did not wish to be seen by his once hysterically applauding people. He had inflicted unspeakable suffering upon the great majority of them and, since the war was clearly lost, they had suffered – the very fabric of Germany had suffered – in vain. He was, moreover, a tattered scarecrow of his former self, in reality physically and mentally damaged beyond repair – and his underlying condition continued to deteriorate. When he used to phone Eva from the Wolf's Lair she noticed his voice had become slow and husky. But when she met him after his return to Berlin on 20 November 1944 she was shocked at the sight of him. He seemed to have aged many years in just a couple of months. His face wore the greyish pallor of death, he could no longer walk properly, just shuffling along, and his hands now shook violently. The man she adored above all others was now a human being nearing the end of his tether.

By now Allied bombing raids had ravaged much of Berlin, the Reich Chancellery included, but Hitler's private quarters in the Chancellery – lounge, library, bedroom, bathroom, small bedroom for Eva Braun, adjoining his – were as yet undamaged, and Eva moved back into her own guest quarters adjacent to his own. But three weeks later, on 10 December 1944, Hitler announced he was leaving Berlin for his command post in the West, where the Germans were about to launch the Ardennes Offensive, the last desperate attempt to throw the Western Allies back to the sea. For the first time Eva scolded him. As far as she was concerned, she told him flatly, his health was more important than some battlefield victory. For a long time he stood and stared at her as she berated him. There was a deep warmth in his eyes, and when he finally spoke his voice was soft and gentle. 'You are the only one who would say that,' he told her. 'You are the only one who cares.'

On 16 January 1945, after it was clear the Ardennes Offensive had failed, Hitler left his command headquarters in the West for the last time and came back to Berlin to prepare for the capital's last stand. From the Reich Chancellery he telephoned Eva at her villa in Munich and as soon as she could she returned to Berlin to be at his side.

'This time you will stay with me,' she informed him when he greeted her in his apartment in the Reich Chancellery. 'I will take care of you. We will not part again.'

During the Allied air raids they took shelter in the Chancellery bunker. By now enemy forces were advancing on the capital from both east and west. The war was clearly lost, but Hitler was in denial – since surrender was not on his agenda, and his own capture was out of the question, there was no other attitude he could adopt.

Early in February 1945 he sent Eva back to the Berghof for her own safety, and she left for Munich by the midnight vegetable train in the company of her sister Gretl. But she had no intention of staying. She was here simply to put her affairs in order, find a home for her dogs, see her family and friends one last time. A few evenings after her arrival she celebrated her thirty-third birthday of a few days back in her little villa in the Wasserburgerstrasse. It was a warm, merry, deeply poignant occasion, and in the early hours, while they partied, Eva made up her mind.

She was not going to take refuge in the Berghof for the rest of the war, she told them all. She was going back to Berlin, to be at Hitler's side, whatever fate had in store for them. Her friends and family were aghast. Long into the early hours they argued with her. Eva would not be moved.

'Death matters little to me,' she said. 'I know the end that is in store for me. Hitler has forbidden me to return. But nothing can stop me. My place is with *him*!'

The correspondence between Eva and Adolf (reckoned to total around 250 letters and cards) might have revealed her state of mind more clearly – the psychology behind her apparent death mission – but the collection was removed from the Berghof immediately after the end of the war and probably destroyed. A final desperate love letter from another adoring admirer, Emmie Mayer, already quoted earlier, reveals a state of mind parallel to Eva's – a state of mind in which death is seen as the final fulfillment of eternal union with the beloved.

Frau Mayer had written to Hitler a few months earlier, when he was still holed up at the Wolf's Lair on the Eastern Front:

> My life belongs with body and soul to you alone. All I want is to stand by your side, and where you go, there shall I go also, for your ways are my ways, and where you are, that is where I must be also. I will follow you to the Front when you travel back. Please do not say no, for I no longer want to be parted from you. Oh, what sort of life would it be not being near you? It was so difficult living far from you. No, I can no longer live without you. So I say once again, take me to the Front, let me always be with you. I want to bear everything with you, share everything with you, please, dearest Adolf, do not leave me alone any more.

But it was easier said than done for Eva to do the real thing and return to Berlin to fulfil her destiny at her beloved's side. The roads were jammed, the trains in chaos, enemy aircraft harried every moving thing. Eva decided to requisition her own personal Mercedes-Benz, which had been garaged since the beginning of the war, and a chauffeur (in the form of a young Waffen-SS officer by the name of Walther Galen) was found to drive it. On 14 March 1945, they set off. She had not forewarned Hitler she was returning for fear he would forbid her.

The long and difficult journey across much of the breadth of Germany was nearly the end for her, at least as Galen was to recount after the war. Three times the journey was imperilled by American warplanes. Near Leipzig, two Mustangs attacked the car, blowing off one tyre before the chauffeur managed to get out of the line of fire beneath a viaduct. Later, outside Dessau, a P-

38 blew up a German army truck in front of them, and Galen decided it would be safer to take cover in the woods and wait for dark before carrying on. Exhausted, they both fell asleep in the car, and it was almost three in the morning before they resumed their journey. At first it seemed their problems were over, but as they neared Zossen, just to the south of Berlin, where the German High Command had their headquarters, a huge armada of Flying Fortresses and Liberator bombers of the American 8th Air Force launched a massive air raid directly across their route to the capital, with more than 500 aircraft over the target, and once again they were forced to pull to a halt and race for a public air-raid shelter alongside the road. But finally, on 15 March she was at the gates of the city.

As they entered the city via the road leading through the gateway of the old Zossen Palace – the other roads were almost impassable because of the bomb craters – Eva Braun was dismayed at how much air-raid damage Berlin had sustained in the short time she had been away. The American Embassy had been destroyed, the central post office was in ruins, the fashionable promenade of the Unter den Linden was almost impassable because of the waterlogged bomb craters and fallen tree trunks, and the Reich Chancellery, when they had finally picked their way through to it, was in a dreadful state, with gaping shell holes on every side. But Hitler's quarters were, for the moment, still intact and it was to his study that she finally made her way.

She was home!

PART 3

Champagne – and Cyanide

Angel of Death

When Eva was at last ushered into Hitler's presence in his Reich Chancellery headquarters he was amazed and overjoyed at the sight of her.

'I told you to go to the Berghof,' he chided her, taking her hands and smiling.

'Who else,' he told his secretaries, beaming with pride, 'would come back to Berlin when they could go to the Berghof?'

The secretaries viewed it rather differently. Why did Eva return to Berlin? At thirty-three she was still a young woman with much of her life ahead of her. She would have been safe in Bavaria. The Americans not the Russians would have captured her and US intelligence would have spent many riveting and perhaps enchanting hours debriefing her. She was not a war criminal – she just slept with one. She would have been interned for a while, certainly – but she would have lived. So why did the damsel come back to the demon king, certain in her heart that she would die in his arms? The answer was obvious, of course. She was in love with the man. She had been in love with him since she first set eyes on him in the Munich photo shop all those years ago. She had always wished to be at his side, go wherever he went – even unto death.

Eva had her own personal suite in the Chancellery close to Hitler's own and soon settled in to life at the side of the Führer in the beleaguered capital of the Reich. The long years of ambiguity as to her status in Hitler's life were at last behind her. Everyone in the closed circle of Hitler's court (though nobody else in Germany or the world beyond) now knew that, one way or another – and no one was ever exactly sure how – Eva Braun was the Führer's woman, in so far as that was humanly possible, and his fate would be hers also.

But Berlin was now a prime target for British and American round-the-clock bombing, and towards the end of March, with most of the housing in the city centre already destroyed, Eva and Hitler were forced to take shelter at nights in the Führerbunker fifty feet below the Chancellery. On Sunday, 15 April 1945, they took up permanent residence in the Bunker, soldiers trundling her little bed and large dresser down from her apartment in the Reich Chancellery to her new home below ground. It was a defining moment. One of Hitler's secretaries, Gerda Christian, recalled:

> Her arrival was greeted in silence. We all knew what it
> meant. We were still wondering whether the Führer
> would leave for Berchtesgaden. I was now convinced he
> would never fly off to the Obersalzberg. Berchtesgaden,
> in the form of Eva Braun, had come to him.

As one SS man in the bunker complex put it: '*Der Todesengel* – the angel of death – has arrived.'

The Concrete Submarine

As for Eva and Hitler, there was no doubting that, both literally and metaphorically, they had come down in the world. Gone was the comfort and grandeur of the palatial Chancellery. They were now cooped up in tiny concrete cells far from the light of day.

For Hitler's Bunker, often thought to be a fortress, was actually conceived as nothing more than an air-raid shelter, though in complexity, facilities and depth of concrete it was to be grander than any air-raid shelter ever built up to that time. The original air-raid shelter was based on Hitler's own plans, drawn up in 1935 shortly after he had come to power, and consisted of a concrete block 70 feet square built under the New Reich Chancellery cellars. Eventually there were a number of other shelters under the Chancellery complex, all of them with subsidiary rooms and connected by a network of passages. In 1944, when the British and American air raids on the capital intensified, a deeper shelter – the Führerbunker proper – was added, with a concrete ceiling over 13 feet thick (as well as 30 feet of compacted earth) and walls almost as thick designed to withstand the heaviest British and American bombs, the whole structure resting on concrete foundations over 6 feet thick set deep in ground water.

It was this Führerbunker that was increasingly to become the command post, personal quarters and last refuge of the Führer himself, and of his closest aides, and the woman of his life – though few Berliners knew of its existence or the whereabouts of their Führer. The Berlin bunker was in fact the thirteenth bunker Hitler had used as a command post during his direction of the war. Though provisional plans had been drawn up for Hitler and his staff to retreat to the so-called Bavarian Redoubt, where they would fight a rearguard guerrilla war of resistance in the Alpine fastness, Hitler himself never showed any real inclination to resort to this option; and though his personal pilot, Hans Baur, had route plans for an escape flight from Berlin to Greenland, Madagascar, Manchuria and other remote refuges,

Hitler was again uninterested. 'Once out of Berlin,' he quipped, 'I'd be like a Tibetan lama without his prayer wheel.' Berlin would be Stalingrad all over again – a Wagnerian finale in which he would go down in glory at the head of his troops, if only within the fantasy of his own traumatized mind. For Hitler was not afraid of death. What he feared was being prevented from stage-managing his own finale.

The Bunker itself was in two parts on two different levels. The Upper Bunker, which could be reached via steps down from the banqueting hall or the kitchen on the ground floor of the Old Chancellery, consisted of twelve closet-sized concrete rooms, six each side of a corridor. Four of these rooms were inhabited by Dr Goebbels, his wife and six children, two were occupied by staff, the remainder were used as kitchens, pantry and wine cellar. At the end of the central corridor, latterly used as a communal dining passage for Hitler's staff and the Goebbels family, was a wrought-iron staircase that led down to a deeper and slightly more commodious bunker – the Führerbunker itself. At the foot of these stairs there was a bulkhead and a steel door, with two armed guards in front of the bulkhead, with more guards halfway down the Führerbunker passageway on the other side of the steel door. In the last few months the Führerbunker could also be reached via the emergency stairs from the garden entrance up top, or via an underground tunnel some 120 yards long from the cellar complex in the Voss-Strasse.

The Führerbunker consisted of eighteen cramped and uncomfortable little rooms arranged either side of a central passageway covered with a red carpet on a flagstone floor which was divided in two by a partition. The corridor on the near side of the partition was used as a general sitting passage, and gave access to the machine room, air plotting room, telephone exchange (with emergency switchboard and telex), toilets and washroom (containing a little kennel for Hitler's dog Blondi and her five pups). On the other side of the guarded dividing door was the inner sanctum, the centre of power, such as it was, of what was left of the Third Reich.

Here the central corridor was used as a waiting room and conference room where Hitler could hold his daily staff conferences. Eight paintings by old masters hung on the left-hand wall here, with a few old armchairs beneath them. Against the opposite wall stood a sofa, two easy chairs and a table.

A door on the left led to the private quarters of Hitler and Eva Braun. This consisted of six rooms – Hitler's antechamber, with one door leading to Eva Braun's bedroom, another door leading to his living room cum office, from which one door led to his bedroom (just big enough for a single bed) and another door led to a bathroom cum dressing room he shared with Eva Braun, which in turn provided another entrance to her bedroom.

The three rooms in Hitler's private quarters were slightly larger than the rest, measuring some 10 by 15 feet. The anteroom contained a small table, a chair, a stool, a grandfather clock and a coat stand from which hung his trenchcoat, his peaked cap, his suede gloves and his dog Blondi's leash. The living room cum office – a tiny place with a depressingly low ceiling, where the Führer lived and worked and ate – contained a blue and white brocade sofa along one wall, a small table in front of it, a small table with a radio to the side of it, a desk to the right of the door from the ante-room, three armchairs with the same blue and white covering as the sofa, two stools, a painting of Frederick the Great on the wall above the desk, a still life above the sofa, and a fine patterned carpet over the stone floor. The carpeted bedroom was furnished with a single bed, a bedside table, a wardrobe, a dresser, two chairs, a bell bush to summon his valet, a safe at the foot of the bed, and an oxygen bottle to help him sleep better if the Bunker air failed.

Eva Braun's bed-sitting room, in which there was barely room to swing a handbag, contained a single bed, a small table, an armchair, a small dresser, a sideboard and a coloured rug. There was no egress from Eva's room to the 'outside world' except via the shared bathroom and Hitler's own suite.

On the right of the corridor other doors led to the rooms of Hitler's valet and duty orderly officer, the staff day room, a first-aid and dressing station, and the doctor's room, later the bed-sitting room of Dr Goebbels (whose wife had heartily abhorred him for years). The last door on the left along the waiting-room passageway led to the military conference room, or briefing room, bigger than most of the other rooms, with a large table where Hitler could sit with his maps and at a pinch up to twenty people could stand side by side and present their reports.

At the end of the passage another gasproof steel door led to an airlock with a guard post and another gasproof door from which four flights of concrete steps, thirty-eight steps in all, led up to the emergency exit (latterly doubling up as an emergency entrance) in the Chancellery garden, housed in a massive concrete blockhouse with yet another steel door, yet another guard – and then light, air, and freedom of a kind (or, depending which way you were going – and when – chaos, fear and confusion).

There were other extensive bunkers and underground cellars in the governmental area – the bunker of the Party Chancellery where Bormann and his staff lived, a bunker for General Mohnke, the Commandant of the Chancellery, and his staff, and another bunker for Dr Goebbels in the cellar of the Propaganda Ministry. All told there were some half dozen big bunkers and half a dozen

smaller ones spread out over whole city blocks – 'the most elaborate labyrinth,' it has been said, 'since the one designed for the
Minotaur in ancient Crete.' From these bunkers, every day, almost
every hour, officers and officials came to the Führerbunker for the
endless rounds of war conferences, along with daily supplies of
food, drink and other provisions for Hitler and his court.

It was a dreary and depressive life they all led in that bleak
catacomb down there, like prisoners in a cave. The ceilings were
low, the corridors narrow, the walls a dull battleship-grey or
rusty-looking brown or orange; the naked light bulbs glared day
and night; in some places the bare new cement was moist or
even mouldy, the air was sometimes warm and humid,
sometimes cold and dank, and before long the place stank of old
boots, sweaty uniforms, acrid disinfectant and (from time to
time) blocked drains. 'It was like being stranded in a concrete
submarine,' recalled one of Hitler's SS honour guard, 'or buried
alive in some abandoned charnel house.' They were, he said, 'like
miserable rats in a musty cement tomb'. For long periods the
only sound was the loud hum of the diesel generator that helped
keep them all alive. None expected to survive.

In this bewildering and claustrophobic complex the last act
of the drama – and the love story – would be played out.

'A madhouse run by the inmates'

Hitler had taken up residence in the Bunker on 16 January and
was destined never again to see a sunrise or sunset. Though he
might occasionally repair to his old haunts in the New Reich
Chancellery or walk his dog Blondi in the Chancellery garden
between air raids at night, Hitler in effect became a troglodyte

in mind and in deed for the remaining 105 days of his life. Rarely, if ever, did he even venture up the twelve stairs from the Lower (or Führer) Bunker to the Upper Bunker. He was seemingly committed to remaining as deep as possible below the capital of his Third Reich on as permanent a basis as possible. None of the other Bunker people lived like this. Few slept there; most ate elsewhere; even Eva Braun would stroll off into the nearby public park. It was not surprising that visitors regarded the Bunker as 'a madhouse run by the inmates' or 'the Isle of the Departed'. A few of the inmates did go off their head, like the sergeant in charge of the Bunker dog kennel, who had to be taken away in a home-made straightjacket.

Hitler's own personal routine determined the routine for all the others in the Bunker. He usually went to bed around 4 or 5 in the morning, but would sometimes still be in session with his secretaries, adjutant or physician as late as 8, read in bed for some of the time, then got up around 10 or 11 the same morning. He had always slept badly and the air raids did not help, though it took a blockbuster landing nearby to make the Bunker tremble and the ceiling lights to swing as in a breeze, a disconcerting experience which led to evening war conferences being scheduled between the departure of the American bombing squadrons and the arrival of the British ones.

For a large part of her time in the Bunker, Eva Braun stayed in her quarters or Hitler's. Day by day the military situation worsened on all fronts and from east and west the vast armies of Germany's enemies closed on the capital. On 19 April Eva wrote to her friend Herta Schneider:

> We already have artillery fire from the Eastern Front and naturally air raids every day [from the West].

Unfortunately I have Hitler's orders to stand at the ready at every alarm, because of the possible danger of flooding.

With almost every hour the atmosphere in the Bunker grew progressively more depressive and paranoid. It was not just the news, which was bad enough. It was also the lifestyle. There was no getting away from the fact that though they were still in the centre of their universe they were all – including the erstwhile absolute ruler of much of Europe from the English Channel to Russia's Volga River – actually buried in a large hole in the ground, detached from the realities of the world up top, deprived of the basic indicators of the passage of time, such as night and day, sunrise and sunset, and deprived (when the Russians shot down the balloon that supported the aerial for the radio-telephone link from the Bunker) of any means of communication with the outside world. Though they were not short of basic creature comforts – booze, food, cigarettes, ventilation, running water, electric light – the unnatural, confining, troglodytic environment (the lights on and machinery whirring day and night, the claustrophobia, the overcrowding, the lack of privacy, the smell of sweat and urine, the sense of encroaching doom, especially when bombs and shells exploded in the garden up top and the walls reverberated and showered them with clouds of dust and plaster flakes and sulphur fumes) got them all down, Hitler especially – all, that is, except Eva Braun.

Eva took to the Bunker like a mole to a burrow. She remained cheerful, attentive to her man, well presented. She changed her dress as often as she could – one visitor said she did it every hour, other Bunker denizens reckoned it was five times a day – kept herself nicely made up and manicured, smuggled hairdressers in and out and when that became impossible washed and waved her blonde hair herself. She was not worried about the war but she was worried about the Führer.

His health was appalling and deteriorating rapidly. His specialist medic, Dr Morell, who had his own room in the Bunker and was on constant call, dosed and injected him daily with a variety of curatives, some of them quack and harmful. It was undoubtedly this steep physical decline, as well as the worsening military situation, that adversely affected both Hitler's often hysterical nervous state and the quality of his decision making. More and more he would rant at his top military staff, screaming and bellowing so much that his voice became hoarse. He even insulted his secretaries. To cheer him up Eva arranged a party for him on 20 April – his fifty-sixth birthday.

This was the last bash of Hitler's court. Russian tanks had now reached the edge of the city and the thunder of the Russian guns carried as far as the Reich Chancellery itself. All the grandees attended for the last time – Himmler, Göring, Goebbels, Bormann, Ribbentrop, Speer – as well as a number of junior officers. In vain they tried to persuade Hitler to leave Berlin. 'The city will soon be surrounded,' they advised him. 'You will soon be cut off and unable to reach the south. There's still time to take command of the southern armies if you go by way of Berchtesgaden.' But Hitler refused. He would await developments, he said, he would remain.

That evening, when they were all squashed together in his study drinking birthday champagne, his secretaries asked him the same question. Would he leave Berlin?

'No, I can't,' he replied. 'I'd feel like a Tibetan lama turning an empty prayer wheel. I must bring things to a head in Berlin – or go under!'

It was now clear to him as it had been to the others that victory was impossible and he and they and everyone would indeed go under. Brooding and depressed, Hitler left the party early and on an impulse Eva suggested the rest of the younger and more junior guests continue the party in her old living room on the first floor of the damaged Old Chancellery. It had been her custom for some weeks, while Hitler was busy conducting his briefings down below, to hold intimate little parties in her own old living room in the Chancellery, where she would drink and dance with anyone and everyone – including, whenever he was around, Hermann Fegelein, her sister Gretl's husband. Eva had always fancied Fegelein, flirted with him, laughed with him, danced with him. Hitler's secretary, Christine Schroeder, sometimes attended these parties, and recalled:

> I have a picture etched in my mind: at the end of a dance Fegelein lifted Eva Braun up with both arms level with his chest. And as she lay in his arms, they gazed into each other's eyes with tenderness and longing. It was obvious that Eva Braun liked Hermann Fegelein very much and felt herself strongly attracted to him . . . From their looks, from their age and from their character they were made for each other.

But this evening there would be no Fegelein – indeed there would be no Fegelein ever again in Eva's presence – for his fate lay elsewhere. Instead the younger Bunker folk, Traudl Junge included, climbed up the stairs laden with food and bottles and a gramophone, and all night they partied in that spectral bare dark room overlooking the jagged skyline of the ruined city, quaffing champagne and laughing and dancing to Eva's single

181

record, 'Blood Red Roses Spell Happiness for You', a pre-war hit with a catchy tune. There was no British or American air raids that night, only the occasional burst of artillery fire, no one spoke of war; instead there was music and merriment – and a brief glimpse of how life had once been and now would be no more.

Traudl Junge remembered:

> A restless fire burned in her eyes. Eva Braun wanted to numb the fear that had woken in her. She wanted to celebrate again, even when there was nothing to celebrate, she wanted to dance, to drink, to forget. Eva Braun carried off anyone she met, all who crossed her path. She whirled everyone away in a desperate frenzy, like a woman who has already felt the faint breath of death. We drank champagne, there was shrill laughter, and I laughed too because I didn't want to cry. No one said anything about the war, no one mentioned victory, no one spoke of death. This was a party given by ghosts.

Eva danced with everyone, her face a picture of joy. They were young, they were doomed, but for this last night they were free. At dawn they all left and Eva retired.

'Do you think I'm *crazy?*'

And still it all continued to fall apart. Hitler was now showing distinct signs of dementia, in part a consequence of his medical condition, in part a consequence of his situation – the Bunker life, the lost war, the growing inevitability of his impending fate. A key feature of his dementia was paranoia. During the course of 21 April he finally turned on his loyal if useless physician Dr Morell, ranting like a madman. Morell recalled:

> He was very dejected. I gave him shots of glucose. I wanted to give him another shot but he grabbed me and lost his temper, shouting that he knew that I was going to inject him with morphine.

Hitler, it seemed, had formed the demented notion that his doctor was going to drug him so that the generals could spirit him out of Berlin against his will. In vain Morell protested his innocence.

'Do you think I'm *crazy?*' Hitler screamed at him.

He continued to rage at Morell, threatened to have him shot, finally ordered him to go home, take off his uniform of physician to the Führer, then 'act as if you've never seen me!'

At this point the shocked Morell collapsed at Hitler's feet, which only enraged the Führer still more.

'Get out of that uniform!' he screamed. 'Put on some plain clothes, then go back to being the doctor of Kürfurstendamm!'

Morell fled and two days later, in the company of a number of other fleeing Bunker folk, flew out of Berlin low over the Russian lines in Himmler's four-engined Focke-Wulf Kondor aircraft bound for the relative sanity and safety of Bavaria, taking with him Eva's jewellery at her request.

The last Anglo-American air raid on Berlin was on the night of 21 April. There would be no more, because now the Russian army was entering the city. The final showdown, the inevitable nemesis, was fast approaching. Even for Hitler the writing was on the wall – and in rather large letters. And then the Russian guns opened up.

The next day, 22 April, the Goebbels family moved into the Bunker on a permanent basis, signalling to all that time was running out. At the main three-hour conference of the day, Hitler broke down utterly, breaking into a rage so violent that it shocked all who were present, the generals and the politicians, even the secretaries and aides listening to the screaming through the plywood wall. Hitler, it seemed, finally saw reality plain and realized he was staring defeat and demise in the face. And he could not handle it. He blamed everyone but himself. He blamed the army, the traitors, all the corruption and failure and lies.

'The war is lost!' he screamed, confronting reality for the first time. His face went white and then purple and knotted; he was berserk, virtually out of his mind, standing there, silent and trembling. And then, exhausted, he slumped down, burnt out, all hope extinguished. It was the end, he said, it was all over, the Third Reich had failed and would perish; its founder had no choice but to perish with it.

Hitler's main personal dilemma was now solved. He would not go to the National Redoubt around Obersalzberg in Bavaria and fight on in the mountains. Anyone else could go if they wanted, but he was going to stay in Berlin, and meet his end here. Entreaties from top ministers and generals had no effect. 'I will never leave Berlin,' he screamed, '*never*!' He would take over the defence of Berlin. He would fight to the last, even though he was physically no longer capable of fighting, and he would die in Berlin, though he would never let himself be taken by the enemy, dead or alive. He ordered the people of Berlin to be informed, and by the next day the news had flashed round the world. Those who had been at this conference, a turning point in the events that were to unfold, were emotionally shattered by it, and some for the first time were distinctly critical.

There was an exodus of top Nazis from the Bunker and Berlin after that. One of them, the Foreign Minister, Ribbentrop, called on Eva to say goodbye.

'You are the only one who can get the Führer away from here,' he told her. 'Tell him you want to leave Berlin with him. You can thereby do Germany a great service.'

'I will not tell the Führer a word of your proposal,' she replied. 'If he thinks it is right to remain in Berlin, I will stay with him. If he goes, I will go too.'

Ribbentrop shook his head, kissed Eva on the cheek, and left. One day he would be hanged.

Later that afternoon, after Hitler had seen to the incineration of his private papers, something extraordinary happened. Hitler met with Eva, his two secretaries, Traudl Junge and Gerda Christian, and his vegetarian cook, Konstanze Manzialy. A plane was arriving in Berlin, he told the women, to take them to safety in Munich. All told some forty members of the Reich Chancellery group and most of the senior army officers would be making their escape that evening.

'All is lost,' Hitler told the women. 'It is best if you leave for the Obersalzberg immediately.'

Hitler turned to leave, and at that moment, as Traudl Junge observed, Eva Braun walked across to him and took both his hands in hers.

'But you know that I'll stay with you,' she said in a soft, consoling voice. 'I'm not letting you send me away.'

And then Hitler's eyes began to shine from within and he did something none of the other women in the room had ever seen him do before. He leaned towards Eva, pulled her face down to his and kissed her full on the lips.

That afternoon there was a long military briefing. After that Hitler could do nothing more. He sat in silence on a bench in the corridor cuddling a puppy on his lap, watching people come and go about their business. Then Eva Braun came out of her room, and on an impulse – another life-affirming, death-defying act – walked out of the Bunker, where it was impossible to tell whether it was night or day, summer or winter, and up into the real world above, a world of sky and breeze and grass and bird-song – and springtime! Traudl Junge and Christian Schroeder went with her. Traudl Junge remembered:

> The air was mild and you could feel the spring. The trees were in blossom, quiet and peaceful. All at once we heard the birds, we saw the daffodils flowering in the grass, and nature waking to new life. Up here in the open air you could breathe more easily, your head was clearer. The dogs romped about on the grass, and we sat on a rock and smoked. Even Eva Braun lit a cigarette.

And then they heard the first air-raid siren wailing and hurried back down again, into the catacomb, the anti-life of the Bunker – and Hitler. Another air raid had started now, more bombs falling, anti-aircraft guns blasting away. In the Bunker the iron door along the corridor was closed, Hitler had the radio on, listening to the news and the air-raid reports. Suddenly Traudl Junge felt terribly sorry for him. 'He was no longer a commander, a politician, a dictator,' she was to record. 'Instead he was a hopelessly disappointed man, toppled from the greatest heights, broken, lonely.'

Then, footsteps dragging, Hitler went out to the officers.

'Gentlemen, it's over,' he announced. 'I shall stay here in Berlin and shoot myself when the moment comes. Anyone who wants to can go now. Everyone is free to go.'

And that was that.

'I am so terribly frightened!'

With most of the army and political staff departed, there was no set timetable any more, no more military briefings, no differences of class or rank – just a kind of casual informality, with people wandering vaguely from room to room, the Goebbels children singing and playing in the corridor, everyone smoking their heads off (not that Hitler cared any more) and losing count of date and time. 'It seemed to me almost incredible,' Traudl Junge recalled, 'that we could still eat and drink, sleep and talk. We did it mechanically. We had become perfectly indifferent in those hours. We'd given up waiting. We sat about talking, smoking, vegetating. You get tired doing that.'

Hitler too began to turn his back on the old formal protocol of the Bunker, with himself at the top of the pyramid and everyone else near the bottom. He was now Führer of nothing, a non-Reich, deprived of power over virtually anything and everything – the increasingly squalid Führerbunker included. If anyone had power of life and death over the Bunker folk now, it was the Bunker's pumping and ventilation engineer, Johannes Hentschel, a highly reliable and responsible man who had worked at the Berlin Bunker since its beginning before the war and alone provided the basic air and water they needed for survival. And it was to Hentschel, in a ruminative moment of man-to-man, chaps-only frankness, that Hitler – wandering about like everyone else in those last days, seeking the companionship of others as an antidote to the imminence of death – unloaded his final considered wisdom regarding another of life's basic requirements, namely men, women and sex. He was down to earth, devoid of romantic illusions, faintly disenchanted, as Hentschel recalled:

> Let me tell you all there is to know about this copu-
> lation business. Follow my advice and you'll never go
> wrong: trust no man, and no woman either, below the
> waist. You know why? Below the umbilicus all men are
> goats or centaurs, horny goats when they are young and
> randy centaurs when they get older. And the women?
> Below those dainty waists they are as hot-blooded as
> Prussian mares in the springtime. Worse than mares.
> All women are in perpetual heat.

Nevertheless, Hitler increasingly spent more and more of his time with the women in the Bunker, his secretaries and even his cook included. He was a man who genuinely liked women, per-petual heat or not, and was at ease in their company. For one thing they were the same gender as the mother he adored to his dying breath. For another, they were not Prussian generals. That evening at dinner, as a token of his affection and esteem, Hitler gave each of the women a potassium cyanide capsule – at least they called it cyanide, though it was almost certainly prussic acid, a poison with which cyanide is almost universally confused but which is infinitely more reliable and far quicker to act. The capsule looked like a rather flashy lipstick holder containing a glass phial with a transparent liquid inside it. Crush the phial between your teeth and the cyanide/prussic acid would cause a virtually instantaneous progression from breathlessness, through paralysis and unconsciousness to death in seconds.*

'I suggest you keep the phial with you from now on,' Hitler told them, 'to use if and when you want to.'

Eva put a brave face on it, and did not lock herself away and brood, or drink or drug herself into a stupor like some of the others. Her main tasks were to keep Hitler happy and prepare as well as possible for the end. She had by now given up all hope of becoming Hitler's wife.

But it was hard. To Traudl Junge she confessed: 'I am so terribly frightened.' To Speer she later confided:

> One needs courage when death is near. I hope that my courage doesn't fail me at the end. How about some champagne for a farewell drink?

Earlier Hitler had expressed to Speer a very different attitude. 'Believe me, Speer,' he said, 'it is easy for me to put an end to my life. One brief moment, and I am free of everything, liberated from this painful existence.'

Eva now felt impelled to write her farewells. To her close friend Herta Schneider she wrote on 22 April:

> My dear little Herta,
>
> These are the very last lines and therefore the last sign of life from me. I'm sending you my jewellery. I hope

---

* The poison was indeed dehydrated prussic acid (HCN with an additive of 2 per cent oxylic acid). Some 4,000–5,000 of these so-called 'self-destructors' were produced in the laboratories of the Reich Criminological Technological Institute in Sachsenhausen concentration camp.

that with this jewellery you'll be able to keep your heads out of water. We're fighting here to the bitter end. I can't tell you how much I'm suffering personally on the Führer's account. Forgive me if this letter is a little incoherent, but Goebbels' six children are in the next room making an infernal racket. What else should I tell you? I can't understand how all this happened, it's enough to make one lose one's faith in God.

I shall die as I lived. It's no burden. You know that. With fondest love and kisses.

Eva

Perhaps everything will turn out happily, but *he* has lost faith.

The next day she wrote to her sister Gretl, due to give birth any day to the baby of her husband, Hermann Fegelein:

My dear little sister,

How sad I am that you're going to receive such a letter from me. But it's inevitable. Every day, every hour, the end may be upon us . . . As for the Führer, he has lost all hope for a happy outcome. But all of us believe that while there's life there's hope. But naturally we're not going to be caught alive.

By the same courier she was sending as a gift to Gretl the diamond bracelet and topaz pendant Hitler had given her for her last birthday, also some tobacco for Papa and some chocolate for Mama. She went on:

> Now, my dear little sister, I wish you lots and lots of happiness. And don't forget you'll certainly see Hermann [Gretl's husband, Fegelein] again. With most affectionate greetings and a kiss from your sister.
>
> Eva

Eva also instructed her sister to look after the correspondence between herself and Hitler, which was kept at the Berghof, and to pack it all in a waterproof container and if possible bury it. Later, however, it seems the SS custodian in charge of the collection, comprising some 250 letters and cards, set fire to the lot and totally destroyed it.

That same day, 23 April, Hitler lost control again, and this time almost went out of his mind. A message was received from Göring announcing that, since it was clear the Führer was going to meet his death in Berlin, he assumed the Führer now expected him to take over the leadership of the Third Reich. Hitler's rage on hearing this premature but not unreasonable sitrep was of a truly apocalyptic order. He had always known Göring was fat, lazy, incompetent, a crook, a drug addict – but now, a traitor! Göring, for so long a grand player in the Hitler legend, was instantly dismissed and stripped of all rank and office.

That day also happened to be the last time Albert Speer would ever see the Führer. Neither Hitler nor anyone else knew of Speer's foiled plan to terminate the Führer, the war and the further destruction of the Fatherland by pumping poison gas down the Bunker's ventilation shaft. Oblivious of this super-treachery, Hitler continued to regard his personal friend and colleague as a source of solace and diversion after the shock of Göring's so-called treachery, and he spent much of his time reminiscing to Speer about the good old days – his principal distraction in the Bunker, which he never left – and the dream future that would never be. He would like to retire to his native Austria one day, Hitler told his architect friend. Speer recalled:

> He would build a house a few miles upstream from Linz, on the Danube. The house would have two architects' studios. I would always be welcome to use one of them. How pleasant it would be, he said, to watch all the power-brokers fading away. He and Fräulein Braun would be so happy to entertain the Speers anytime, as weekend guests.

Later that evening Hitler began to scream and rage again about the 'traitorous Göring' and this time it was left to Eva to calm him down, not by placation but by a diversionary tactic.

'Look,' she said, walking over to him. 'You're really rather dirty.'

She pointed at the soup and mustard stains on Hitler's grey field uniform jacket.

'But this is my work suit!' the Führer retorted, forgetting the traitor Göring. 'I can't go to a conference wearing an apron!'

When Hanna Reitsch, the famous woman pilot, flew Göring's replacement, General Ritter von Greim, into Berlin, she was impressed how calm Eva was – much the calmest in the Bunker – and how charming, thoughtful and attentive to the ailing Führer's needs, and how attractive looking in those grim circumstances.

'I want to be a pretty corpse'

The same day as Göring's apparent treachery, Hitler began to make plans for his end. He explained to his valet, Heinz Linge, in the presence of Eva, how he wanted all his personal effects to be destroyed after his death, how he aimed to shoot himself and take poison at the same time, and how he wanted his body to be burned.

Eva walked out of the room then. She was resolved to die with Hitler but was full of dread at the prospect. A little later she told Traudl Junge, 'I want to be a pretty corpse. I'm going to take poison. I wonder if it hurts? I'm so afraid of having to suffer for a long time.'

Late on the evening of 23 April Speer returned to the Bunker. The only person still up was Eva Braun and for two hours they sat talking in her bed-sitting room over champagne and cookies, with Hitler asleep in the next room. Outwardly at least, Speer perceived, Eva seemed to be the only Bunker inmate who was actually happy – serene, composed, normal, content that she was going to her death with the man she loved. But inwardly she was different. 'Frau Junge,' Eva told Hitler's secretary later, taking her hands, her voice husky and trembling, 'I'm so dreadfully frightened. If only it was all over!'

On 26 April there was another critical twist in the plot, the bi-product of an event that only tangentially involved them. Eva and Hitler attended a double wedding of two Waffen-SS orderlies and their brides in the ruins of the Führer's apartment in the Chancellery above the Bunker – a high-ceilinged room dimly lit by candles. Outside, the guns known as Stalin organs made their own kind of terrible music, inside the newly weds and the guests danced to the music of a fiddle and accordion – 'as if they were dancing,' in the words of one who was present, 'on the edge of a volcano'. It was apparent to other guests at the wedding that both Eva and Hitler were deeply moved by the ceremony.

A day or two later Eva received a thank-you note from one of the orderlies. She immediately took it to Hitler in his study and read it aloud to him. 'If I am killed in battle now,' it went, 'I will die happy because I was permitted to marry my sweetheart.' Hitler nodded and Eva said, 'I am so happy for them.' At that point Hitler got out of his chair, went over to Eva, and whispered something in her ear. Traudl Junge was at the other end of the room, and saw Eva step back and stare at Hitler in utter disbelief. Hitler nodded reassuringly, then went to the door and called for Goebbels, while Eva walked towards Traudl Junge, her eyes glistening.

'Tonight you will certainly cry,' she said to Traudl.

Traudl thought she meant the end had come and Eva and Hitler were going to kill themselves that evening. She went out into the corridor. As Gauleiter of Berlin, Goebbels had been given the task of locating someone in the terminal chaos of the capital with the authority to marry the Führer and his bride. She could hear Goebbels giving orders to Waffen-SS soldiers to locate a certain Walter Wagner, an official in the Berlin city council now serving with a Volkssturm detachment in the Friedrichstrasse.

So why did Hitler wish to marry now? He had once told Traudl Junge, 'I wouldn't be a good head of a family. I would consider it irresponsible to start a family when I cannot devote myself to my wife sufficiently. Besides, I want no children of my own. The offspring of geniuses often have a hard time in the world. They are mostly cretins.'

And there was another consideration. Hitler had always exerted an intense fascination among German womanhood that could almost be described as sexual infatuation on a mass scale. Hitler had ascribed his own loyalty to German womanhood and their loyal support of his own charismatic self as the reason he chose to remain a bachelor. This is what he meant when he told the teenage Eva Braun at his very first meeting with her, 'I am married to Germany.'

But these reservations were no longer relevant. Children were no longer an issue. The women of Germany had receded into the outer darkness of a defeated Germany. Hitler now felt free to break his monastic rule, perhaps – free, even, to marry the woman of his life. So was marriage a last-minute reward for loyalty and services rendered, an opportunity to rectify the ambiguity of her ambiguous position at the Führer's court at a moment when it no longer mattered one way or the other? The evidence of other women present in the Chancellery and the Bunker suggests it was more than that.

'I only ever saw Adolf Hitler shed tears twice,' his secretary Traudl Junge was to recall. 'The first time was when she refused to leave the Bunker. The second time was when they got married.' It seems clear that in the latter years – the toughest times – Hitler was devoted to the girl, full of admiration for her, still attracted to her; in a word, he was in love with her. In Albert Speer's view she was not a mere floozy, not the shallow, banal, trivial wench that some (mainly other women) made her out to be. Speer recalled:

She was a modest woman, endowed with common sense, extremely calm and quite the bravest and most intelligent woman in the Bunker. She wanted to stay there, and she wanted to die there – which you can understand if she really loved him. And there was no doubt Hitler had the greatest respect for her, and her love was very significant for him.

According to Speer, the sexual relationship between Eva and Hitler in the past had been 'perfectly normal'. But Speer did not inspect the sheets. The wife of Hitler's administrator at the Berghof *did* inspect the sheets – *and* Eva's and Adolf's dirty linen – and so did all the chambermaids, and at no time could any of them ever detect the slightest indication of any trace of a normal male-female sexual union between the two. There were others whose instinct told them that whatever this relationship might be – a love match, maybe, a meeting of souls of a kind – it was not an overtly sexual one. Heinrich Hoffmann, who had known them both from the day they first met, was adamant: 'I believe Hitler's relationship with Eva Braun was strictly platonic.'

But sex was no longer an issue. For Hitler to marry the woman and tidy up the relationship once and for all was now but a step – and it was now or never.

'A collection of German arseholes'

By 28 April the Battle of Berlin was reaching its bloody climax. The distance between the Eastern Front and the Western Front, German soldiers quipped, was now one tube stop on the Berlin subway – not that it was running any more. Russian forces now stood at the northern, southern and eastern perimeters of the government quarter in the city centre, and the battle for the Tiergarten, the public park whose eastern end fringed the Reich Chancellery, had reached a climactic stage with some of the bitterest fighting since Stalingrad. By now the Chancellery itself was under continuous shellfire. Explosions nearby caused the whole mass of the cement membrane of the Bunker to shake due to the rapid transmission of shock waves in the sandy soil, and with each explosion Hitler would start in his chair, while the sulphurous reek of cordite was sucked down into that underground warren by the Bunker's ventilation system.

Hitler and his remaining staff could only follow the progress of the battle by calling random numbers on the telephone, but often Russian voices answered the calls, and increasingly the lines were dead. Not that it mattered. Hitler himself shuffled up and down the Bunker corridors, clutching a Berlin petrol station street map that was falling apart in his clammy, trembling hands. His power was now so shrunken that it covered no more than a few square yards of disputed city streets, yet still he clung to hope and life, still he cherished the fantasy that the army of General Wenck (itself a fantasy) would fight its way to Berlin and throw the Russians back.

Hitler's main preoccupation was increasingly his own fate – he was obsessed that he would be captured alive by the Russians, 'squeezed until the pips squeak and then displayed in a cage in a Moscow Zoo.' It was clear to all but a faithful few that the Führer must die. It required a new development to persuade the Führer himself to think so too. At 9 p.m. the BBC broadcast the news that Heinrich Himmler, without any reference to Hitler, had offered unconditional surrender to the Allies. Hitler was seized by an almost apoplectic fury over what he saw as Himmler's treachery. Himmler was beyond the reach of his vengeance, but a substitute was close at hand in the form of Himmler's liaison officer at the Bunker, who was none other than SS Brigadeführer Hermann Fegelein, who was the husband of Eva Braun's sister was therefore Hitler's prospective brother-in-law.

Fegelein had never quite been what he seemed. Charming and debonair to most, including Eva Braun above all, he was in reality, in the view of German historian Anton Joachimsthaler, 'one of the most evil and disgusting careerists within the Nazi elite, the SS'. Formerly he had been in command of the SS cavalry brigade, who utterly detested him and whose lives he recklessly and brutally squandered. His SS file portrays a corrupt and incompetent officer, servile to those above him, arrogant to those below, with a criminal bent that included the theft of money and luxury goods from a military train from the East, for which he only escaped court martial by the intervention of the head of the SS, Heinrich Himmler himself. Fegelein was also an unscrupulous and compulsive womanizer, with a smug, inveigling leer and invasive charm that won numerous unwary women's hearts. He had been engaged to a number of German girls and in May 1941 was arraigned before an SS court on the charge that he was 'suspected if not proved to have maintained sexual relations with a Polish woman in Krakau, made her pregnant and then induced her to have an abortion'. The case was quashed on the direct intervention of Himmler, and Fegelein's murky career continued upwards until by March 1944 he found himself working as Himmler's liaison officer with Hitler and on occasion lunching at Hitler's table at the Berghof – often in the company of Hitler's lady, Eva Braun. Hitler's secretary, Traudl Junge, was later to describe his impact:

> At the beginning he only came for briefings, but after he had quickly made friends with Martin Bormann and others he quickly became the focus of attention – the

life and soul – of Berghof society. Fegelein was the archetypal romantic hero. He was incredibly cheeky and wore the Knight's Cross with Oak Leaves and Swords, and it was therefore not surprising that he was accustomed to have women throw themselves at him. He was also entertaining and habitually told funny and risqué stories without the slightest sign of embarrassment . . . The handsome Hermann succeeded in gaining Eva Braun's favour so astonishingly quickly; on the other hand it is not really astonishing if one took into account how fresh, funny and amusing Fegelein could be when he wanted to.

That Eva was strongly attracted to Fegelein there is no doubt. But in a curious twist to this burgeoning plot, it was Eva who contrived to arrange the marriage of her sister Gretl to the lecherous Hermann – so effectively that within a month they were engaged to be married and within three months (on 3 June 1944) were duly celebrating their marriage in the Salzburg City Hall and on the Obersalzberg. 'I want this marriage to be as beautiful as if it were my own,' Eva had declared. And sure enough her own star rose in the Hitler entourage from this point on. Now there was an element of security in her life. Now she was somebody. Now she was Fegelein's sister-in-law. Traudl Junge noted:

Young, zestful Eva, who had to live such a withdrawn and demure life, was overjoyed when she finally had a brother-in-law (or boyfriend) with whom she could dance and flirt to her heart's content without running the risk of gossip.

Hitler's other secretary, Frau Christa Schroeder, was quick to note the impact of this lecherous and beguiling new presence.

> Eva Braun was attracted to Hermann Fegelein as a man, and that he liked the pretty girl very much – who was much better suited to him than to the old man [Hitler] – could not have escaped the attention of any observer who was present at the small, intimate parties that Eva Braun arranged in her room in the Chancellery before and after air raids during the final weeks of her life.

But by 26 April 1945 Fegelein had not been seen in the Bunker for two days – he clearly had no intention of perishing at his Führer's side. Eva Braun was surprised and seemingly a little upset that her friend and brother-in-law Hermann Fegelein had not been in touch with her. No one seemed to know where he was or what he was up to. Then, during the night of 26 April, he telephoned Eva from his Berlin apartment at 4 Bleibtreustrasse ('Stay Faithful Street') and told her, 'Eva, you must abandon the Führer if you can't persuade him to leave Berlin. Don't be stupid – it's a matter of life and death.'

Not long afterwards Fegelein was arrested in his apartment by the Gestapo as he was preparing to leave. With him was his latest mistress – a young Hungarian redhead who managed to slip away on some pretext or other. Fegelein had changed into civilian clothes and had packed a suitcase containing over 200 pieces of silver and other valuables (including a diamond watch belonging to Eva) with which he had been intending to decamp across the German border into neutral Switzerland.

Fegelein was summarily bundled out of the apartment and brought back under guard to the Reich Chancellery to stand trial for desertion. Before leaving the apartment he telephoned his sister-in-law in the Bunker again. There had been a misunderstanding, he told her. Could she possibly use her influence with the Führer to help sort it out? But Eva would not – and probably could not – help her brother-in-law. Her answer was a curt no. He should come back to the Bunker forthwith. And as Fegelein was being marched back to meet his fate, she publicly declared, 'Poor, poor Adolf! Deserted by everyone, betrayed by all! Better that ten thousand others die than that he be lost to Germany.'

Eva had always fancied Fegelein, flirted with him, danced with him. It was Fegelein, through his marriage to her sister, who had established her credentials at Hitler's court, provided a raison d'etre for her presence at Hitler's side. It was Fegelein who so often danced with Eva at her intimate little late-night parties up in the Chancellery. No one will ever know which was the bitterest blow for Eva – news of Fegelein's betrayal of the Führer through his complicity in Himmler's peace-feelers, or news of his betrayal of herself and her sister through his affair with his new mistress in Berlin.

SS General Wilhelm Mohnke, military commander of the citadel area, was in charge of Fegelein's court martial in the second bunker. He was to recall later:

> Roaring drunk, with wild, rolling eyes, Fegelein kept blubbering that he was responsible to Himmler, not Hitler. He refused to defend himself. The man was in wretched shape – bawling, whining, vomiting, shaking like an aspen leaf. Then he began urinating on the floor. He really was drunk. He tore off his epaulettes and threw them on the floor. He called us a collection of German arseholes.

Mohnke decided the accused was not in a fit condition to stand trial and the other judges concurred. He was led away in handcuffs to face interrogation in the Gestapo cellar and Mohnke never saw him again. The following evening, when Hitler heard that documents incriminating Fegelein in Himmler's clandestine and treacherous peace-feelers had been found in his briefcase in the Chancellery, he ordered him to be executed immediately on the grounds of high treason. Exactly how or where Fegelein died is not entirely clear – possibly in the Gestapo cellar where he was held, more probably up in the Chancellery garden. What is clear is that Hitler postponed his wedding for about an hour until he received confirmation that the bride's brother-in-law was dead. Eva too was informed of his death, but as Gerda Christian noted after the wedding: 'There were tears in her blue eyes, but they were tears of radiant joy.'

While Fegelein was being tortured or (more likely) shot to death – 'shot like a dog,' as Traudl Junge put it, 'in the Park of the Foreign Office under the blossoming trees' – shortly before midnight on 28 April, his sister-in-law was getting ready for her great moment. When she was eighteen she had taken a bath, put on her best knickers and gone to meet Adolf Hitler for her first rendezvous. Now, at thirty-three, preparing for her last rendezvous, she took a bath, washed her hair, waved it herself, perfumed herself, put on her best knickers, then selected the most appropriate dress to wear from the wardrobe in her little bunker room – Hitler's favourite, a black dress (her own favourite colour), silk taffeta, wide skirted, with two gold clasps on the pink shoulder straps. On her feet she wore black suede shoes with modern wedge heels, round her neck a pearl necklace, round her wrist a platinum watch with diamond numbers, and in her hair a gold clip. She was pale, lovely, calm, happy, if not radiant. When Traudl Junge caught a glimpse of her, she looked so beautiful that Traudl felt impelled to whisper to Gerda Christian, 'Why is she dressed so well to die?'

Wagner at the Opera

The big occasion had begun with a supper party in Hitler's study, the table festively laid with food and champagne glasses for the bride and groom to be and their guests – the Führerbunker veterans Goebbels and his wife, Axmann, Bormann, Generals Burgdorf and Krebs, secretary Gerda Christian and cook Constanze Manziarly. Traudl Junge was not there. Hitler had taken her to the small map room to dictate to her his political testament – 'the last page in the history of the Third Reich,' as she put it – and his private will. All this she took down in shorthand, and when Hitler eventually returned to his wedding supper she went and sat in the conference passage and began to type it out.

The conference room now became the wedding room in which Hitler and Eva Braun would be formally married, with Goebbels and Bormann present in addition to the bride and groom and the marriage official, Walter Wagner. Herr Wagner was the mystery man at the wedding, an unknown face to all except Dr Goebbels, thirty-seven years of age, married with a baby son he had never set eyes on (and never would), Wagner was a Nazi Party member of long standing, and a local council member who as head of the main department of legal affairs for the Gauleitung staff in Berlin was personally known to Dr Goebbels as possessing the necessary registrar and notary credentials to conduct a wedding. With some difficulty, and sometimes under enemy fire, the bewildered bureaucrat had been brought to the Chancellery inside an armoured car and then led down into the bowels of the earth to officiate at one of the last and bizarrest set-pieces in his Führer's life. His first encounter with his legendary hero would prove not only awesome but shocking.

For Hitler was in dreadful shape for such an occasion. Professor (Colonel) Schenk, a surgeon who ran an emergency operating theatre in the main Chancellery cellar, up to his elbows in entrails, arteries and gore, and surrounded by buckets of blood and human limbs, had met him earlier that day and was amazed at the decrepitude of the once mighty Führer. Since his narrow escape from assassination by disaffected German army officers in the 20 July Bomb Plot of the previous year, very few photos or newsreel shots of Hitler had been seen by the German public, and the sight of him now was shocking. For a start, his uniform was sloppy and stained with food. His head was sunken in 'like a turtle', his spine hunched, his curved shoulders twitching and trembling. He hardly seemed to be able to shuffle two paces at a time and looked in danger of losing his balance. His eyes seemed unfocused and filmy, the whites bloodshot. His face was yellow and grey, puckered, expressionless, immobile. Droopy black sacks hung under his eyes, deep lines ran past his pulpy nose to his mouth, and his lips trembled and drooled saliva. His handshake was a flappy, listless gesture.

'I was profoundly shocked,' Schenk recalled. 'At fifty-six the Führer was a palsied, physical wreck. The man, I am sure, was senile.'

Two hours later, Schenk was able to observe Hitler again, seated at a table. He was clutching the table with his left hand in an effort to stop the violent trembling and shuddering that ran up the whole of his left arm, and had wrapped his left leg round the leg of the table to try and stop his leg shaking uncontrollably. 'These are the classic symptoms of *paralysis agitans*,' Schenk was to comment later, 'what in English you call Parkinson's disease.' Unknown to Schenk, Hitler's former physician, Dr Morell, had already diagnosed this disease and was administering two drops a day of a medication he described as 'Homburg 680, a Bulgarian-Italian drug manufactured in Kassel'.

What Schenk did not mention was how smelly Hitler could be. He had suffered for much of his life from flatulence, sometimes farting and belching abominably, and for many years had been addicted to anti-gas pills whose toxic ingredients may have contributed to his final dementia. To make matters worse, new research recently published in the *Journal of Forensic Science* reveals that Hitler was tormented by tooth decay, abscesses and gum disease that caused 'terrible bad breath'. As one of his secretaries, Frau Schroeder, remarked later, 'I would never have wanted to kiss Hitler. He had very yellow teeth and his breath smelt.'

This, then, was the wrecked human being who had rallied millions by his rhetoric and dynamism, the Führer in eclipse whom Walter Wagner was presented to, the pitiful lover Eva Braun was about to marry. Not that Hitler did not still have the power to electrify. 'He was still the Führer, Chancellor, Supreme Commander-in-Chief of the Armed Forces,' Schenk recalled. 'My whole body seemed to freeze. A chill went up and down my upper spine.'

If that was the effect on Schenk, a surgeon professor and 'a mere colonel' (as he put it), how much greater the impact on Walter Wagner, a local government official and a 'mere' platoon commander in the local Home Guard – and confronted, moreover, not just with Hitler, but with Goebbels and Bormann as well – an awesome trio, each one of them endowed with the power of life and death. Indeed, Walter Wagner was so fazed by the circumstances he found himself in that for several minutes he stood fumbling with his papers. Marrying people, especially Führers, was not his normal line of business.

'You can call me Frau Hitler if you like'

'Herr Wagner,' Eva Braun said at length, 'can we get on with the ceremony? It's getting late.'

Wagner nodded and laid the two pages of the marriage document on the table in front of him in the conference room. He was painstaking, almost (in Eva's view) plodding. He would ask a question, then fill in the relevant section of the document, then ask another question. Though it was late in the evening and dark up top, the Russian artillery kept up its relentless pounding, and shells continued to land in the Chancellery garden above them, shaking the concrete bunker structure and showering flakes of white cement on to the bridal pair like wedding rice.

'Herr Wagner,' Eva cajoled the struggling marriage maker. 'Please hurry.'

Wagner was doing his best to shortcut the whole nerve-wrenching thing. He missed out the names of Hitler's father and mother, and when it came to proof of Hitler's identity he simply scrawled 'Personally known'. He did, however, ask to see Eva's identity card.

Wagner had been told to get through the marriage service with the minimum of delay. He therefore married them as a 'war couple' under special laws, 'considering the war situation and special circumstances'. Embarrassingly, however, he could not legally avoid asking first the Führer and then his bride two excruciating questions. He turned towards Hitler, who had annihilated millions of Jews and other non-Aryans to date, along with a goodly number of congenital idiots and incurables.

'My Führer, Adolf Hitler,' he asked, 'do you affirm that you are a third-generation Aryan? And do you also affirm that you have no inheritable diseases that would exclude you from marriage?'

Hitler duly affirmed, naturally, and so did his bride.

'Ich komme nunmehr,' declared Wagner, *'zum Feierlichen Akt der Eheschliessung.'* (I now come to the ceremonial act of marriage.) He spoke with a typical metropolitan Berlin accent. It was to chime melodically, like an instrument in a string trio, with Eva's pleasant Bavarian chirp and Hitler's thick Austrian twang.

He turned again towards Hitler.

'In the presence of the witnesses mentioned under sections three and four [of the marriage document] I ask you, my Führer, Adolf Hitler – are you willing to take Fräulein Eva Braun as your wife? If you are, answer "Yes".'

'Ja,' replied Hitler. 'Yes.'

'Now,' Wagner continued, 'I ask you, Fräulein Eva Braun, are you willing to take our Führer, Adolf Hitler, as your husband? If you are, answer, "Yes".'

'Ja,' Eva replied. 'Yes.'

'Both newlyweds having stated their intentions,' Wagner went on, 'I declare this marriage as legal before the law – Berlin, 28 April . . .'

Wagner, glancing at his watch and realizing that it was now gone midnight and the start of a new day, corrected himself.

'Berlin, 29 April 1945.'

'With a pedantic scribble,' Eva was to relate to Gerda Christian afterwards, Wagner changed the date on the marriage certificate and passed it across for Hitler, Eva, and the witnesses Goebbels and Bormann to sign. Hitler's palsied hand shook so violently that his signature was virtually illegible. Eva was clearly as distrait as Wagner, for when it came to her turn to sign she wrote 'Eva B . . .' then corrected herself and continued with a bold 'Hitler geb Braun' (Hitler nee Braun).

Though Hitler was rather subdued, Eva was elated. She had known the man who was now her husband for nearly half her thirty-three years, she had loved him and honoured him dearly and now – miracle of miracles – she was Frau Hitler, the First Lady at last of an Empire that had virtually ceased to exist, and like herself and her beloved had only a few more hours to go.

Schenk met her a few hours later and was amazed at how unconcerned she seemed about her likely destiny. 'A lithe, well-dressed blonde,' is how he perceived her. 'On any other occasion it might have been a mildly titillating occasion for me.' He had never heard of her before, never knew there was such a thing as a Frau Hitler. She was chatting away in a chirpy but agreeable Bavarian accent with a group sitting at the table in the Bunker corridor, seemingly oblivious of the looming future: 'the real life of the party – like a Rhineland carnival queen – not drunk but well on her way to it, tossing her glass back regularly. But she was not the sweet, simple woman she seemed to be. She was deeply neurotic, fighting back hysteria.'

The wedding over, the bride and groom now walked out of the map room into the conference passage where the guests were waiting to congratulate the newly weds. Traudl Junge was amazed to see that Hitler was in tears – the second time she had seen him in this unusual condition, and again for the same reason, she reckoned, his love for Eva. As for Eva herself, she seemed full of joy. When it was clear no one seemed quite certain how to address her, she smiled and told them, 'You can call me Frau Hitler if you like.' But somehow nobody did, not even her husband, for whom she remained to the end as she had always been – Fräulein Braun or Fräulein Eva.

The happy couple shook hands with everyone, then retired into their private suite, where they were shortly joined by the rest of the wedding party, some dozen guests in all.

Someone put Eva's favourite record on the gramophone. 'Blood Red Roses Spell Happiness for You,' went the ditty once again, 'Happiness for You, Happiness for You . . .' There was champagne and sweet wine to drink, sandwiches and sweets to eat, and the little wedding supper went on for some hours. Hitler, a partial abstainer for much of his life, broke his usual custom and took a glass of sweet wine to celebrate the occasion, raising his glass along with the others as they toasted his wife.

Then he made a short speech – a whimsical reverie as to what might have been. He had always had a wish, he said, to retire to his old home town in Austria and settle down with his wife Eva and live a life of peace and contentment as an ordinary citizen, unburdened by the onerous duties of state. During the war he had several times searched for a place to build a home, but never found what he was looking for. Now it seemed he never would. National Socialism was finished, he declared, and would never be revived – death would be a relief now that he knew his best friends (meaning Göring and Himmler) had betrayed him.

Walter Wagner, a relative nobody from the outer dark of embattled Berlin, now found himself in a no less embattled situation at the Führer's bunker wedding party, and was still shocked and bewildered by his abrupt change of circumstance and the terrifyingly exalted company that was now quaffing and munching around him in the Führer's small concrete cell beneath Berlin.

For it was not exactly his kind of party. He was somebody – a relative nobody – picked off the barricades, middling job, middling rank, never commanded an army, never advised a Führer (till a minute ago). Nobody knew who the hell he was or where he came from (Goebbels excepted) – but he knew who *they* were, and it was awesome. And he also knew that the Russians were still up there in the streets – as he would soon find out when this little job was over.

After twenty minutes of supping champagne, gobbling liverwurst sandwiches, and trying to make sense to the rulers of the Reich, Wagner was ushered out, job done, moment in history over, and taken to the steps that led up to the Bunker exit. Here, breathing a sigh of relief – and the cordite-fumed night air of Berlin in flames – he left the nightmare of the Bunker nether world and stepped out into the shellfire and hellfire of the massed Russian guns – the *Götterdämmerung*, the Twilight of the Gods at the end of Wagner's 'Ring' cycle, the final extinction of the symbols of might and power that would consume them all. And within a few hours or so he would be dead.

Transcendentally Wicked

Meanwhile Hitler himself kept coming along to see how Traudl Junge was getting on typing out his last will and political testament, while Eva retired to her room. It was not till the early hours of 29 April that Junge finished typing up the Führer's dictation. There were three copies of each document. Hitler took the clean copies, to which he appended a feeble and contracted signature, for his hands now shook so badly he could hardly write.

The personal will was a simple document. In it he gave the reasons for his marriage of an hour or two ago and the impending death of himself and his new wife in a few hours from now.

> Although during my years of struggle I believed I could not undertake the responsibility of marriage, I have now decided at the end of my life's journey to marry the young woman who, after many years of true friendship, came of her own free will to this city, when it was already almost completely under siege, in order to share my fate. At her own desire she will go to her death with me as my wife. This will compensate her for what we both lost through my work in the service of my people.

He went on:

> What I possess belongs, in so far as it has any value at all, to the Party. Should this no longer exist, it belongs to the State, and should the State also be destroyed, any further decision from me is no longer necessary.

Hitler concluded:

> My wife and I choose death to avoid the disgrace of defeat or capitulation. It is our wish to be cremated immediately in the place where I have done the greatest part of my work during the course of my twelve years service for my people.

In his political testament, aimed at his successors in the Party and the State, and containing his final overview for the benefit of history and posterity, Hitler named Grand Admiral Doenitz as Reich President in a successor government, with Dr Goebbels as Chancellor and Martin Bormann as Party Minister. Both Göring and Himmler were condemned as traitors and thrown out of the Party. Hitler denied all responsibility for the war, which he claimed he had never wanted. Instead he blamed it on 'international statesmen who were either Jewish or who worked for Jewish interests' and lamented the fact that a peaceful accord with Britain had proved impossible, due to the machinations of 'international Jewry'.

Hitler went on: 'Centuries may pass, but out of the ruins of our cities and monuments in the end hatred will arise and be constantly renewed against the people responsible – international Jewry and its assistants.' He exhorted the new government to continue the war by any and every means, at all times bearing in mind his own fundamental and unalterable tenet: 'Unrelenting opposition against the poisoner of all nations, international Jewry'.

Perhaps Eva's bridegroom was not clinically insane, but he remained transcendentally wicked to the bitter end.

When each of the three top copies of the will and testament had been countersigned, three couriers were designated to carry them through the Russian ring round Berlin to their ultimate recipients, and on the afternoon of 29 April, after the usual midday situation conference, chaired by Hitler, they set off on their perilous mission. Eva, too, had written her own last farewell in the form of a missive to her sister Gretl, the letter being flown out in the last plane to leave Berlin just after midnight on 29 April – and just after the death of Gretl's husband and Eva's

Taken 1948 in Uffing on Staffelsee

Ernst Hanfstaengl
Jan 1973

Signed photo of Ernst Hanfstaegl – Hitler's early associate
and later enemy, back home in Germany after the war

Eva Braun and Adolf at the tea house near the Berghof

Hitler bestowing his affectionate greetings on his long-term mistress Eva Braun

Inside Eva Braun's bedroom at the Berghof, with the portrait of her lover opposite the bed and door to his bedroom on the right

Eva and Adolf leaving an official function side by side

The future wife of the Führer of the Third Reich
in an unexpected pose beside a Bavarian lake

Walter Wagner – the first portrait ever published of
the mystery man at Hitler's wedding in the Bunker

HITLER'S BUNKER

KEY TO PLAN OF HITLER'S BUNKER

LOWER LEVEL

1–2	Dr Stumpfegger's room and surgery
3	Goebbels' bed-sitting room
4	Emergency switchboard, telephone exchange and air-plotting room
5	Machine room (heating, ventilation and electrical)
6–7	Corridor (with 7 serving as Conference room)
8	Guards' day room and 'dog bunker'
9	Small conference room
10	Hitler's office
11	Eva Braun's bed-sitting room
12	Toilet
13	Hitler's bedroom
14	Hitler's living room
15	Bath and dressing room
16	Electrical switchboard

UPPER LEVEL

17–18	Pantry and wine cellar
19–22	Kitchens (plus toilets and washroom)
23	Communal dining room/canteen
24–27	Rooms of the Goebbels family
28–29	Rooms for personnel
30	Unfinished concrete tower
31–32	Emergency exit to the garden of the Foreign Ministry
33	Exit to the Reich Chancellery
34	Emergency exit to the Reich Chancellery garden

Inside Hitler's quarters in the Bunker after the fall of Berlin

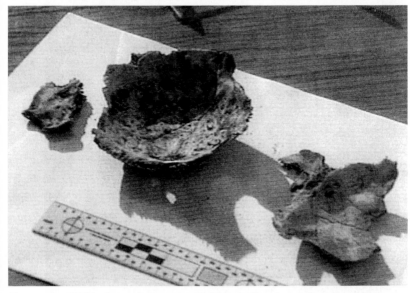

Four parts of Hitler's cranium as revealed by the Russian authorities in Moscow, with a spot of light shining through the bullet hole onto the table top

Hitler's giant window at the Berghof at the end of the war – the glass has gone but there is still a dog around the place

own wedding. The letter never reached Gretl, for Hanna Reitsch, who piloted the plane, tore it up after reading it, believing it to be too dramatic and self-serving, though she was later to claim she remembered what it said, which was broadly as follows:

> I must write you these words so that you will not feel sad over our end here in the shelter. It is rather we who are filled with sorrow because it is your fate to live on into the chaos that will follow. For myself I am glad to die here; glad to die at the side of the Führer; but most of all glad the horror now to come is spared me. What could life still give me? It has already been perfect. It has already given me its best and its fullest. Why should I go on living? This is the time to die; the right time. With the Führer I have had everything. To die now, beside him, completes my happiness. Live on as well and as happily as you can. Shed no tears over our deaths. It is the perfect and proper ending. It is the right ending for a German woman.

There was no reference to her brother-in-law – her sister Gretl's husband, the father of her soon-to-be-born baby – in the letter, which Hanna Reitsch (who did not much care for Eva) decried as 'so vulgar, so theatrical, in such poor adolescent taste'.

And so, that night, for the first time – and the last – Adolf and Eva retired together as man and wife, united by a single name and a common fate. It would probably not be exaggerating to say that theirs had been one of the strangest weddings in nuptial history, and for that matter the history of Führers, Emperors and Kings.

'The Russians will be able to spit in our windows!'

It is doubtful that Hitler slept much – if at all – during that final night. When General Mohnke was summoned to Hitler's suite in the Bunker to give the latest situation report at six o'clock on the morning of 30 April, he found the Führer seated on the edge of his bed, which looked – significantly perhaps – as though it had not been slept in. Hitler was wearing a black satin dressing gown over his white pyjamas and patent-leather slippers on his feet. He looked a nervous wreck, Mohnke noted, with the frail, unsteady movements of a prematurely aged man.

The news Mohnke brought amounted to the Führer's death sentence. Russian troops were now only four blocks from the Bunker. They now ringed his own positions in the Potsdamer Platz, only 300 yards away. They had got into the underground railway tunnels just outside the Chancellery. They were everywhere, in overwhelming strength.

'My Führer,' Mohnke said, 'as soldier to soldier I can no longer guarantee that my battle-weary troops can hold for more than one day. I now expect a frontal, massed-tank attack at dawn, 1 May – May Day. You know what May Day means to the Russians.'

Hitler knew only too well. He was also aware that his life was at an end and that if he was going to die it would have to be soon, before the Russians came clattering down the Bunker stairs. He seemed curiously disinterested, his gaze fixed on the wall behind Mohnke's head. He had hoped to last until 5 May, he told the young general, the date Napoleon died on St Helena. After that, he had no desire to live. 'We were both men born before our times,' he said. 'So much the worse for Europe.'

For an hour the Führer kept the busy general from returning to his command post, sitting there twitching in his dressing gown, pouring out whatever was uppermost inside his head. He reviewed his whole career, what he called the dream of National Socialism and why and how it failed. The German people had, in the end, proved unworthy, he complained, just not up to the supreme challenge. The war had been forced upon him by the Anglo-American plutocracy, the Marxist-Bolshevik world conspiracy, Jewish international finance, the Freemasons and the Jesuits. He had been betrayed right and left, he lamented. Even Göring, Himmler and Speer had betrayed him, and the Führer Headquarters leaked like a sieve. 'As he said this,' Mohnke was to recall, 'his voice rose, his fist clenched, his face turned white. It was obvious that the thought of treachery almost drove him mad.'

Finally Hitler gave Mohnke typed copies of his last will and testament, which he hoped the general – now effectively his fourth messenger – might be able to carry safely out of the Russian encirclement, and when the general left he began to put in order the last day of his life.

Later that morning, at the last war conference in the Bunker (and for that matter the war), the city Commandant, General Weidling, presented an even bleaker report. There was no ammunition. Hope was at an end. They could perhaps hold out for another twenty-four hours. But by May Day 'the Russians will be able to spit in our windows.' Hitler then reaffirmed to the Commandant that he himself would stay in Berlin. He did not want to have to wait for the end 'somewhere under the open sky or in a farmhouse'. He was not prepared to be caught wandering about the woods like a common criminal. He would end his life here.

By now there was no other choice. Russian artillery had already let loose a ninety-minute barrage on the Reichstag. In the streets above the Bunker an apocalypse was taking place, primordial and surreal, like a vision of hell by Hieronymus Bosch. Shell holes exposed corpses lying several layers deep in the subways. The screams of soldiers undergoing amputation without anaesthetic punctuated the massive thunder of the guns. An escaped lion had been seen loping past Gestapo Headquarters, a zebra was grazing in one of the city's cemeteries, and not far from the ruined Chancellery lay the body of another escapee, an Amazon ocelot. On iron bedsteads in the burned-out ruins of the Elizabeth Hospital lay the charred bodies of Russian soldiers and the German nurses they were in the act of raping when the building went up in flames.

'If we go under,' Goebbels, a propagandist to his last breath, had declared, 'then the whole German nation will go under with us so gloriously that even in a thousand years' time the heroic apocalypse will have pride of place in the history of the world.' Well – this was it.

Götterdämmerung

Hitler now planned for the imminent suicide of himself and his wife of one night. 'There are two ways of judging a man,' he had once told a close associate in the early days of the struggle for power – 'by the woman he marries and the way he dies.' Now the time for judgement had come.

The Bunker might be short on hope and euphoria, but by way of compensation two commodities it was not lacking were champagne and cyanide, and both were to be used by the Bunker folk as convenient ways of escape.

The first step was to kill the dogs. No formal reason was ever given. Undoubtedly it would have been to test the poison, but it could also have been kindness, the right thing to do for the four-legged members of the family. At 7.00 p.m. one of the guards saw Eva Braun emerging from the Bunker exit, explaining: 'I want to see the sun one more time.' Hitler's faithful canine friend, Blondi the Alsatian, was the first to go, put to death by cyanide in the Bunker loo that afternoon. Blondi's five orphaned puppies were then shot, as were three other dogs belonging to the Bunker household, one of them Eva's own.

A good few hours later, around half-past two the next morning, 30 April, orders came for some twenty officers and women to assemble in the dining passage of the Bunker – the Führer wished to say goodbye to them. He duly arrived and walked slowly and silently down the passage, shaking the hands of all the women in turn. He looked as though he had retreated deep inside himself, his gaze was abstracted and some of them thought he had taken drugs. All were sure this was Hitler's long goodbye and that his suicide was now imminent. And then, after he had gone, something unexpected happened. The mood of the Bunker people suddenly lifted. SS generals cheerfully slapped lower ranks on the back. In the Chancellery canteen the soldiers and orderlies danced. There were no tears. Nazi rule, Nazi life, Nazi values, it was perceived, were over.

The preparations were already in hand. Hitler was keen for his body to be reduced to ashes, to cease to exist. 'I don't want to be put on exhibition in a Russian waxworks,' he told his adjutant, Günsche. Around lunchtime as much spare petrol as could be found was brought to the emergency exit of the Bunker. After lunch – Hitler's last, spaghetti and salad at the small table in his study in the company of his secretaries, his cook and an SS orderly – Traudl Junge popped in to see Eva, who had not attended. Eva was sorting out her clothes to give away as parting presents. To Traudl she gave her valuable silver fox fur. 'When you put it on,' Eva said, 'always remember me.'

Around 3.15 p.m., Hitler stepped out into the Bunker corridor with Eva on his arm. 'The time has come' he said, 'It's all over.' This was their very last goodbye, this time to the court's inner circle. While Hitler's face remained solemn, Eva was smiling – whatever else she was, she was a brave lady – but her moist eyes betrayed her inner sadness.

'Farewell,' Traudl Junge said.

Eva nodded, then she kissed her. 'Tell everyone in Munich farewell,' she told Traudl. 'Tell my parents I love them.'

Then Hitler took Eva by the arm again and led her into the study for the last time. It was now between 3.20 and 3.25 p.m. As the fireproof, gasproof, soundproof steel door was closing, Eva turned and looked back at Traudl Junge, and then she smiled. It was the end. Or so those outside the door believed.

Minutes went by and then there was an extraordinary intrusion – Magda Goebbels, frantic, almost hysterical, rushed past Hitler's adjutant, burst through the door and pleaded with Hitler to escape to Berchtesgaden while there was still time. Magda had been deeply (but discreetly) infatuated with Hitler for years, though most probably it was the lives of her children rather than her love for the Führer that provoked her last-minute attempt to head off destiny. But Hitler, preoccupied with the imminence of his own extinction, refused even to converse with her. It was too late, he told her, and she left, weeping and trembling. And now the door closed for the last time. There had been no sign of Eva Braun-Hitler during this intrusion, Guensche noticed, and he reckoned she was probably in the bathroom – powdering her nose, so to speak, before destroying her brains.

No one knows what passed between Hitler and his wife of just a day and a half in those final moments together. Each was all the other had left and it could be said that they died as a loving couple. For Hitler especially, killing himself by a shot through the head presented a tricky technical problem, especially as his hands shook so badly that he could not even shave himself, let alone reliably fire a gun. He had to take his time; he had to get it right; he simply could not afford to fail. For Eva it was a rather simpler matter. 'Bite the capsule,' she had been advised, 'as soon as you hear a shot.'

It was later claimed that within a minute or two a single pistol shot was heard. This is what Kempka claimed and what the world press was soon to report. Traudl Junge, who was busy trying to cheer up the Goebbels children at the time, remained adamant that she heard a shot. 'Suddenly there is a shot,' she recalled, 'so close that we all fall silent. It echoes through all the rooms.' 'Bull's-eye!' shouted one of the children. But in fact none of those waiting outside Hitler's door heard anything at all.

At 3.40 p.m., unsure what was happening, Bormann, Goebbels, Guensche and Linge, Hitler's valet, opened the door and entered the room. They found it filled with a choking mixture of toxic cordite and the strong bitter almonds smell of cyanide fumes (or strictly speaking prussic acid). Hitler was slumped at one end of the couch, eyes open, head canted to the left, dark circular spot on his right temple, puddle of blood about the size of a medium-sized plate. Eva was reclining at the other end of the sofa. It is practically certain they had died almost simultaneously, which had been Hitler's wish. But just exactly how Hitler died has been to some degree a matter of conjecture.

That he had received an instantaneously fatal bullet wound in the head was unquestionable – blood was still running down his face, soaking the sofa and dripping on to the floor. But not even those present were in agreement as to how the fatal shot was inflicted. Axmann and Kempka thought Hitler had shot himself through the mouth, Gunsche and Linge felt sure Hitler had shot himself through the right temple with his Walther 7.65 pistol. Years later a learned American professor, having studied all the conflicting evidence, went as far as to suggest that Hitler could only have been shot by his wife. No bullet was ever found, probably because it had lodged in the left temple under the skin, and may later have fallen out during the removal of the corpse to the bunker garden. Whether Hitler had also taken cyanide (prussic acid) is a matter of conjecture and increasingly doubted. Hitler's adjutant, Otto Günsche, for example, has testified that while Eva Braun smelt strongly of bitter almonds, Adolf Hitler quite definitely did not. Nor did poison conform to Hitler's psychological make-up and system of values. On the table beside the late Führer was a photo of his mother, perhaps the one real love of his life, and on the wall his favourite painting of his inspiration and hero, Frederick the Great.

Eva, sitting at the other end of the sofa about two feet from her husband, dressed in a blue chiffon spring frock, with her shoes off and her legs tucked up, looked as though she was asleep. Her revolver lay near her, unfired. She would have superseded her husband just long enough to have heard the shot that blew out his brains and ended an era in history. Her empty cyanide phial was lying on the floor below her left foot. Her nostrils were discoloured and her mouth tight shut, but though she was dead there was still the hint of a smile on her face. Her third and last suicide attempt had proved successful. It was the sixth suicide or attempted suicide by women at one time close to Adolf Hitler. 'Greater love than this hath no woman . . .' She was thirty-three years of age.

Eva Braun had been a reasonably nice, almost ordinary younger woman in love, in her way, with a not very nice and totally unordinary older man. In many ways they complemented one another. Even here, now, in death. And yet, and yet . . .

Historian Anton Joachimsthaler was to declare:

> Eva Braun's life was a struggle for success and recognition according to the glitter of her imaginary Hollywood world. She was an 'actress', and her life was but one big play. Through Fegelein she found a role at Hitler's court and continued to play this role even after she discovered Fegelein had cruelly disappointed her. When Fegelein died, she was also dead. And a broken Eva Braun realised that only one more role remained to her: the end at Hitler's side.

Only yesterday these two people had taken part in a wedding. Now these same people would take part in a funeral – two funerals, to be exact – and a cremation.

So perished the third most demonic and murderous specimen of that flawed and lethal species of ape labelled (perhaps erroneously) homo sapiens. The squalor and cowardice of his death, not at the barricades fighting to the last for a nation and its people, but in a neatly furnished little room in a hole in the ground beside a pretty young woman by whom he was adored, spells out, perhaps, the essential equation of his life. Absolute power, it has been said, corrupts absolutely. In Hitler's case, it can also be said, absolute power seduces universally. But the suspicion has always remained that it was Hitler's failure, relative or absolute, to consummate the seduction that fuelled the drive to maintain the power – and the rage and the violence and the genocide and universal destruction with which he manifested it. At the end of the day, it would seem, his father had a lot to answer for.

Hitler's true love was his mother, Klara. His passion had been his half-niece, Geli Raubal. Eva Braun was not the passion of his life – but she was his true companion, even unto death.

As for his love life, it can also be said that the exterminator of the Jews, the enslaver of the Slavs, the creator and destroyer of the Greater German Empire, allowed the occasional pretty woman a privilege that millions of the downtrodden and dead would have loved to share – to piss in his face and crap on his head.

And here he lay dead.

For several minutes everyone was too shocked to speak. Hitler's valet picked up a Dresden vase of spring tulips and daffodils which Hitler had knocked over when he slumped forward, examined the vase for cracks, refilled it with the flowers and set it back on the table. Then an army surgeon arrived and pronounced the two bodies to be dead. Linge and another SS man then wrapped Hitler's body in a blanket, taking care to cover the disfigured head, though the ex-Führer's black trousers, black silk socks and black leather shoes were plain to see, and carried it out into the corridor. There two other SS men carried it up the four flights of stairs and out into the garden. Bormann then took Eva's limp body into the corridor – 'clutching her breast with his ape-like paw', one eye-witness recalled with disgust – and from there a relay of SS officers carried it up the stairs and into the garden to join the corpse of her husband.

The bodies of Adolf and Eva Hitler were laid side by side on the sandy soil in a shallow depression less than ten yards from the Bunker exit and soaked in some fifty gallons of petrol. Hitler's head and chest were by now uncovered and a passing security guard noted that the skull was partially caved in and the face encrusted with blood, though still recognizably Hitler. Attempts to light the cadavers with matches failed, then Linge made a paper spill (which he lit with his cigarette lighter) and handed to Bormann. At his second attempt Bormann landed the spill in the trench. There was a gigantic whoof of brilliant leaping flame and a thick black puff of smoke, and then, since the garden was under intensive Russian artillery fire, all the six principal mourners, including Goebbels and Bormann, swiftly retreated to the shelter of the Bunker exit, where they briefly stood to attention and with arms raised gave the Hitler salute. Hitler's cadaver meanwhile was observed to raise its legs and the upper part of its body in an upward movement caused by the intensity of the heat. The Russian shellfire provided the only touch of Wagnerian awesomeness to an otherwise hole-in-the-corner occasion, for no word was said, no flag flown, no music played to honour the passing of the Führer of the Third Reich and his Frau. It was, so Hitler's SS adjutant, Otto Günsche, was to relate later, 'the most terrible experience of my life'.

Eva had had beautiful legs, but now, observing the cremation through a slit in the closed bunker door, Linge noticed that the flesh of one of her knees was already being roasted. 'I want to be a pretty corpse,' she had said. Well, here she was, bubbling and blackening like a sucking pig on a spit. Then something utterly grotesque happened, or so Linge claimed. 'Eva Braun's once trim figure had jack-knifed, under rigor mortis, into what the morticians call an "equestrian posture",' he recalled. 'That is, she was now sitting upright as if riding in a saddle. Both arms were outstretched and her hands seemed to be holding imaginary reins.' As the first flames died down an eyewitness was able to see in the midst of the blaze her husband's shattered head. It was, he said, 'a sight repulsive in the extreme'. More petrol was thrown over the bodies, and the incineration continued apace. It was a little past 4 p.m., Sunday, 30 April 1945.

Down in the Bunker there was bedlam. Hardened politicians like Goebbels were hysterical, tough front-line generals like Mohnke openly weeping. Among the lower ranks in the Chancellery cellars, however, the reaction was different, and as if to celebrate their sudden sense of new-found freedom a special concert was put on in the soldiers' canteen, a loudspeaker blaring out American jazz and swing music and patriotic British numbers like 'Tipperary' and 'The Lambeth Walk'. Then came a popular German ditty with a message more pertinent than Wagner's ever was:

'*Es geht alles vorüber, es geht alles vorbei*' (Everything passes, everything has its day).

'Hitler's death,' Traudl Junge was to remember, 'was like the end of a state of collective hypnosis for us. Suddenly we discovered the light, a mad desire to live, to revert to our former selves, to return to a normal human state, took possession of us. Hitler no longer interested us.'

Up in the garden from time to time SS men came to pour more petrol on the smouldering, bubbling bodies. Before long the stench of burning flesh became insufferable. That night an SS detail was assembled with the task of burying the torched remains of Adolf and Eva Hitler, and what was left of the burnt-out corpses – little flesh but some skeletal parts probably still intact – was dragged across to a deeper trench dug out of one of the bomb craters in the Chancellery garden where other bodies and parts of bodies, some of them from the underground hospital, had been tossed in the previous few days. Then the trench, not far from the emergency exit of the Bunker, was filled in with earth, debris and planks – and that, it seemed, was that.

So the political genius and psychopathic lunatic, with an historic destiny and a devoted following to the moment of his demise, perished in a manner fitting for a man of his status and depravity – like a slaughtered bull steer infected with foot and mouth, with a bullet through his head and his body in flames on a patch of sandy waste ground – 'the most powerful man in the Reich a few days ago,' as Traudl Junge put it at the time, 'and now a little heap of ashes blowing in the wind'.

This makeshift funeral and backyard burial was not quite what the erstwhile Führer of the Greater Reich had had in mind for himself and his wife in his days of triumph and glory. But it was better than any discernible alternative now – capture by the Russians, for example, a cage in Red Square, a public hanging. And the man who had the blood of 40 million dead on his hands had gone to his own death happy in the certainty that he himself was blameless, that the British were to blame for starting the war, the German people for losing it, and the Jews for everything.

These were the first two interments, but there would be four in all, for Dr Goebbels, the prophet to Hitler's messiah, planned a similar exit for himself and his wife. Four funerals and a wedding – a totally Wagnerian day.

Time to Get Out – or Die

As long ago as March, Goebbels had confided to an aide: 'Neither I nor my wife nor a single one of my offspring will be among the survivors of the coming debacle.' His last official act on the morning of 1 May, as the new, short-lived Chancellor of a Reich that had all but vanished, was to reject the Russian demand for the unconditional surrender of Berlin. The Russians' reply was to let loose on the Reich Chancellery an artillery bombardment so heavy and sustained that it created panic among the occupants of the Bunker – and in the Chancellery cellars an hysteria of a special kind. By now some 2,000 soldiers, civilians and wounded had sought shelter in the halls and corridors and the overcrowding reached nightmare proportions. The lights were flickering, the water pressure falling, the toilets blocked, so that everywhere there were puddles of urine that began to stink. Still people poured into the cellars until even the stairways were jammed solid. Then the air ventilation failed, followed by the fresh water supply. Many died, particularly the wounded, and their bodies were carried up into the Chancellery garden and tossed into shell craters or covered with dirt.

Aware that their lives could be snuffed out at any moment, a mass hysteria inflamed by drink and terror overtook many of the men and women in the cellars and the Chancellery, and they copulated together in a kind of ritual bacchanalian celebration of life's most life-affirming act. 'It came as a bit of a shock,' recalled Professor Schenk, still operating on the teeming wounded, 'to see a German general chasing some half-naked signalwoman between and over the cots.' The Führer's dentist chair in the dental clinic, especially, became a kind of sacred altar of love, and random couples queued up to have sex in it in all kinds of positions as if performing a primal but holy ritual.

In the Führerbunker it was time to get out – or die. In the early evening of that day, as the Goebbels' six children, aged four to twelve, were getting ready for bed, Magda Goebbels summoned an SS medic to come and give them each a shot of morphine (or possibly a soporific drug called Finodin), and once they were all unconscious, Dr Ludwig Stumpfegger, Hitler's own doctor in the last days, crushed a prussic acid capsule inside the mouth of each one of them. The eldest girl, Helga, seems to have fought for her life, for several bruises were found on her body subsequently. They had been, by any standards, very beautiful and bright and life-loving children, and the awfulness of their mass infanticide at the hands of their doting and inconsolable mother in the nightmare depths of the Bunker must stand as a haunting symbol of the depravity of their beloved Führer and the world he had created and now destroyed. Afterwards, ashen-faced, red-eyed, barely able to speak, almost out of her mind with grief, Magda Goebbels sipped champagne and chain-smoked cigarettes until it was her own turn to die. General Mohnke watched the Goebbels go:

> Going over to the coat rack in the small room that served as his study, Goebbels donned his hat, his scarf, his long uniform overcoat. Slowly, he drew on his kid gloves, making each finger snug. Then, like a cavalier, he offered his right arm to his wife. They were wordless now. So

were we three spectators. Slowly, steadily, leaning a bit
on each other, they headed up the stairs to the courtyard.

At 8.30 p.m. they stepped out into the garden for the final
act. There, standing in the dark under a sky glowing molten red
from the fires consuming Berlin, Goebbels' wife bit on a cyanide
capsule and, as she sank to her knees, her husband blew her
brains out. Immediately afterwards Goebbels bit on a cyanide
capsule, squeezing the trigger of his pistol as he did so. To be
doubly sure, a soldier fired twice at Goebbels' body, and then
Goebbels' adjutant and driver emptied four cans of petrol over
both bodies (most of it over Frau Goebbels, it would seem) and
after setting them alight retreated to the safety of the Bunker.
The two bodies burned all through the night.

In the Bunker it was now a case of *sauve qui peut*. Only three of
the inhabitants – General Burgdorf, General Krebs and Colonel
Schädle – decided to call it a day and put an end to their lives. The
rest chose to make a run for it, in ten escape groups organized by
Mohnke, aiming to strike north through the city's subway system
and surface beyond the Russian ring. Traudl Junge, clad in tin hat,
trousers and boots, carrying no papers, no money, no provisions or
clothes, just a lot of cigarettes and a few photos she couldn't bear
to part with, was in the first escape group, led by Mohnke himself,
who had earlier ordered an unsuccessful attempt to set Hitler's
quarters on fire. She recalled later:

One after the other we left that horrifying place. For
the last time I passed the door to Hitler's and Eva's
apartments. His grey greatcoat was still hanging on a
metal coat-rack; above it were his cap with the gold
insignia and his leather gloves. The dog's lead was

there, hanging like a noose from the gallows. In Eva's bedroom the wardrobe doors stood open, and I caught sight of the silver fox fur coat she'd given me. But what could I have done with a coat like that in the hands of the enemy? I was more likely to need my poison capsules.

Missing from Hitler's suite by now, it should be said, was his favourite painting of Frederick the Great, which his pilot, Captain Baur, had taken pains to remove from its frame, roll up and make off with as a final souvenir gift from the Führer. (Before long it would be 'liberated' by a Red Army soldier and probably today still graces the wall of a cottage or flat in far away Russia, its historic provenance unknown).

All through the hours of darkness the breakout groups scuttled through the darkened streets and tunnels of Berlin. The whole city seemed to be ablaze. The ruins of the Chancellery stood out gauntly against the flames and there was gunfire everywhere. All but a hundred or so escapees survived. Most were taken prisoner by the Russians, including Mohnke himself. Among the few to get clean away to the west were Hitler's secretaries (including Traudl Junge disguised as a man), his chauffeur, the Hitler Youth Leader, and Goebbels' aide – and the three special messengers who had earlier been burdened with the responsibility of spiriting Hitler's last will and testament out of Berlin.

The Three Messengers

The three messengers had left the Bunker at noon on the day Hitler and Eva Braun had got married, each carrying copies of

Hitler's personal and political testaments, and his marriage certificate. The three men picked for their unenviable missions were Major Willy Johannmeyer, Hitler's army adjutant, who was to deliver his copies of the documents to the new C-in-C of the Army, Field Marshal Schörner; SS Standartenführer Wilhelm Zander, Bormann's personal adviser, who was to deliver his copies to Admiral Dönitz, Hitler's designated successor at the naval base of Flensburg on the north German coast; and Goebbels' representative, Heinz Lorenz, an official from the Propaganda Ministry, whose task was to escape to Dönitz's HQ, or failing that, anywhere in British or American territory, in the hope that one day the documents could be taken to Munich, the cradle of the Nazi movement, and preserved there as testimony of the Heroic Age. Accompanying them as guide would be a corporal called Hummerlich.

They were a mixed bunch, in motley dress, without money, papers or food, and they were faced with a nightmare mission, for on their way to the north and west they had to negotiate three rings of encircling Soviet forces. At ten that night they took two boats and crossed Lake Havel, making for the Wannsee bridgehead in the south, which was still in German hands. From there Johannmeier radioed Dönitz's headquarters asking for a plane to be sent to pick them up.

For much of 30 April – the last day of the Führer's life – they rested, then in the evening sailed to Pfaueninsel, an island in the lake, where they would rendezvous with the plane. It was then that they realized they were not the only emissaries from the Bunker who were on the move in these perilous times. For following the total breakdown of telephone communications between Berlin and the rest of the country, three adjutants and ADCs to the army commanders, followed later by Hitler's air force adjutant, had sought Hitler's permission to break through the besieging Russian forces and as a matter of overwhelming urgency try and contact the commander of the German relieving army, General Wenck. None of them knew that Wenck's army did not exist and would never come, nor did they know that the author of the testaments in their possession on this near-suicide mission was no more.

While the burning embers of the torched cadavers of the bodies in the Bunker garden cooled, the three emissaries with Hitler's testaments waited in vain for a plane from Dönitz. All through the day of 1 May they waited to no avail on Pfaueninsel, and when night came the Russians shelled them, forcing them to take to a canoe and paddle out into the lake out of sight of the guns. Here they boarded a yacht, but there were no sails to sail, and in any case a burning munitions ship turned the lake as bright as day.

Then, to their huge relief, the plane sent by Dönitz came in and landed on the water. They could hear its engines roaring and see its shadow on the water. While Johannmeyer signalled the plane with his pocket lamp, the other three paddled out to it in two canoes. Shouting at the tops of their voices over the din of the engines, they explained to the pilot that there was another member of their party still to come. The pilot shouted back that they should bring him over. And at that critical moment Zander upset his canoe and fell into the water. Valuable minutes were spent rescuing the man, and by the time they had set off to fetch Johannmeyer the Russians were alerted and began bombarding the plane. The pilot had no option but to take off immediately, reporting to Dönitz later that he had been unable to locate the Führer's emissaries.

The emissaries themselves, meanwhile, after spending another day on the Havel, finally landed at Wannsee swimming pool, and disguised as foreign workers made their way into the territory of the Western Allies. By now there was no purpose in trying to carry out their assignment. Dönitz had surrendered and before long would himself be captive. The war was over. Johannmeyer went back to the family home in Iserlohn in Westphalia (Ruhr) and buried his documents in a bottle in the garden. Zander headed south for Bavaria, hiding his documents in a suitcase in a house in the village of Tegernsee. Here he turned his back on his old life and his past beliefs, changed his name to Wilhelm Paustin and began a new life as a new person with a new woman, his friends putting it about that Zander was dead. Heinz Lorenz, too, vanished into the maelstrom of post-hostilities Germany, eventually surfacing in Hanover.

Two of the three adjutants and ADCs to the Berlin generals – Rittmeister Gerhard Boldt and Major Baron Freytag von Loringhoven – also succeeded in evading the Russians, as did Hitler's air force adjutant, Lieutenant Colonel Nicolaus von Below. For all of them it was a nightmare. Moving westwards towards the British positions, they hid in woods by day, moved on at night, swimming rivers, ducking Russian patrols. Von Below gave up all hope of fulfilling his mission, burned the documents he was supposed to have delivered to the army chiefs, then made his way home to Bonn, where he optimistically planned to start afresh as a law student at the University. Boldt tried to kill himself with a morphine overdose but was made to sick it up by von Loringhoven. Both finally succeeded in becoming prisoners of the British. They were safe.

As for the fourth messenger, General Mohnke – an opportunistic afterthought on Hitler's part – though his breakout group succeeded in getting through the Red Army ring round the Bunker area, Mohnke himself and a number of his companions were finally captured by Russian forces in north Berlin on 2 May, so the copies of the last will and testament bequeathed to him by Hitler never got through.

Last Man Out

Back in the Bunker, meanwhile, there was only one man left alive in the place by four in the morning of 2 May – Johannes Hentschel, the man in charge of the ventilation and water-pump systems for the Bunker and the Chancellery cellars, where several hundred wounded German soldiers depended on him for survival. The Bunker was a spooky place now, dark and silent, a lonely lost world full of ghosts. Hentschel was petrified, and when he saw the dead Goebbels children stacked two by two on three folding bunks he vomited.

Early that dawn, 2 May, not long before the Commandant of Berlin signed the German capitulation agreement, Hentschel made his way up through the eerily empty Bunker to the garden for a breath of fresh air. It was not very fresh. A kind of dense Saharan dust cloud, a bi-product of battle, hung orange and lemon over Berlin. The air was full of gritty rubble dust that made his eyes sore. In the distance he could hear a spattering of rifle fire and the occasional mortar or rocket. There were eight or nine corpses sprawled around the garden, he noticed, some with their heads cut off and limbs lying around. Goebbels' body had been roasted, he observed, and his face was a deep purple. Flocks of mallard ducks, taking advantage of the city's sudden relative quiet, were flying overhead in triple formation – 'like Messerschmitts' – towards their spring nesting grounds in the Tiergarten. Spring! He had almost forgotten. The perfume of jasmine and hyacinth wafted across from Hitler's glassless greenhouse. Hentschel went and picked a bunch of tulips to cheer up his post in the abandoned bunker, then returned to the catacomb below, and waited for the worst.

Resigned to his fate, just doing his job, Hentschel pottered about, peeping into rooms. checking the bulkhead doors. Sometime someone would find his way down here, he knew. And it wouldn't be a German and it wouldn't be a social visit. He had expected the clatter of boots and rifle butts any time, or worse – flame-throwers, perhaps, grenades, tear gas, mines. He was therefore taken aback when he heard the patter of brisk footsteps approaching along the Chancellery tunnel, and cheerful, chattering voices. It was not what he expected. For a start the voices were the wrong gender, and they were also in the wrong mood. Then he saw them, a dozen beaming, bustling young women in uniform – Russian army medics and interns. In a lightning strike, using remarkable initiative, they had arrived at the very heart of the former enemy empire – and they didn't have a gun between them. They stopped when they saw Hentschel, weighing him up. He didn't have a gun either. What's more his hands were as high in the air as they would go.

'Where is Adolf Hitler?' demanded the leader of the group, a blonde, buxom, round-faced woman of around thirty, who spoke German with a Berlin accent.

'Where is Gitler's Frau, Gerr Gentschel?' asked another woman, pronouncing 'h' the Russian way.

What they really wanted to know was where, after months in the field, they could find any nice civilian ladies' clothing in this abandoned place.

Hentschel led them to Eva Hitler's boudoir and they dived inside. Later he saw some of the women scurrying back down the tunnel burdened with Hitler's monogrammed silver, SS daggers, helmets, gas masks, crystal glass, a copy of *Mein Kampf*, an accordion and a telephone. A little later still he saw another half a dozen or so of them emerging from the Bunker's emergency exit 'whooping like Indian squaws in one of those Western movies, waving above their heads at least a dozen black satin brassières trimmed with lace'.

Shortly afterwards a score or so gung-ho Red Army front-line combat officers, as jolly as the women, found their way into the Bunker depths. Some stared in horror at the dead bodies of the Goebbels children. Others struck the neck off a bottle of champagne with a bayonet and danced round Hentschel as if he were King of the May, singing Russian drinking songs as they drank and danced. Hentschel, too, drank and danced, and when he felt dizzy and sat on the floor, the Russians poured a bottle of champagne over his crew-cut head. And then they left. And by mid-morning Hentschel, the last survivor of the last days of Hitler, was under arrest and being frog-marched through the Chancellery gates towards a waiting Russian truck and a waiting Russian prison camp.

Hour Zero

At 3 p.m. on 2 May the guns finally fell totally silent. The ravaged city was enveloped in an uncanny quiet. Only the distant cheers of the Russian soldiers could be heard, as they hugged each other among the ruins. If the great rape of the Berlin women by the Russian soldiery was about to reach its crescendo – some 90,000 women suffered this fate – at least the British and American bombing had come to an end. 'Better a

Russian on your belly,' the Berlin women quipped stoically, 'than an American on your head.' (A variant of this, turned into a song, went: 'I'd rather have a Russian on my belly, Than a British bomb on my noggin.')

'*Gitler kaput!*' the Russian soldiers yelled. '*Voyna kaput!*'

Voyna kaput. The war was over.

Long before *die Stunde Null*, hour zero, Hitler had declared: 'We may be destroyed, but if we are, we shall drag a world down with us – a world in flames.' Now the survivors chalked their derision on the walls of the ruined cities: '*Das verdanken wir Hitler.*' For this we thank Hitler.

Like the Fall of Rome and the Sack of Constantinople in ancient times, the Battle of Berlin marked not only the fall of a capital city but the end of an empire, an era, and a world. Caught up in this Armageddon, the German people, whom Hitler had not only misled but betrayed and finally traduced, had paid a monumental price for their misplaced loyalty.

For Germany now was a surrealist tableau of disasters, a land of ruins peopled by ghosts, without government, order or purpose, without industry, communications or the proper means of existence. Eight million German civilians were on the move from east to west. The statistics of destruction and deprivation read like a litany of awfulness, of absolute negation. In the Battle of Berlin alone some 150,000 German civilians lost their lives, while the German military casualties are incalculable. More than half of all German males in the 21-year-old age group had been killed or wounded, and in Germany as a whole nearly 7 million people had died or were soon to die. Many of the towns and cities were no more. In Hanover 99 per cent of the houses were damaged, in Dusseldorf 93 per cent were uninhabitable. It was calculated that the devastated areas of Germany lay under 400 million cubic feet of rubble – equivalent to an area of 100 square miles completely covered in rubble to a height of several feet. Within a month or two Germany would seem to be on the verge of the worst scourge of pestilence and famine since the Middle Ages. 'More than 20 million Germans are homeless or without adequate shelter,' ran the official Allied report. 'The average basic ration is less than 1,000 calories. The ability to wage war in this generation has been destroyed.' And over all hung the pervading stench of putrefaction.

> Those to whom evil is done,
> Do evil in return.

But now that the war was over, the quest could begin. 'Like Alaric, buried secretly under the riverbed of Busento,' one British intelligence officer was to comment on the fate of Adolf Hitler's corpse, 'the modern destroyer of mankind is now immune from discovery.'

Or was he?

If Adolf and Eva's wedding had been a strange one, their posthumous honeymoon (so to speak) was to prove even stranger. Not for them music, gifts and flowers, dead or alive. Instead they would be turned into refuse mixed up with the rubbish of their last home and resting place. And yet the ex-Führer would pose almost as much a threat to the stability of the world when he was just bits and pieces as he did when he had been whole.

Part 4

End Game

'There are legs here!'

After the Red Army revellers, high on victory, it was the turn of the heavy mob to enter the Bunker – agents of SMERSH (military counter-intelligence) and the NKVD (secret police). They were interested in only one thing – the fate and whereabouts of Adolf Hitler. They were very serious and relatively thorough. There was an overriding reason for this. Their orders came from the highest level – from Stalin himself. Stalin had a special interest in Hitler (which is not surprising) and a special agenda (which was).

Leader of one of the first search teams was Lieutenant Colonel Ivan Klimenko, Commander of the Counter-Intelligence Section, 79th Rifle Corps, Third Shock Army. Klimenko was not exactly Sherlock Holmes, rather the reverse, but he never gave up. He first arrived in the Bunker on 2 May, looked around and, first time lucky, found the body of Dr Goebbels, which was immediately removed to his HQ in a prison in the city suburbs. That afternoon, during his absence, another search team discovered Hitler, or so they thought, inside a big old wooden water barrel packed with other bodies. With pride and satisfaction the Russians put the body on display in the main hall of the Reich Chancellery. The quest, it seemed, was over almost as soon as it had begun. Here he was. Hitler was now theirs.

The following day, 3 May, Klimenko went down into the Bunker and found the bodies of General Burgdorf and the six

Goebbels children. The next day he came back again. With him was a certain Private Ivan Churakov. Klimenko watched as Private Churakov, an adventurous lad, clambered into a shell crater full of bazookas and burned paper and began to nose around.

'Comrade Lieutenant Colonel!' he shouted suddenly. 'There are legs here!'

They started to dig and pulled out the badly-charred bodies of a man, a woman and two dogs – a German Shepherd dog and a puppy – or so the story goes. In the opinion of Klimenko, not of the brightest, this did not look a very promising find, so he ordered the corpses to be wrapped in blankets and re-buried.

That same day Marshal Zhukov and his staff visited the Chancellery.

'Where is Hitler? Show him to us!' they demanded of the Russian commander of the Chancellery.

'He has escaped, the dirty pig,' the commander replied. 'Into the hereafter, but still escaped.'

They made their way to Hitler's quarters. 'All these years we had sworn we would enter the very den of Fascism,' one of Zhukov's staff was to comment, 'and now we had reached our goal. It was in fact a den; to call it accommodation would have been misplaced.'

Two days later, on Saturday, 5 May, Colonel Klimenko had a sudden thought and on an impulse rushed back to the Chancellery garden. There, he began to dig feverishly in the newly filled shell crater till he had successfully exhumed the two human bodies in the blankets he had recently re-buried – or so he claimed, thereby earning himself, in the fullness of time, the Hero of the Soviet Union medal and a place in the history books.

According to a Soviet account of this incident first published in Germany in 1968, Klimenko was now convinced he had found the remains of Adolf Hitler and his wife, and took the bodies back to headquarters, where he was advised to take them on to the 496th Field Hospital at the SMERSH base in Berlin-Buch. It was thus by a curious twist of fate that, just as Walter Wagner had come to Hitler's home in the Bunker to officiate at his wedding, the cadaver the Russians believed might be Hitler's arrived less than ten days later at Wagner's home base in a block of flats at Buch in north Berlin to undergo his dissection – or so it was claimed. The Russians had set up a makeshift mortuary in the clinic here to carry out the autopsies of the Goebbels family and others. In charge of the Russian autopsy medics was a senior forensic pathologist with the suitably spectacular name of Dr Faust Shkarvaski.

The Russian autopsy report on the remains assumed to be Adolf Hitler – 'a male corpse disfigured by fire and delivered in a wooden box' – claimed that the corpse was greatly damaged and smelled strongly of burnt flesh, though it still managed to sport the remnants of a yellow jersey resembling a hand-knitted undervest and seemingly fire-proof. Pathologically speaking, the corpse was not an easy proposition in its present condition. The hands were burnt crisp like bacon, so there would be no fingerprints available, and the skin on the face was missing. The brain was fire damaged, and the charred tongue was now firmly locked between the teeth of the upper and lower jaws. Through a hole in the abdomen a good view could be had of the right lung, liver and intestines, but the left foot had dropped off somewhere and much of the flesh of the legs was gone. The penis of the former Führer, so the good doctors duly noted, was scorched, the scrotum only singed, and no matter how hard they looked they could find no sign of a left testicle (posthumous proof, perhaps, of the claim of that old British wartime marching song, 'Hitler has only got one ball') – though it has to be said that the family doctor who examined him when he was a boy found nothing lacking in that direction.

According to the Russian autopsy a crushed glass ampoule in the mouth and the marked smell of bitter almonds were a clear indicator of the cause of death – there was no mention of a gunshot wound.

The autopsy on the remains assumed to be Eva Braun came to a similar conclusion as to the cause of death, though the cadaver was even more extensively damaged, probably due to incoming shellfire during the burning in the Bunker garden.

Significantly, part of Hitler's cranium could not be found. In the absence of fingerprints, the only hope of identifying the corpse in the crate as Adolf Hitler would be by means of the jaw and teeth. Until two of Hitler's former dental technicians could be found, Hitler's jaw and teeth were entrusted to the care of a young Red Army interpreter by the name of Elena Rzhevskaya. And so it was that on 7 May 1945, the day the war ended, 24-year-old Elena found herself toasting victory with a glass of cheap Rhine wine in one hand and a little red box containing the jaw of the man who had started it in the other. She recalled this bizarre episode recently: 'My God, can this really be?' she wondered. 'The day Germany capitulates, here I am celebrating with Hitler's teeth under my arm!'

When she slept, his teeth were on the shelf by her bed. When she ate, they were on the floor by her feet. All day they were in her little red box under her arm as she and her team rushed round the ruins of Berlin looking for a dentist who could identify them. It was not a posthumous situation Hitler could ever have dreamed he might end up in, but given his disposition, the scourge of mankind might well have thought there could be worse places than in the protective hands of a pretty 24-year-old Muscovite called Elena.

So far so good. That is what the Russians were thinking, or claimed they were thinking, with regard to the whereabouts of the defunct Führer in early May 1945. But there is a more recent school of thought that will have none of this. That Adolf Hitler and his wife of a day and a half had committed suicide in the Bunker in the way that those close at hand had described was not in doubt. That their corpses had been carried out into the Chancellery garden and set on fire was not in dispute. That a young Russian woman called Elena ended up with Hitler's teeth on her bedside table in Berlin is not in question. That part of Hitler's cranium was also in Russian hands was also very possibly the case. But what remained in contention, growling away beneath the seemingly universal unanimity of most historians, was the actual fate of the bodies and the claim that Hitler's and Eva's bodies had been found in the way Colonel Klimenko had reported. Leading the dissidents (so to speak) was a persevering German historical investigator by the name of Anton Joachimsthaler, who doggedly carried on his investigation through the 1980s and into the 1990s.

Joachimsthaler's conclusion was that the generally accepted version of the cremation of Adolf and Eva – that the bodies were laid in a trench and only partly consumed by the fire, just like Goebbels – did not hold up. There were witnesses who affirmed that the bodies were hastily dumped on a flat stretch of sandy ground and thus (unlike bodies laid in a hole or ditch) were totally vulnerable to the full intensity of the fire (constantly replenished from an abundant stock of petrol) and to the fury of the incoming Soviet artillery and mortar fire, including napalm, pouring into the Chancellery garden.

Under such circumstances the freshly dead corpses would react according to a well-established pattern – the pressure of steam generated in the subcutaneous tissue would soar dramatically, causing the body surfaces and the skulls to burst; the muscles would shrink, causing the arms to lift up and the legs to contract; the fat would melt and ignite; the carbonated torso would shrink substantially; the soft tissue would be consumed almost totally, leaving only charred, calcified and fragile bones with burnt bits of tissue adhering. Such cadavers, after a lengthy and intense burning, would be so fragile that they could almost be blown away in the wind, and certainly not buried whole.

As far as can be ascertained, this is what some of the eyewitnesses observed after the bodies had been burning for nearly two and a half hours. Thus Hermann Karnau, a security guard, testified on his return from Soviet captivity in 1954 that by five in the afternoon the two bodies were just piles of white ash that disintegrated when he nudged them with his foot and blew upwards in flakes in the wind. 'I believe then,' he went on, 'that the remains were scattered by the continuing heavy fire and bombing.'

Anton Joachimsthaler concluded:

> Let us now try to envisage the picture that the evidence so far presents of Hitler's departure from the world stage. The Chancellery is in ruins, the buildings burning from bombing attacks and shellfire. The Russians are firing heavy guns, mortars and dreaded 'Stalin organs'. High explosives and napalm shells are detonating in the garden, fountains of earth are rising and falling, craters form and are covered up again. A truly infernal scene! And this bombardment continued not only during the

whole of 30 April but well on into 1 May – in other words for one and a half days. It is small wonder that the Russians never found his corpse. Yet from the very beginning, they claimed they had! . . . Where are the authentic photographs? Where is the picture of Hitler's skull with an upper and lower jaw? Where is the allegedly lead-lined box with Hitler's identifiable corpse?

Where indeed? So – according to this thesis – no corpse in a hand-knitted yellow undervest, no tongue sticking out between the teeth, no cyanide ampoule in the mouth, no lung, liver and bowel putting on a good show through a hole in the abdomen, no fire-damaged brain, no singed penis, no ball, missing or otherwise. As Otto Guensche, who was there, later pointed out:

> The Russians were never in a position to display the remains of Hitler's body, which they certainly would have done if they had found it. But they did find Goebbels' corpse, shrunk together and barely recognisable, which they did display.

Not long after the war a US 'semi-official' investigator by the name of Michael A. Musmanno, a judge and US navy captain who had interviewed some 200 members of Hitler's entourage over a three-year period, was finally persuaded to this view, declaring, 'It is no secret that Hitler's corpse was never found.'

It followed that the same could be said for the lady of his life (and death) Eva Braun.

What was not known at this time was that the Russians had indeed found *parts* of the corpses of Hitler and Eva Braun-Hitler – though they could not be sure about this immediately. It seems that they had begun an intensive new search for Hitler's body (and anything else of interest) in the Chancellery garden and in the process gathered up the corpses and body parts of some thirteen to fifteen bodies so that they could be examined and hopefully identified. So intensive had been the Russian bombardment in the last hours of hostilities that most of the bodies had been blown to bits and widely scattered, so to collect them together the Russians put them through a double sieve system, consisting of two enclosures – one with a wire mesh like a chicken coop, the other with a finer mesh like a garden sieve, so that by shovelling earth and detritus first through the one and then through the other they reckoned to collect even small remains of human bodies.

On 9 May, the day after this collecting exercise, Frau Käther Heusermann, 36, who had been an assistant to Hitler's former dentist, Dr Hugo Blashke, was taken by Elena Rzhevskaya and her Red Army boss, Colonel Vasily Gorbushin, to Schwanebeck (near Buch) where they showed her four fragments of human remains – a gold bridge with porcelain facets from an upper jaw, a complete lower jawbone with teeth and bridges, a small gold filling, and a bridge from a lower jaw made of synthetic resin with a gold crown. Frau Heusermann was immediately able to identify these items as having belonged to Adolf Hitler and Eva Braun. Later in May, Frau Heusermann was taken to a wood near Finow, some 30 miles from Buch. She was to recall:

> Here, in the presence of a General and many officers, I was shown seven crates with human corpses and one crate with the corpses of two dogs. All of these crates were in a hole that was about one metre deep. I was made to climb down into the hole and inspect the

corpses. I clearly recognized the corpse of Dr Goebbels, and the other six corpses were those of his children. Dr Goebbels' corpse was hardly burned at all. The head was easily recognisable, as was the crippled leg. The children lay in their crates with their mouths open. They were dressed in pyjamas which were open at the front. All the bodies, including that of Dr Goebbels, showed autopsy cuts that had been sewn up.

The body of Frau Goebbels, she was told, was so badly burned that it was no longer recognizable. The same must have been true of the bodies of Hitler and his wife, or she would undoubtedly have been shown them too. Instead, she was taken back to Finow in July and shown all that could be found of them by way of identifiable remains – all of them now stowed in a cigar box. In addition to the jaws and dental parts, the Russians now included such personal effects of Hitler's as had survived the cremation, including his Iron Cross 1st Class, a gold Party badge, a gold watch and a few small pieces of cloth.

At the same time as Frau Heusermann, but separately from her, Hitler's dentist's technical assistant, Fritz Echtmann, was shown the same items by the Russians and was able to carry out a more exhaustive examination of them. 'I had no doubts whatsoever,' he reported, 'that the dental segments shown me originated from Hitler's and Eva Braun's bodies.'

During his examination Echtmann noticed that Hitler's lower jaw showed small remnants of singed and carbonated tissue and was also introduced to the Russian expert who had removed the dental fragments from the corpses.

The Russians themselves had thus proved beyond all reasonable doubt that Hitler and Eva were dead. Amazingly, moreover, the testimony of Heusermann and Echtmann was published in the London *Times* for all to see on 9 July 1945 – though few especially noticed it or (if they did) believed it. And on the plane that took Heusermann and Echtmann and others to Moscow and many years of captivity in the Soviet Union, Red Army soldiers gleefully passed around the cigar box with Hitler's remains inside, laughingly shouting, 'Here is the Führer!'

But though it was now a proven fact that Hitler was dead, even to the Russians, Stalin did not want to know and had no intention of revealing the fact to the world at large. Though the Russians some years later produced a photo of a coffin-like box with some unrecognizable dark object inside it which they claimed was Hitler, all that was actually left of Hitler could in reality fit into a cigar box. And though this was sufficient to prove that Hitler was dead, Stalin resolutely declined to admit this.

'Ashes in my hand'

While their main prize had been found and identified, Russian investigators continued to search the Bunker complex for clues, and by now they had over thirty of Hitler's entourage as potential witnesses in their hands. It was a month before the first Westerner was allowed to visit the Bunker, soon after the Allies entered Berlin in June 1945. This was a British army liaison officer by the name of Lieutenant-Colonel Wilfred Byford-Jones, an investigative foreign reporter in his peacetime profession, who now, as a British military liaison officer, had unique access to the Soviet sector of Berlin and the Russian military.

Byford-Jones had last been to the Chancellery nearly six years earlier, a few weeks before the outbreak of war, and had looked on as Hitler and Goebbels came out on their way to Berchtesgaden. There were smart Prussian Guards there then. Now there were Mongolian Russian guards in filthy uniforms, standing by shabby sentry boxes adorned with pornographic graffiti. A Russian intelligence officer took the Englishman in, both of them still looking, rather ambitiously, for Hitler's bones amid the Chancellery ruins.

'Have you ever seen such a mess?' said the Russian, eyeing the shattered debris all around.

They went into Hitler's library. There were books strewn all over the floor. One of the pages, with a quote from Spengler, caught the Englishman's eye: 'To such beasts as we, eternal peace would be like intolerable boredom.' He showed it to the Russian, who howled with laughter.

'See here,' he said, wiping the tears from his eyes, 'it is all so magnificently ironic. See . . . books on Charlemagne, Frederick the Great, Bismarck. Is life not funny?'

They went into what had been the Chancellery garden and later a battlefield. The debris of the carnage was still lying around – steel helmets, broken weapons, shells, bloody uniforms, new unmarked graves – and everywhere the stench of death. Littering the place too were some of the contents of the Chancellery, a random scattering of law books, sports equipment, female clothing, copies of Hitler's speeches, a photo of a girl in a bathing costume.

A concrete block with big steel doors led to the Bunker. They went down several flights of steps and stood for a moment in the dark and the heavy silence. The timber was scorched black, the floor was covered with three inches of water. They went into Hitler's bedroom. There had been no fire here. On a broad settee there were signs of blood. Byford-Jones was later to record:

My Russian friend and I examined the settee carefully. The signs were consistent with someone who sat in the corner of it having committed suicide by shooting, for the blood had run down the three-inch square arm of the settee and dripped on to the floor, where there were dark stains. On the wall were several splashes of blood, which could have been accounted for by a wounded head having come into contact with it.

They went on into Eva Hitler's bedroom and the adjoining bathroom she had shared with her husband of a few hours. It was as though the woman had just popped out for a coffee. Her towels marked 'A.H.' were still neatly hung on the chromium-plated rails, the bedroom cabinet was still stocked with cosmetics and medicines, her hairpins and two empty powder boxes still lay on the table.

The Russian officer and the British officer sat side by side on Eva's bed, lost in thought, staring at the wisps of hair that lay on the carpet from the last time Eva had combed her blonde locks. They sat there, trying to reconstruct it all in their minds, but it was all too fantastical. After a while they left and went down a deep tunnel, as long and as wide as a street, to the Chancellery bunker headquarters area – a subterranean fortress honeycombed with hundreds of enormous offices, each office guarded with a huge steel door weighing a ton, along with a kitchen that could prepare meals for a thousand people.

They went back to the surface. The sun was going down over the Bunker garden. By a shallow trench near a conical block-house the Russian stopped. That, he pointed, was where Hitler and Eva Braun were supposed to have been burned.

'The trench was black with ashes,' Byford-Jones reported

later. 'I bent down, took up some of the ashes in my hand, and put them into an empty tobacco-pouch. They might have been the remains of a cremated Hitler.'

Byford-Jones believed Hitler was dead, but his Russian companion was not so sure. 'We want more proof than I have seen up to now,' he told the Englishman. 'All we know is that he *was* here.'

Other visitors from the West came to see Hitler's lair. The British war leader, Winston Churchill, only managed two flights of steps down and then gave up. The Canadian Prime Minister got as far as Eva Braun's bedsit and noticed 'a vase with a twig in it that had obviously been a flower'. A writer-photographer team from *Life* magazine ventured through the damp chill and sodden squalor of the Bunker to the former Führer's quarters and confirmed that an attempt had indeed been made to set fire to the briefing room and antechamber – the strong smell of burning, the charred pictures on the wall proved that – though Hitler's living room was unscathed. 'The debris and rubbish in the bunker,' the reporters noted, 'defied description.'

James O'Donnell, reporting for *Newsweek* magazine, echoed this. Moving carefully through the labyrinth by the light of a kerosene lantern, along corridors three or four inches deep in muck and slime, he noted: 'Everywhere the floors, corridors and duckboards were littered with glass shards, bottles, rusty picture frames, German Army cheesecake photos, dented air-raid-warden helmets, empty first-aid kits, bloodied bandages, tin cans, empty pistol clips, scattered playing cards, cigar and cigarette butts, slimy condoms.' Even worse was the stench of the place – the stench of stale air, dead rats, clogged toilets, 'the distinctive malodour of the rubble of war'. The only way the Russian sentries survived in that atmosphere was by wearing gasmasks and changing guard every quarter of an hour. More extraordinary still was all the documentary material of Hitler's former headquarters scattered about the place: army reports, phone records, Hitler's desk diary and Bormann's and Goebbels' personal diaries included – priceless intelligence data that the Russians had totally ignored. Later O'Donnell discovered the reason for this apparent neglect of duty. Under direct orders from Stalin the search team were looking for one thing only – Hitler's body.

'The beast has escaped us!'

Ever since the completion of Hitler's autopsy the previous month Soviet officials had known that Hitler was dead. But it was then that the fun and games began. These would later be given a code name – *Operatsiya Mif* (Operation Myth) – though the reasoning behind it was never made known. Locked away in the Soviet secret archives in Moscow for half a century or more, the files on this clandestine operation have only recently been released. According to the latest CIS/CIA review of these files, Operation Myth was totally Stalin's invention. A product of his obsession with his arch rival Hitler, it had begun the day Nazi troops swarmed across the Soviet frontier four years ago and it did not finish when the war came to an end. When Marshal Zhukov telephoned Stalin from his HQ outside Berlin on 1 May 1945 to tell him of Doenitz's broadcast informing the German people of Hitler's death, Stalin did not dance with glee at the demise of his arch rival, instead he snarled at Zhukov, 'So the beast has escaped us! Have you found the body?'

Shortly after Hitler's autopsy, Stalin sent his fearsome chief of the secret police, Beria, to Moscow to review the autopsy findings and bring all relevant evidence, including the bodies, back to Moscow. Bizarrely, however – by the standards of the Stalin era – the SMERSH team had removed and reburied the corpses and refused point blank to dig them up and hand them over to Beria and his secret police. Nevertheless, Stalin rejected the autopsy outright. From now on the truth of the matter – *his* truth – was that Hitler had escaped and was alive.

At a Kremlin meeting with former President Roosevelt's chief adviser Harry Hopkins on 26 May, Stalin stated point blank that he believed Hitler was alive and in hiding in the West. 'Stalin was not making diplomatic small talk,' commented a later CIA review of the matter, 'he was launching a disinformation campaign that he had personally devised and directed.' Two days later, *Time* magazine ran a cover picture which featured Hitler's portrait with a large cross through it and an account of Hitler's escape through a secret tunnel in the Bunker.

On 5 June, at the first meeting of the Allied Commanders in Chief in Berlin, senior Russian officers affirmed they had exhumed and identified Hitler's body. Stalin immediately sent Andrei Vyshinski, the notorious prosecutor of the Moscow show trials, to put Zhukov right on a few things. On 9 June, in a public statement to the press, Marshal Zhukov duly performed a complete volte-face. He knew nothing definite, he pronounced. No body had been identified. Hitler could easily have flown out of Berlin at the last moment. He might very well be alive. 'My opinion,' Zhukov went on, 'is that Hitler has gone into hiding and is somewhere in Europe – possibly with General Franco in Spain.' Shortly afterwards he said the same thing to General Eisenhower in person.

At the summit conference of the Big Three in Potsdam in July, Stalin went further. He told the US Secretary of State he had reason to believe that Hitler was in Spain or Argentina. He told President Truman's military adviser that Hitler had probably left Germany for Japan.

Theoretically it was possible. There were ways out. The Vatican was known to be quite obliging towards Nazi fugitives. Some of the most wanted Nazi war criminals – like Adolf Eichmann, the organizing administrator of the Holocaust, Auschwitz death camp doctor Joseph Mengele, and Klaus Barbie, the Butcher of Lyons – would all succeed in making their getaway to South America. But as far as the Russians in Berlin were concerned – from the investigators in the Bunker all the way up to the C-in-C Marshal Zhukov – there was absolutely no doubt that Adolf Hitler was well and truly dead, and later some Russians would even claim that the monster's body had been located, identified, photographed and autopsied.

There were even certain officers in Allied Intelligence who knew Stalin could not possibly be telling the truth, for the interception by the British of Goebbels' telegram to Doenitz on 1 May 1945, which referred to the Führer's Testament of 29 April, spelled out the Führer's intended demise.

So why was Stalin putting about the myth that Hitler had survived? Why did he have some 800 people, including over thirty members of Hitler's entourage, locked up and endlessly interrogated and beaten in Berlin and Moscow for years in an attempt to compel them to reveal the truth about Hitler's escape? Why did he have Hitler's and Eva Braun's suicides re-enacted time and again in the hope of finding a flaw in the evidence? Was he just plain wrong? Misinformed, perhaps? Or simply irrational, issuing summary diktats in his role as the infallible dictator who brooked no argument? As the CIA review suggested: 'The fantastic effort carried out under the rubric of *Mif* suggests that Stalin was trying to bend the evidence to conform to his own distorted version of reality . . . not attempting to mislead someone else but trying to prove his own delusion – or at least destroy the evidence that contradicted it.'

Perhaps also there was an underlying strategic motive, aimed at confusing the Western Powers who would soon (he knew) turn from wartime Allies into future Cold War enemies. It is a fact that for thirty years the FBI was kept busy investigating every report about Hitler sightings and claims that he was alive in a file that ran to 734 pages. It was reported that Hitler had been seen living as a hermit in a cave near La Garda, as a shepherd in the Swiss Alps, as a monk in the monastery at St Gallen, as a croupier in a casino at Evian, as a head waiter in a restaurant in Grenoble, as a fisherman on the Aran Islands off the Irish coast. Perhaps there was a political motive, aimed at forcing the Anglo-Americans to maintain their suppressive hold on Western Germany for fear of a Nazi revival – a hold that would ensure Germany could never again pose a threat to the USSR. Perhaps some of the claims were simply from nuts, like the claim that until a few years ago, when he was involved in a shooting accident, Hitler was living quietly in the town of Tetbury, in Gloucestershire, under the name of Hunton Downs.

Or perhaps the motive was closer to home? As an absolute and paranoid ruler, Stalin was always quick to squash anyone whose popularity or status could threaten his own – as for instance the victorious Soviet generals, above all the supreme commander Marshal Zhukov, the architect of the final defeat of Nazi Germany. Only a few days after Zhukov's 'Hitler is dead' statement, General Eisenhower was advised that 'the Russian

government intends to control General Zhukov completely.'
And eventually Stalin did indeed remove him from Germany
and all high command, sending him into virtual exile as the
relatively lowly military governor of the small port of Odessa on
the Black Sea coast of Ukraine.

Stalin had gone further. At his behest a senior Kremlin
official publicly stated that Hitler and Eva Braun were not only
alive and well, but living in Germany protected by the British.
The fate of the erstwhile Führer was now linked to Soviet
accusations about British leniency towards Nazi war criminals.
And not just Soviet accusations – in America, too, suspicions
had been aroused when Himmler managed to kill himself while
in British custody.

Oxbridge Spy in Specs

It was Stalin's intransigence that finally led to the unravelling of the
facts about Hitler's final days. For as it happened, during the middle
of all this mounting controversy, the British Intelligence chief in
Germany, Dick White (later head of MI5 and MI6), invited an old
colleague to stay for a weekend at his place in Riehlkirchen in the
British Zone of Germany. The name of the colleague was Hugh
Trevor-Roper, a 31-year-old former history don at Oxford
University whose main wartime role had been to monitor the
German Intelligence Service, the Abwehr, for the British Secret
Intelligence Service (SIS/MI6) by intercepting and decoding radio
signals between German agents and their controllers. White was
clearly furious about the current Soviet stance on Hitler.

'The Russians refuse to tell us about Hitler's fate,' he complained to Trevor-Roper. 'We've had stories that he was

murdered in Berlin replaced by accounts that he's alive on a Baltic island or escaped to South America in a submarine. Now it's worse.'

As a result of his own investigation in Berlin he was convinced that Hitler was dead. Now he suggested that Trevor-Roper undertake his own investigation and produce the definitive report once and for all. And so Hugh Trevor-Roper – a trim, perky, clean-shaven English public school and Oxbridge intellectual cum spy in specs – set off on his epic quest through darkest Germany, like Theseus on the trail of the Minotaur, tracking down a bunch of yahoos in a spectral and ruined land. Throughout September and October of 1945, with tenacity and cunning, he hunted for clues and sought eyewitnesses out in the chaos of the erstwhile Reich (the Soviet Zone excepted).

Many of the personnel involved in the last days in the Bunker were interrogated by him – many, that is, except the dead, the missing and those in Russian hands. Hitler's deputy, Martin Bormann, who had escaped from the Bunker, was among the missing, as was Bormann's adviser, Wilhelm Zander (along with certain important documents he had taken from the Bunker), and Hitler's wedding official, Walter Wagner.

Nor was Hitler's family (such as it was) of any use. He had disowned them all and they knew nothing. Some, like Adolf's half-brother Alois Hitler, who had run a pub in Berlin's Wittenbergplatz – much to Adolf's disgust – had simply vanished. When American reporter William L. Shirer went to look for him in November 1945 he found the place under new management, though beneath the new name on the pub sign he could still make out the old name – 'A. Hitler'.

Those relatives who remained were not spared the Russians' wrath. Hitler's cousin, Maria Koppensteiner, a harmless

Austrian peasant woman, was arrested (along with three of her brothers) by SMERSH agents in May 1945 purely because she was related to Adolf Hitler. Relentlessly interrogated in Moscow, she was sentenced to twenty-five years' imprisonment in one of the worst Soviet camps and cruelly mistreated, dying suddenly eight years later, possibly by lethal injection. Similarly Leo Raubal, son of Hitler's half-sister Angela Hitler, was sentenced to twenty-five years after his capture at Stalingrad on the grounds of 'being a relative of the main war criminal, Hitler', though in his case he gained release in 1955.

As for Eva Braun's next-of-kin, though her parents never fell into Russian hands, they never received the jewellery she had sent them in the final weeks to help tide them through the lean years to come, and within a year or so of the end of the war Hitler's father-in-law was slaving away as a common labourer to survive.

Trevor-Roper was not alone in his quest. As one British liaison officer observed at the time: 'Never have there been so many "detectives" on any case.' One day in the Chancellery grounds he counted forty-five separate parties from at least four nationalities, all armed with torches, pencils, notebooks, cameras and diagrams, all hoping they would hit upon a clue. But by the beginning of November the facts meticulously assembled by Trevor-Roper and his team already proved conclusive enough for the British to call a press conference in Berlin designed to totally refute Stalin's claims that Hitler had survived the war – a gathering keenly attended by the Russians. So on a foggy evening in the British press headquarters in the Hotel-am-Zoo in Berlin's once fashionable and now ruined Kürfurstendamm, Trevor-Roper presented his case. 'The evidence,' he began, 'is not complete; but it is positive, circumstantial, consistent and independent.' By the end he left no one in any doubt that Hitler was dead and any opinion to the contrary was purely mischievous. Then came the questions.

'Is there any danger of Hitler being alive?' one questioner asked.

'We are satisfied in our own minds,' came the reply, 'that Hitler is dead.'

The matter of Hitler's marriage cropped up – and an oblique reference to Walter Wagner.

'Who actually performed the marriage?' another questioner asked.

'A member of the Ministry of Propaganda,' came the erroneous reply. 'As a matter of fact, somebody did ring up and try and get another marriage performed, and the person who answered said, "What a pity you did not ask two days ago – you could have had the same man who married Hitler and Eva Braun."'

As one British officer in attendance commented later, 'This is one of the many inconsistencies in the story told by the British Intelligence Service. Later it was revealed that a city councillor named Walter Wagner performed the ceremony, but he could not be found.'

The Berlin press call did not mark the end of Trevor-Roper's quest and he carried on into the following year. Of special interest was Hitler's testament and marriage certificate, countersigned by Walter Wagner. Of Wagner himself there was still no trace, though Wagner's wife (or widow), Cordula, did receive a visit from Trevor-Roper's team on the island of Föhr. Nor was there any trace of the special messengers who some four months previously had slipped out of the Bunker and through the Russian lines in the hope of delivering Hitler's last words to whoever survived him – and to the world at large.

The Three Messengers Revisited

Searching for three men in the chaos of Germany in the autumn and early winter of 1945 was a nearly impossible task. Millions of homeless people were on the move or dossing down with strangers in cellars and ruins and air-raid shelters. None of the wanted men were well known and it was therefore a stroke of luck that one of them eventually made a false move that led to his apprehension.

This was Heinz Lorenz, the former confidant of Goebbels in the Propaganda Ministry. Hoping for a job with the British, he had tried to pass himself off as a Luxembourg journalist with special knowledge of such topical human interest stories as life in Hitler's bunker, about which he seemed unusually well informed. Arrested in Hanover early in December 1945 on suspicion of using false identity papers, Lorenz then underwent a routine search. 'It was the crinkle of paper in the shoulder of his coat,' a British intelligence officer explained, 'that caused us to rip the coat open. There were the documents, cleverly concealed.' The Lorenz set contained not only Hitler's personal will and political testament, but an appendix written by Goebbels.

With one of Hitler's messengers in Allied custody, the other two were soon tracked down. Next to be apprehended was Major Willy Johannmeyer, who was found living with his parents at Iserlohn, in the Ruhr, a few hundred yards from British Army Headquarters. Johannmeyer proved to be a patriotic ex-soldier, a holder of the Ritterkreuz with Oak Leaves, who felt disinclined to help his country's conquerors. He flatly refused to co-operate, claiming he knew nothing about the mission of Hitler's messengers, as he had merely been their guide.

It soon became clear to Major Trevor-Roper that if he was to break Johannmeyer he would have to find Wilhelm Zander, the remaining messenger. Zander had been a dyed-in-the wool Nazi who had renounced the cause and elected to begin a new life under a new identity. He was not exactly the brightest or best-educated ex-Nazi on the run, but he had cunning and resolve. His home was in Munich, but it was soon evident he had never been there since the end of the war and had gone to ground. 'Investigations then started to locate Zander in the Hanover area,' Major Trevor-Roper confided to Colonel Byford-Jones at this time. 'His wife gave me the address of his parents. She put up a splendid screen, because she knew his whereabouts, but she had told his parents that he had died. I set off to Bavaria, and found evidence that Zander had been in hospital at Tegernsee as a result of walking from Hanover. He had been treated by a Nazi doctor, who has since been arrested for removing identification marks from SS men.'

Bavaria was in the American zone of occupation and Trevor-Roper could only proceed with the authorization and co-operation of US military intelligence in the form of the 3rd US Army Counter Intelligence Corps. Local evidence began to indicate that Zander had assumed the false name of Friedrich Wilhelm Paustin and had been working variously as a gardener and janitor in Tegernsee, near US Third Army headquarters. A raid on his home in Tegernsee proved fruitless, however, and Trevor-Roper and CIC special agents Weiss and Rosner learned he had left a few days previously with his 22-year-old girl-friend Ilsa Unterholzner (who had been Bormann's secretary) in order to spend Christmas at Ilsa's sister's house in the little village of Aidenbach near Vilshoven on the Austrian frontier.

At three o'clock in the morning of 28 December, Trevor-Roper and his team launched a raid on the house. According to one of the American agents, Zander resisted arrest and a gun-fight ensued. Zander was quickly overpowered, however, and taken to Munich for interrogation. There he revealed that he had given his suitcase (with the Hitler papers hidden inside) to his girlfriend's other sister, Irmgard, in the house in Tegernsee. This was voluntarily handed in, though an initial search by CIC Special Agent Ernst Mueller revealed nothing but clothes. Subsequently, however, he noted a bulge in the lining and found a secret compartment containing a cloth envelope from which dropped a packet of documents topped with an official gold seal.

As a souvenir of his momentous find, Special Agent Mueller took a set of photos of Hitler's will and wedding documents with his 'liberated' German camera. These are now in the Sayer archives – the only contemporary photos of these historic documents in private hands. Now, however, to the consternation of Trevor-Roper, who considered the quest for Zander and the Hitler papers was a British 'show' under his control, the Americans chose to retain the papers, then forwarded them to Washington for FBI forensic analysis of the paper and ink to confirm their identity.

For the Americans the find was not only an event of historic importance but a valuable public relations coup in an otherwise quiet sector of American-occupied Germany. 'Hitler's Private Will Found; Affirms His Suicidal Plans' splashed the front-page headline in the *New York Times* of 30 December 1945. General Lucien E. Truscott, commanding the US Third Army, was outspoken in his praise of the co-operation between British Counter intelligence and the CIC operatives who made the discovery. 'It was teamwork of the highest order,' he proclaimed, adding that the documents were of 'inestimable value' in piecing together the closing days of the Nazis' downfall.

Trevor-Roper now returned to the unyielding Johannmeyer, and another round of relentless interrogation. Finally the dogged German gave up.

'*Ich habe die Papiere,*' he admitted at last. 'I have the papers.'

'He accompanied me by car to Iserlohn,' Trevor-Roper was to record,' and there led me into the back garden of his home. It was dark. With an axe he broke open the frozen ground and dug up a buried bottle. Then, breaking the bottle with the axe, he drew out and handed to me the last missing document: the third copy of Hitler's political testament.'

But doubters remained, most of them ill-informed. When Hitler's testaments and marriage certificate were published in the British press, various authorities on German matters cast doubt on them. 'Hitler's marriage certificate is a patent forgery,' wrote one such expert in a British newspaper. 'It was clearly typed on a non-German machine by a non-German. The registrar who is supposed to have officiated, "Walter Wagner", proves unknown to the Chief Registrar in Berlin.'

Though the quest was to all intents over and the facts about Hitler's final days virtually complete, the enquiry continued with a momentum of its own. Later that January, Lieutenant Colonel von Below, the last man out of the Bunker before Hitler's death, was found quietly studying law at the University of Bonn and promptly apprehended. During the spring and summer other eyewitnesses were located, most importantly Hitler's two secretaries, Traudl Junge and Gerda Christian, and all of them were interrogated.

Of those close to the centre during Hitler's final hours, only Martin Bormann, Hitler's Deputy, and his wedding registrar,

Walter Wagner, remained unavailable for questioning. It was alleged that Bormann had been seen lying dead in the vicinity of the Lehrter railway station around 2 May while trying to break through the Russian lines in Berlin, and this proved to be correct when in 1972 his corpse (complete with splinters from a glass cyanide capsule lodged in the jaws) was accidentally exhumed during construction development near that same station. But as to Wagner, half a century and more was to pass, and still nothing was publicly known about his whereabouts. And as to the final resting place of the remains of the Bunker dead – Adolf and Eva Hitler, Joseph and Magda Goebbels and their six children – there was not a single clue.

Nevertheless the dossier was complete, the case closed. Major Hugh Trevor-Roper and the Western Allies were right, the Soviets were wrong and Stalin was proved a calculating and culpable liar.

Humanoid Gunge

It was not until after Stalin's death, when other eyewitnesses to these events were released from Soviet captivity and returned to Germany, that the matter was finally resolved in any official sense.

So concrete were the facts as to the place, date and mode of the deaths of the erstwhile Führer and his wife that on 25 February 1956 – after an investigation that lasted more than three years and ran to over 1,500 pages of witness statements – the West German Federal Court in Berchtesgaden finally issued Hitler's official death certificate, concluding:

There can no longer be the slightest doubt that on 30 April 1945 Adolf Hitler put an end to his life in the

Chancellery by his own hand, by means of a shot into
his right temple.

And on 28 December 1956 Hitler (still officially recorded
under the job title 'Führer and Reich Chancellor') was entered
on the 'Register of Declared Dead' in the Federal Records Office
in West Berlin.

The more recent opening of the former secret Soviet archives
completes the story – after a fashion. On Stalin's orders, it
seems, SMERSH reburied the remains of Adolf Hitler and Eva
Braun (less the jaws and teeth which they sent on to Moscow),
together with General Krebs and the Goebbels family, first in
Rathenow, then in Stendal, and finally, in February 1946, in
the courtyard of an apartment house in Magdeburg com-
mandeered by the Red Army as a counter intelligence base ('36
Westerndstrasse, near the southern stone wall of the courtyard,
25 metres straight to the east from the wall of the garage, at a
depth of 2 metres'). There the bits and pieces of Adolf and the
lovely Eva and the others remained until April 1970, when,
with the newly formed East German government about to take
over the area, KGB chief Yuri Andropov (with Politburo
approval) ordered a KGB team, on the pretence of looking for
long-lost Nazi archives, to excavate and remove once and for
all the remains, including Hitler and Eva Braun, plus two
dogs. According to the KGB report, these remains were now
a 'jellied mass'. This humanoid gunge was first pulverized,
then soaked in gasoline and completely burned up. Afterwards
the ashes were mixed with coal dust and taken just over 6
miles north of Magdeburg, where they were dumped into the
Bideriz, a tributary of the Elbe River and outflow of the city's
sewage system.

And so what little was left of the Führer of the Third (and last) Reich, Founder of the Heroic Age, Purifier of the Aryan Race, respectful husband of the erstwhile Reich's 'First Lady', Eva Braun, ended not as he or she had wished, enshrined in a glorious sarcophagus in the national mausoleum of his dreams, but as a slurry of soot drifting seawards like sludge. His Thousand Year Reich had lasted just a fraction of that time, and during that short period he had destroyed half a continent and slaughtered some 40 million human beings from over twenty nations.

So far so good. But more recently the picture has grown even more confusing and it seems possible that one other fragment of the monster has mysteriously remained. For what it was worth, the 1945 Russian autopsy report on Hitler had stated in a footnote that part of the skull was missing. Recently released former Soviet files now reveal that early in 1946, when Stalin's Operation Myth was at its height, a SMERSH team was sent back to the former Chancellery garden in Berlin where Hitler's remains had previously been found. Here, in a bomb crater that had been turned into a makeshift grave, the team found four human skull fragments, the largest measuring some 3 inches by 4, with a bullet hole on one side. These fragments, it turned out, appeared to fit the rest of the skull that had been examined during Hitler's autopsy.

The remnants of Hitler's cranium were then forwarded to Moscow, where it was rumoured in the Red Army Officer Corps that the largest fragment, roughly the size of a man's cupped hand, was used by Stalin as his ash tray – it would have been appropriate, one tyrant stubbing out his butt-end inside the head of another. For most of the intervening years, however, the skull was kept in a cardboard box in the KGB archives until it was finally made public in April 2000 at an exhibition at the Russian State Archives commemorating the 55th anniversary of the Red Army's capture of Berlin and victory over Nazi Germany. To Maria Sountsova, the present authors' researcher in Moscow, the exhibition director confirmed that 'we are 99.9 per cent sure the skull is Hitler's' – though the official who had stood guard over the exhibit for a week told her he had grown sick of the thing, and couldn't believe it was Hitler's skull, 'it looked more like a dog's than a man's.'

Today Hitler's head rests, not in peace but on two sheets of Kleenex in a floppy disc storage case. Assuming that the skull is authentic – DNA testing will ultimately resolve the matter – it may shed one further light on Hitler's final moments: the exact manner of his suicide. It has always been assumed that Hitler shot himself in the right temple. How he managed this so skilfully given the fact that his hands trembled so wildly and had so little grip has always posed a quandary (though it is known his right hand trembled less that his left). Recently, however, his skull has been the subject of fresh expert examination in Moscow by Professor Viktor Zyagin of the Federal Centre of Medical Forensic Examination. His conclusions were, inter alia, that the skull had the typical grey-blue bone colour of a vegetarian, that finger-made depressions indicated inner cranial pressure typical of a person suffering from persistent headaches, and significantly – but confusingly! – that the bullet hole is in the parietal area of the cranium, indicating that the shot was most probably made through the underside of the chin.

So much for such evidence as exists concerning the deaths and final disposition of the bodies of Adolf Hitler and his bride of a few hours, Eva Hitler, together with his acolyte and propagandist Joseph Goebbels, his wife and six slaughtered children.

The final truth of the matter may never be known for sure and the exact fate of Hitler's remains may stay as great a mystery as the nature of his drive to power and the workings of the inside of his head.

Today the Bunker where these apocalyptic events took place is no more. Anxious that the site of Hitler's last stand should not become a neo-Nazi national shrine, like Frederick the Great's summer palace, Sans Souci, the Russians decided in 1949 to remove all vestiges of the Chancellery and the Bunker. The Chancellery was blown up and the ground levelled. It proved impossible to blow up the Bunker, however, and the remains were simply topped with a mound of grass-covered earth. Then in the late 1980s the thick concrete roof was removed layer by layer, the Bunker was filled in, and eventually a road and apartment buildings built over the top. Today even the very name of Hitler has been expunged, and no such word is to be found in any telephone directory anywhere in Germany.

Sic transit horror mundi.

PART 5

Postscript
The Unsolved Puzzle

The Mystery Man

But what of the fate of the mystery man at the heart of the climactic events in the Führerbunker on the night of 29/30 April 1945, Walter Wagner – career Nazi, staunch patriot, street fighter, former rubbish clearance official, registrar at the Führer's wedding, devoted husband, adoring father, missing person, one of the last unsolved puzzles in the last days of Hitler?

For the first time the full facts can be made publicly known. When in August 1963 *Stern* magazine claimed that it was believed Walter Wagner was still alive and had been seen in the outskirts of Frankfurt, it had done so partly in the belief that it was impossible for someone who had been temporarily so prominent and close to the central debacle in Berlin to have vanished utterly into thin air. No one, it seemed, had witnessed his demise or reported it, no body had been found. In fact, the truth of the matter had lain in the archives of the Hamburg City Court for more than half a century, only coming to light as a result of the authors' present enquiries in the summer of 2003. What happened was this.

When Berlin fell and Germany finally surrendered in May 1945, Walter Wagner's wife Cordula and his seven-months-old son Michael were still living in the former Flying School hostel at Wyk on the tiny island of Föhr. Almost immediately they were confronted – like millions of other German civilians who

273

had survived the war (nearly 4 million had not) – with the awful reality of life in the post-war ruins of the Reich during the so-called hunger years.

The once mighty Fatherland had been divided into four zones of occupation and was now governed by the armies of the four victorious Allies – Berlin, the former capital, likewise. Food was in desperately short supply and before long the average daily calorie intake per person in the British Zone (which took in the whole of north-west Germany, including Wyk) would fall to a near-starvation level of 1,040 calories and less. Most basic commodities – soap, candles, sanitary towels, matches – were virtually unobtainable. Cordula, like many others, was eventually hauled before a denazification court, cleared of any misdemeanours while a member of the Nazi Party, and allowed to pick up the threads of her life.

These, on a tiny offshore island with a grounded air force facility and an extinct holiday and spa trade, were not especially promising, though there was always the allotment to live off in the growing season. She struggled along, doing her best for her son, resigned to the fact that her husband, the man with whom she had spent barely more than six months of her life together, would never come home to her. In the midst of this desolation, the British arrived.

The Last Card

They came in the form of British Military Intelligence – specifically Hugh Trevor-Roper's team, still hot on the trail of anyone and everyone involved in Hitler's final days. They were polite but firm. Did she know the whereabouts of her husband, Walter Wagner?

they asked her. When had she last seen him? When was he last in touch? Did she have any correspondence from him?

They did not explain why they were looking for her husband. They gave no hint of his presence in the Führerbunker or of his last-known movements, all of which remained completely unknown to her. She handed them her little sheaf of postcards and letters – love letters mostly – from her husband. They riffled through them, selected the postcard written from Berlin on 29 March, wrote 'THE LAST CARD' in English on the front of it, and took it away with them.

As it happened, the card was to prove of absolutely no help at all to Trevor-Roper in his quest. But nearly fifty years later it was to resurface and come into the possession of Ian Sayer and his Second World War document centre – and this in turn would lead to the present final unravelling of the story of the mystery man in the Bunker in Hitler's last hours.

Early in 1947, in the coldest winter ever recorded in Germany, Cordula and her son finally abandoned Wyk and moved to the brighter prospects of the nearest big city – the north German port of Hamburg, bombed by the British, conquered by the British, run by the British, but offering improving prospects for employment, a reliable food ration, medical care, and nursery care for Michael. Life remained hard and bleak, but they were surviving, she had a job in a Hamburg Central Station restaurant, life could be worse. It was then that she first got word about her husband.

At the end of February 1947 Walter Wagner's sister, Elly Wagner, got in touch with Cordula to say that she had encountered a certain Frau Illing, the wife of Walter Wagner's company commander, Erich Illing, in the final battle for Berlin. Erich Illing had been made prisoner by the Russians and was now a Soviet captive in a 'so-called internment camp' somewhere in the depths of Russia. He had now made contact with his wife to confirm that, though he had not seen it with his own eyes, he was practically certain Walter Wagner had been killed in front-line street combat with Red Army units in Berlin on the last day of April 1945. From the Displaced Persons Division of the Allied Military Authorities in Berlin, Cordula later received confirmation that there was no evidence her husband had survived the war.

Finally, in the summer of 1949, four years after the end of the war, Military Government by the three Western Allied Powers stepped down in favour of an elected democratic West German government with a new capital in Bonn. For Cordula Wagner, like many in West Germany, life was returning to post-war normality. And in due course, like many other German women in that vast army of German war widows, Cordula at last felt free to fall in love again – sufficiently in love, in fact, to want to take her new man for her second husband. And there lay the crucial problem – a problem that would lead eventually to the final unravelling of this story.

Cordula Wagner could not remarry, officialdom declared, because as things stood she was still married to a man called Walter Wagner – at any rate there was no hard evidence that she was not. Michael Wagner, now aged six, knew little of these matters. All he was sure of was that in course of time a new father arrived in his home – a West German civil servant and former Wehrmacht paymaster by the name of Ernst Jessel. The event did not move Michael greatly. 'Both my parents were Nazis,' he told Ian Sayer recently.

Then he recalled one thing. In order to remarry, his mother had to petition the Hamburg Court for legal permission, and this permission could only be granted if she could prove incontrovertibly that her first husband was deceased. To do that the lawyers advised her in 1951 to submit several affidavits as proof of the circumstances of her husband's demise. These affidavits had never been made public, Michael explained, but perhaps if he applied to the Hamburg Court for their release he might discover once and for all how his father – the mystery man in Hitler's dying days – had met his end.

Recently these affidavits have been released. They are not eyewitness reports but testimonies from three people close at hand who had spoken to eyewitnesses at the time. Now they can be made public, revealing for the first time the known facts about the death of Walter Wagner, the man who married Adolf Hitler and Eva Braun. From this it would seem he outlived his Führer and his bride by only a few hours, died facing the enemy, and has no known grave.

Death at the Barricades

When Wagner finally emerged from Hitler's Bunker – shocked, confused and short of sleep – and was let out through the steel doors of the emergency exit into the horrendous night of a Berlin under fire, his aim was to get back to his Volkssturm company (the 'Gauleitung' company) in the central square known as the Potsdamer Platz. This was not straightforward. Though there were as yet no Russian troops in Berlin's inner citadel, there were no lights to guide him (only fires) and the whole area was ceaselessly pounded by artillery and rocket fire. By the time he regained his company, the final massive Soviet onslaught on the capital's citadel was already under way.

The role of the 'Gauleitung' company was to defend the Potsdamer Platz and seal off the two approach avenues that led to it. As the day advanced, Russian tanks and infantry were reported to be advancing along one of these approach avenues, the Saarlandstrasse, and elements of the Volksturm, with Erich Illing in overall command and Walter Wagner in command of No. 1 section, were despatched down this avenue to head off the approaching Russian forces. Halfway down the avenue, just to the north of Anhalt railway station, they formed a defensive position.

If the conditions in the Potsdamer Platz had been hellish, at Anhalt station they were apocalyptic. 'The station looks like an armed camp,' an eyewitness recorded. 'Women and children huddling in niches and corners listening to the sounds of battle. Shells hit the roof, cement is crumbling from the ceiling. A terrible sight at the entrance of the subway station: a heavy shell has pierced the roof, and men, women, soldiers, children are literally squashed against the walls.' There were so many wounded that young women made a Red Cross flag using sheets and lipstick but it did not stop the Russians firing on them.

Here Walter Wagner had to hold his ground against the might of the oncoming enemy. The German Home Guard was no match for a battle-hardened spearhead of the Red Army triumphant. As another Volkssturm unit trying to put up a tank barrier in nearby Hohenzollerndamm nearby was advised by a sceptical bystander: 'It will take the Russians two hours and four minutes to knock that thing down. Two hours roaring with laughter, then one gun to knock it sideways.' The Russians were not long in coming, in numbers and firepower they were overwhelming, and the fighting was desperate. Erich Illing recalled:

In the course of the combat I was severely wounded by

Russian tank fire. Walter Wagner took over command and I was carried back to a first-aid post. From there I was in continuous communication with the company. Twenty-four hours went by and then I got news that my successor, Walter Wagner – an outstanding comrade and a good friend – had been shot in the head and killed in an action with a small group in the direction of the Anhalt railway station. Further details I do not know. I was taken prisoner by the Russians, finally returning to Berlin in 1950.

A female auxiliary attached to Illing's company, a young woman by the name of Luzie Leuenberg, confirms this:

According to testimonies of several wounded coming back to the Potsdamer Platz, Wagner and several comrades were killed on the near side of the Anhalt railway station. Because of the severity of the fighting it was not possible to recover the bodies. For this reason I never saw them. Sadly I can't name any eyewitnesses as they were all taken into captivity.

What happened shortly afterwards was recalled by a third witness, Frau Vera Kroeckelberg, a civilian who was stuck in the Potsdamer Platz because the Russians had already occupied the district where her home was. She wrote in a letter submitted to the Hamburg Court in 1951:

I heard from several members of the detachment after it was pulled back that Walter Wagner was among those who were killed. Later the Russians broke

through and the collapse of the defending forces
followed. As a result, the whereabouts of the bodies in
the confusion that reigned was unknown to me.

Wagner's body was never recovered. Probably it was
bulldozed into the rubble of the ruins of the city where he was
born, served, and met his death, or perhaps burned on the giant
funeral pyres where the Russians incinerated tens of thousands
of corpses to prevent pestilence in the first days of the peace.
Whatever the facts of the matter, the Hamburg Court was
satisfied with Cordula's petition and the facts of the death of her
first husband, declaring: 'I recommend therefore that the
Petitioner be allowed to take another husband.'

It was only later that Cordula discovered her former husband
had been in the Führerbunker in the final hours of Hitler's Reich
when she chanced to see a photo of Hitler's marriage certificate
with Walter's signature at the bottom.

Such are the known facts about the life and death of Walter
Wagner. What exactly made him tick, and what kind of man he
would have been to meet, one can only guess. Perhaps he was
indeed, amid the infinite permutations of human characteristics,
that not entirely unknown phenomenon – the nice Nazi, the
loyal and loving family man, the city councillor doing good
works, who yet supported an evil cause.

For no one could Walter Wagner present a more enigmatic
image than for his son Michael, now a lawyer in Mannheim.

He confided to us at the completion of this investigation:

'Walter Wagner was my father. I never ever set eyes on
him. All I knew was that he was a Nazi – the mystery
man who for a moment stood at the heart of the Third

Reich, who came out of the dark to marry Adolf Hitler, then went back out into the dark and was never seen again. But now I know, from those letters I could never read till now, that after all he was a Nazi with a human face. Now I know how much he truly loved me and my mother in those dark and terrible days when I was a little boy. And now I know that in the end I miss him – Walter Wagner, the father I never had, whose name I bear.

The Last Letters of
The Man who Married Hitler

Berlin, 18.12.1944

My dearest Cordula!

Enclosed is my Christmas letter, which I would ask you to open at 4 p.m. At that time my thoughts will be firmly with you. Any hopes of my coming to Wyk have now vanished. We will just have to accept it. The main thing is that you and Michael are healthy and in good spirits. Let's hope that the great offensive in the West now brings about a change in our fortunes of war. For the time being no details whatsoever are being announced. You should therefore remain unperturbed by any news, be it positive or negative, and believe only the announcements made in the Wehrmacht reports. This afternoon Party Member Schach [Gerhard Schach, Deputy Gauleiter of Berlin] and I spent about an hour with the Minister of Justice [Otto Thierack]. It goes without saying that it was very interesting. I achieved everything I set out to achieve. I would so much like to discuss everything with you in detail, but alas, it is not possible, of course.

Tomorrow I shall post a parcel of small Christmas candles, which I hope will still reach you in good time.

Hans [Walter's brother, a private in the army] told us yesterday that he is going to send you some butter, which I'm sure will come in very useful. I was very touched by his kindness and caring.

Today we had a very pleasant surprise. Hermann [Cordula's brother, a private in the army, killed in Copenhagen in 1945] rang, passing through. We missed each other, as I wasn't here at the time. However, with great difficulty I managed to get in touch with Traudel [possibly his wife?].* Of course we were very happy that he'd been granted leave for Christmas. After the events of the last few weeks it must be an indescribable joy for him and his family, not least his encounter with his son, Andreas. How we both worried about him, and now everything has ended so well. Let's hope that his – and Carl's – soldier's luck continues! Mother will be so pleased to have at least one of her sons home for Christmas. After all the worries and anguish she had to endure over the last few months, she will now have a lovely Christmas. I just wish that her arm will recover fully and speedily.

I shall go home now and straight to bed, as I am dog-tired, having slept badly last night. I wonder if there will be a letter for me tomorrow morning? I have not had any news at all since Saturday. Just as well that I can go home on Sunday.

Lots of love

Walter

*Queries in [square] brackets are the translator's.

Berlin, 19.12.1944

My dear, beloved Cordula,

A whole year has passed since we sat facing each other at the Christmas party in Posnan – strangers, but not indifferent to each other. I remember so well the morning of Christmas Day, laying on my bed in the Posler [?] hotel room, thinking about the past and the future. A second stage in my own life and that of my two siblings had been brought to a close by the loss of our flat. That was the first Christmas we could not spend together. You can imagine what a sad Christmas it was, under the circumstances. To us, Christmas had always been a family celebration – both before and after the deaths of our parents. Some of the loveliest memories of my youth are linked with Christmas. Now all this was suddenly gone. A year on, and in this dejected state of mind, I suddenly imagine how nice it would have been if I could have gone to Wyk with Miss Kroepels. But what a difference a year has made. Miss Kroepels is now Mrs Wagner and no longer alone. This year, again, I cannot be in Wyk, but I feel, happily, that someone else will ably stand in for me – our dear little Michael. To be sure – it is very sad that we cannot spend the first Christmas of our married life together, but let us remember the past year, and we will have to admit that we have no reason to complain. It was a most fortunate year, my dearest, that brought us together the way it did. Isn't it strange to think how fate took a hand and brought such fundamental change to both our lives! I would never have thought that I could find such a sweet and good companion with whom to share my life. With your life you have given my life a very special meaning, and you have made me very, very happy. My thoughts are with the many hours we have been able to spend together, hours of blissful happiness and quiet reflection in Wyk, Hamburg and Buch. Also my thoughts are with our dear little Michael, who had made our lives together richer still. Our son, born by you in pain, but conceived in love and trusting faith. In this hour, I want to thank you, my dearest Cordula, for all the love and trust you have given me over this past year. Also, I want to thank you for your loving, devoted care for our Michael. In this hour I also want you to know that my heart is yours forever, and I love you very, very much and that I will always love you. Whatever fate may have in store for us – all the things we cannot know. One thing we do know for sure is that we will be bound together in true love until we draw our last breath. My dear, good Cordula, our life together is yet to come, and we shall live it as we began, in love for each other and unconditional trust for each other. Let us celebrate this wartime Christmas 1944 in this spirit [?] in the hope that we may be reunited and happy a year from now. May the momentous events which started in the West on Saturday be a good omen for our future.

Now, my dearest, best Cordula, let me wish you, Michael and Mother a very happy Christmas. I do hope you enjoy the holiday season. I think and I hope that our dear little Michael will be completely better very soon and give you much happiness. I am sure that the best present for Mother will be the good news from Frau Hungen. I wish with all my heart that this will continue.

At this moment, as you read this letter, Cordula, sadly I cannot be with you, but in my thoughts I am – more than ever.

With the very best wishes for Christmas and many loving kisses

I remain, dearest Cordula, your ever faithful Walter.

Best Christmas wishes to Mother, and a little kiss for Michael from his father. Season's Greetings also to Grandma and the aunts.

Berlin, 4.3.1945

My dearest, best Cordula!

Again it is your birthday and, contrary to all the wishes and hopes I held out last year, I cannot be with you this year either, to convey my best wishes in person. My thoughts in these March days travel back to last year, and in my mind I relive every detail of those indescribably beautiful days in Wyk, which were so crucial for our life together. It is true that we could not celebrate your birthday together and in style, but at least on your birthday I was on my way to you – albeit under dramatic circumstances. Again I see myself on 8 March at Sczecin station, caught in an air raid and trembling for the departure of the train. Everything went wrong and yet came to a most agreeable conclusion, as it often does for you and me. How wonderful was our meeting in Dagebüll, the merry steamship cruise and, finally, the "get-together" of our two clans. What followed was an abundance of incredibly lovely, harmonious and joyful hours and days. I can see it all before me, so vividly as if it had been only yesterday. A year has passed since we started our life together, and I think we both can say that it has been a happy year. I started our marriage with high expectations, and I can say that my expectations were not disappointed, but were exceeded many times over. With all your love and devotion you have made me the happiest man alive. I don't know how to thank my good fortune that I have found you, my dear, good Cordula. I can thank you, however, for all the happiness that you have given me in this first year of our marriage. In this hour I want you to know that I love you with all my heart, that I shall love you for ever, and that my thoughts are with you, full of deepest longing. May the day come soon when we are together again, this happy hour when I can hold you, my darling, in a loving embrace. This hour will come and prove to you once more that you have remained what you were to me during the first year of our marriage, and what you will always be – my faithful wife, my affectionate lover, the caring mother of our dear little Michael, my best companion. We both know that these are not merely empty and big words, but an unconditional and unshakeable profession of faith in our deep and pure love, according to which we live our lives. In my birthday wishes to you last year I wrote that I was hoping to be able to celebrate this year's birthday with you and that, maybe, it would no longer be just the two of us. Sadly, my first wish has remained completely unfulfilled. You have to celebrate another birthday without me, but you are not alone – apart from Mother. Rather, I have found an able deputy. *My* son Michael will convey my best wishes to you on 8.3. On this day, his sweet eyes will beam at you in the morning, and he will tell you lots of things in a *loud* voice. It is entirely up to you to collect the little kiss from him and from me. My dear, good Cordula, we wish you all the very best for this new year of your life. May you remain in good health throughout this year. Most of all, your two men wish that you may be able to celebrate your next birthday in a time of peace – a victorious peace for our country. Our wish for all of us is that we may be happily reunited on this day. Maybe the three of us will not be alone any more, because a little Susanne has joined us. As you see, Michael and I will never ever allow our [. . .] to be taken away. Michael also gives you his solemn promise that he will "mend his ways" and hurry up about his cradle cap, so that your enjoyment in him is totally unclouded and your loving care of him is finally rewarded. I hope that you will spend your birthday as happily and peacefully as possible.

With these good wishes, my dearest Cordula, I will finish my letter.

Keep loving us, just as we are going to love you forever.

With all my love and many loving kisses – your faithful Walter.

Berlin, 16.3.45, 22.00 h

Dear Cordula!

Again the intended letter has to remain unwritten. All I can manage is a card, which makes the letter I received from you all the more special. Our "outpost" – to quote today's accommodation report – has not suffered in any way. It happened further "out" still, not in our direction. Tomorrow, Saturday, I shall be in the bunker again [i.e. the local air raid shelter] until Sunday 13.00 h. After that I have to bicycle from Gustel [?] to B. [Buch]. The afternoon is when my Sunday really starts: my phone call to Wyk and, hopefully, a letter to you at last. Best wishes from me until that phone call.

Your Walter

Dear Cordula! We have just come through another air raid. It is almost unheard of now for us not to be stuck in the cellar at 8.30 [a.m.] Unfortunately I could not get through to Frau Dr Solden [?] today during her consultation hour. Lots of love to you, aunt [. . .] and Michael.

Best wishes to all of you up there from your Gustel [his sister Auguste]

Postcard to Frau Cordula Wagner

Buch, 18.3.1945

My dear, good Cordula!

I have just reached Buch, with some difficulties, at the end of my shift in the bunker. There was quite a lot going on in Berlin today, but everything is perfectly alright in Buch and in my section. We Berliners are as determined as ever not to be defeated under any circumstances. Sadly, I had to abandon the letter I had started in the bunker [ie. the air raid bunker near his home in Buch, where he was an air raid warden] during a short period of peace and quiet, when the "turmoil" started. Quite honestly, after my marching performance, I am a little too worn out to continue writing. I hope I'll find some time tomorrow. My thoughts are with you more than ever, my dearest. Keep on loving me and think of me as often as I think of you. No need to worry about me. I send you all my love, dearest, best Cordula.

Your ever faithful Walter

Lots of love to Mother and a little kiss to Michael. How is the boy? I was going to ring today, but now you have to make do with this card.

19. 3. 1945
8.15 p.m.

My dearest Cordula,

I have just arrived in Buch by bicycle, after a very vigorous march this morning. The Berliners will not be defeated. It is the same Buch you have seen many times before. All in all, things were looking a lot friendlier already. We had a good supper, for "technical" reasons in House 14, and are now expecting our evening visitors [British bombers]. Nothing has happened here and in the surrounding area, but a lot of damage was done in the district of [indecipherable]. My boss Schach, too, was bombed out completely. His family are moving in with the Droefes [?]. I wonder if I will be able to finish my letter to you today. It depends on our "visitors". Lots of love, your Walter.

'The Last Card'

Addressee: Frau Cordula Wagner, 24 Wyk auf Föhr, Südstrand, Fliegerheim (House No. 24, Wyk on Föhr Island(s), South Beach, Air Crew Centre)

Sender: Walter Wagner, 1 Berlin-Buch, Wiltbergstrasse 50, 3rd Floor

28.3.1945

1300 hours

My dear Cordula,

After the visit [American air raid] this morning, here at the office and at the house, everything is fine. I am still not absolutely sure what has happened.

I have received your letters of the 24th, 16th and 30th of March, and they give me much joy, especially regarding your description of our little Michael. Apart from the cradle cap he certainly seems to be all together. Thanks to both your letters I can at least get an idea of what he's like. I hope the cradle cap goes soon. I wish for all of you, and for me, that Wyk stays the quiet place it is now.

In Berlin nothing has changed. In the next few weeks we can only stick it out and must not lose our nerve. Here in Berlin we must stand by our Man.

As far as I am personally concerned everything remains OK. On Friday and during the Easter holidays I will probably not be on duty and I hope I can get a little rest if nothing special happens in the meantime. Hopefully I will be able to call you with early Easter greetings.

Now, my dear Cordula, do spend time with Mother and Michael during the festive occasion and take it easy. With heartfelt greetings to you three. I am yours, as always. Thinking of you.

Walter.

How is your farming going? Have you written to the Group? You can ask Krings whether you need to get permission.

This scribbled postcard was the last communication Cordula ever received from her husband. A little over thirty days later Berlin fell to the Russians and the war was over. Wyk became part of the British Zone of Germany and in due course British Intelligence, searching for clues to the last days of Hitler, visited her at her home on the little island of Wyk and took the card, writing in English on the front 'THE LAST CARD'.

The authors would like to express their gratitude to Michael Wagner, of Mannheim, Germany, for locating and submitting the letters, photos and documents relating to his father, and to Walter Herrmann, of Weilheim, Germany, for translating them into English from their difficult old-style German handwriting. The authors would also like to thank Marielle Williams, who first conceived the idea of turning Walter Wagner's last card into a book, and whose own birthday anniversary, appropriately, falls on the publication day of the first English edition.

Bibliography

Anonymous, *A Woman in Berlin* (London, 1955)

BBC News Online, 'Russia displays "Hitler skull fragment"' (26 April 2000)

Beevor, Antony, *Berlin – The Downfall 1945* (London, 2002)

—, The Mystery of Olga Chekhova (London, 2004)

Bezymenski, Lev, *The Death of Adolf Hitler – Unknown Documents from the Soviet Archives* (London, 1968)

Boldt, Gerhard, *Hitler's Last Days – An Eye-Witness Account* (London, 1973)

Botting, Douglas, *In the Ruins of the Reich: Germany 1945–1949* (London/New York, 1985)

Botting, Douglas, *The Aftermath: Europe* (Time-Life History of World War II) (USA, 1983)

Braun, Eva, *Diaries 1935* (Special Collections of the Library of Congress, Washington DC)

Bromberg, Norbert, and Small, Verna Volz, *Hitler's Psychopathology* (New York, 1983)

Bullock, Alan, *Hitler – A Study in Tyranny* (London, 1952)

Burleigh, Michael, *The Third Reich – A New History* (London, 2001)

Buxell, Dag, *Notes and Comments on Mohnke* (Caracas, Venezuela, 2003)

Byford-Jones, W., *Berlin Twilight* (London, 1947)

Carr, William, *Hitler – A Study in Personality and Politics* (London, 1978)

CIA History Staff, 'Hitler, Stalin, and Operation Myth' (Benjamin

Fischer, Center for the Study of Intelligence Bulletin, issue No. 11, Summer 2000)

Counter Intelligence Corps (CIC, US Army, Germany): OI Special Report 36 (2 April 1947) – 'Adolf Hitler: A Composite Picture': Report 4 – Eberstein – 'Women Around Hitler': Report 6 Haselbach (f) 'Eva Braun'

Counter Intelligence Corps (CIC): 'Reports on Zander et al' (Munich December 1945–January 1946)

Cross, Colin, *Adolf Hitler* (London, 1974)

Dolgov, Anna, Russian museum displays fragment of Hitler's skull (Associated Press, 26 April 2000)

Fest, Joachim C., *Hitler* (London, 1974)

Franchetti, Mark, 'Russian interpreter tells how she hid Hitler's jaw for Stalin' (*The Sunday Times*, London, 6 Oct 2002)

Frank, Johannes, *Eva Braun* (Oldendorf 1988)

From, Bella, *Blood and Banquets – A Berlin Social Diary* (London, 1942)

Galante, Pierre, and Silianoff, Eugene, *Last Witnesses in the Bunker* (London, 1989)

Gollancz, Victor, *In Darkest Germany* (London, 1947)

Gun, Nerin E., *Eva Braun: Hitler's Mistress* (London, 1968)

Hanfstaengl, Ernst (Putzi), *Hitler – The Missing Years* (London, 1957)

Hayman, Ronald, *Hitler and Geli* (London, 1997)

Heiden, Konrad, *Hitler – A Biography* (London, 1936)

Heston, Leonard L, and Heston, Renate, *The Medical Case Book of Adolf Hitler* (London, 1979)

Highfield, Roger (Science Editor), 'Dental detective work gets to the root of Hitler mystery' (International Campaign for Real History, London, 26 Oct 1999)

Hitler, Adolf, *Mein Kampf* (London, 1974)

Hitler, Adolf, *Hitler's Table Talk 1941–44 – His Private*

Bibliography

Conversations (Introduction by Hugh Trevor-Roper) (London, 1973)

Hitler, Paula, Interrogations by US Intelligence (National Archives, Washington DC – Modern Wars Department and Military Section – 1945)

Hoffmann, Heinrich, *Hitler Was My Friend* (London, 1955)

Hughes, John Graven, *Getting Hitler into Heaven – The Memoirs of Hitler's Valet* (London, 1987)

Imperio Argentina, 'Imperio Argentina died, star of the Thirties, adored by Hitler' (Internet, 2003)

The Times, 'Imperio Argentina – Argentine singer and actress who befriended Hitler' (2003)

Infield, Glenn B., *Eva and Adolf* (New York 1974)

Infield, Glenn B., *Hitler's Secret Life – The Mysteries of the Eagle's Nest* (New York, 1979)

Irving, David, *Hitler's War* (London, 1977)

Irving, David (ed.), *Adolf Hitler – The Medical Diaries* (The Private Diaries of Dr Theo Morell) (London, 1983)

Joachimsthaler, Anton, *The Last Days of Hitler: The Legends – The Evidence – The Truth* (London, 1996)

Jenks, William A., *Vienna and the Young Hitler* (New York, 1960)

Jetzinger, Franz, *Hitler's Youth* (London, 1958)

Jones, J. Sydney, *Hitler in Vienna 1907–13* (London, 1983)

Junge, Traudl, *Until the Final Hour – Hitler's Last Secretary* (London, 2003)

Kershaw, Ian, *Hitler* (London, 2000)

Knopp, Guido, *Hitler's Women – And Marlene* (Stroud, 2003)

Kohler, Pauline, *I Was Hitler's Maid* (London, 1939, 1973)

Krueger, Dr Kurt, *Inside Hitler* (New York, 1941)

Krueger, Dr Kurt, *I Was Hitler's Doctor* (New York, 1942, 1943)

Kubizek, August, *Young Hitler* (London, 1973)

Bibliography

Kuby, Erich, *The Russians and Berlin* (London, 1968)

Langer, Walter, *The Mind of Adolf Hitler – The Secret Wartime Report* (New York, 1972)

Lewis, David, *The Secret Life of Adolf Hitler* (London, 1977)

Lewis, David, *The Man Who Invented Hitler – The Making of the Führer* (London, 2003)

Machtan, Lother, *The Hidden Hitler* (Oxford, 2001)

Maser, Werner, *Hitler: Legend, Myth and Reality* (London, 1973)

Maser, Werner, *Hitler's Letters and Notes* (London, 1974)

Mauch, Christof, *The Shadow War Against Hitler – The Covert Operations of America's Wartime Secret Intelligence Service* (New York, 2003)

McKale, Donald M., *Hitler – The Survival Myth* (New York, 1983)

McKnight, Gerald, *The Strange Loves of Adolf Hitler* (London, 1978)

Mayer, Emmie, *Love Letters to Adolf Hitler* (unpublished manuscript – Spandau, 8 August 1942 to 15 March 1943)

Misch, Rochus (as told to Simon Finch), 'I heard Hitler shoot himself' (*Sunday Telegraph*, London, 30 April 2000)

Mosely, Leonard O., *Report from Germany* (London, 1945)

Musmanno, Michael M., *Ten Days To Die* (New York, 1950)

New York Times, 'Hitler's Private Will Found' (New York, 30 December 1945)

O'Donnell, James P., *The Berlin Bunker* (London, 1979)

Owings, Alison, *Frauen – German Women Recall The Third Reich* (London, 1995)

Payne, Robert, *The Life and Death of Adolf Hitler* (New York, 1973)

Petrova, Ada, and Watson, Peter, *The Death of Hitler – The Final Words from Russia's Secret Archives* (London, 1995)

Peis, Gunther, 'Die unbekannte Geliebte' (*Stern* 24, 1959)

Pryce-Jones, David, *Unity Mitford – A Quest* (London, 1976)

Public Records Office, Kew, UK:

Bibliography

File No. WO 208/3781

US Intelligence report on Hitler's teeth, also Eva Braun's

Statement by Erna Flegel (German Red Cross nurse) re last days of Hitler and Berlin

File No. WO 208/3787

p 30/31 – typed field report by Trevor-Roper re current position at Nov 45 re death of Hitler, plus further recommendations

pp 32 ff – The death of Hitler

– sources

– evidence from available sources

– incorrect versions

– suggestions for next Quadripartite Conference

– list of persons in the Bunker

pp 67–81 Last days of Hitler in the air raid shelter by Hanna Reitsch (interviewed by Robert E. Work) Airborne Division, HQ US Forces in Austria, 8 Oct 45

pp 93–112 Hitler as seen by his doctors (20 sections) US Military Intelligence, 15 Oct 45

P 133 Top Secret

(some rough notes on Hitler's diary by Lt Col J.L. McEwen) 18 Sept 45 File No. WO 208/3790: Secret Timetable of Events in Hitler's Bunker on 29 April 45

File No. WO 208/3791

pp 33–39 re various escapes from Bunker (by von Loringhoven, 12 Jan 46)

pp 89 ff re various Hitler survival reports

Lagebesprechung 27 April 1945 (verbatim reports of conversations by Hitler, Krebs, Goebbels, etc)

pp 137–158 A Berliner's account of last days by Dr Karl Scharping (Fritsche's deputy and former broadcaster and political commentator on German radio) 1947

Bibliography

pp 188–194 – Frau Gerda Christian Interrogation Report (US Military Intelligence, 20 April 1946)

pp 219–223 – various interrogations e.g. Boldt and others

pp 228–30 – Interrogation Report of personal servant staff at Berghof, 19.4.46 – Antonia Sternig (Eva Braun's maid at the Berghof, b. 1924), also Liesl Ostertag (Eva Braun's special chambermaid), also Resi Steingassinger, Wally Bernegger and Erika Treutler (b. 1923).

USFET interrogation report of Gerda Christian, 25.4.46, re Hitler's marriage.

Rauschning, Hermann, *Hitler Speaks* (London, 1939)

Redlich, Fritz, *Hitler – Diagnosis of a Destructive Prophet* (New York, 1999)

Reiter, Mimi, 'I was Hitler's lover' (*Sunday Pictorial*, London, May–June 1959)

Riefenstahl, Leni, *A Memoir* (New York, 1993)

Rosenbaum, Ron, *Explaining Hitler – The Search for the Origins of Evil* (New York, 1998)

Ryan, Cornelius, *The Last Battle* (London, 1966)

Sayer, Ian, and Botting, Douglas, *Hitler's Last General – The Case against Wilhelm Mohnke* (London, 1989)

Sayer, Ian, and Botting, Douglas, *America's Secret Army – The Untold Story of the Counter Intelligence Corps* (London, 1989)

Schenk, Ernst Gunther, *Patient Hitler* (Dusseldorf, 1989)

Schenk, Ernst, 'Ich sah Berlin sterben – als Arzt in der Reichskanzlei' (Herford, Germany, 1970)

Schroeder, Christa, 'Er war mein Chef: Aus dem Nachlass der Sekretärin von Adolf Hitler', ed. by Anton Joachimsthaler (Munich, 1985)

Sevruk, V. (ed), *How Wars End* (Moscow, 1969)

Shirer, William L., *The Rise and Fall of the Third Reich* (London, 1973)

Bibliography

Smith, Bradley F., *Adolf Hitler – His Family, Childhood and Youth* (Stanford, USA, 1967)

Sountsova, Maria, Report on Hitler's head in Russian State Archives, Moscow (University of Kazan, Tatarstan, 2003)

Speer, Albert, *Inside the Third Reich* (London, 1970)

Strasser, Otto, *Hitler and I* (London, 1940)

Toland, John, *The Last 100 Days* (London, 1966)

Trevor-Roper, H.R., *The Last Days of Hitler* (London, 2002)

Trevor-Roper, H.R., *The Last Days of Hitler* (*Life Magazine*, 17 March 1947)

Wagner, Gottfried, *He Who Does Not Howl With The Wolf – The Wagner Legacy* (London, 1998)

Wagner, Walter, Documents relating to professional career and NSDAP associations of Walter Wagner and Cordula Wagner 1934–1944 (Bundesarchiv, Berlin)

Wagner, Walter, Documents testifying to the death of Walter Wagner near the Anhalter Bahnhof, Berlin, on 29 April 1945 (Amtsgericht, Abt 54, 1951/1963)

Wagner, Walter, Letters to Cordula Wagner from Berlin-Buch 18 Dec 1944 to 28 March 1945 (originals from Michael Wagner, Germany, and Ian Sayer, UK)

Waite, Robert G.L., *The Psychopathic God – Adolf Hitler* (New York, 1977)

Wallace, Irving and Sylvia, and David Wallechinsky, *The Intimate Sex Lives of Famous People* (London, 1981)

Warlimont, Walter, *Inside Hitler's Headquarters 1939–45* (London, 1962)

Zoller, Albert, *Hitler Privat* (recollections by Hitler's 'secret secretary' Schroeder) (Dusseldorf, 1949)

Index

Index

Hamburg 275

Hanfstaengl, Erna 31, 105

Hanfstaengl, Ernst ('Putzi') 18–19, 46, 51, 58, 66–70, 77–8, 102, 106–8, 112, 113–14, 128, 129–30, 156

Hanfstaengl, Helena 31, 67, 156

Haug, Ernst 33, 105

Haug, Jenny 33, 105

Haus Wachenfeld 34, 44, 99, 121–2, 145

see also Berghof, the

Havel, Lake 230, 231

Heiden, Konrad 48–9

Helm, Brigitte 105

Hentschel, Johannes 187–8, 233–5

Herrmann, Walter 294

Hess, Rudolf 55, 59, 70–1, 77

Heusermann, Käther 248–9, 250

Hewel, Walter 108

Himmler, Heinrich 148, 180, 183
Führer File 32–3, 57
offers unconditional surrender 197–8, 201, 202, 209, 212, 215
suicide 258

Hindenburg, President Paul von 137

Hitler, Adolf
character and attributes
anti-Semitism 20, 94, 212, 215, 222, 225
appearance 10, 11–12, 13–14, 28–30, 39, 111, 141, 204–5, 214
aversion to medical examinations 88
contempt for human life 93–4
eccentricity 93–5
egomaniac 91, 129
fear of intellectuals 32
health 157–8, 162–3, 164–5, 180, 182–4, 204–5, 214
love of Wagner 112–14
obsession with astrology 125
personal routine 94–6, 155, 178
pet likes and dislikes 93–4, 141
psycho-analysis of 90–2, 129
psychopathic 92–3
smelly 205
social inadequacies 27–8
vegetarianism 65, 95
views on children 148, 157, 194–5
views on suicide 61–2, 189, 216, 220, 264, 266–7
early life
as art student 19, 20
childhood 16–18

in First World War 14, 21–3
blinded in gas attack 14, 22
his death
cremation 223–5, 237, 245–6, 252–3
escape theory 255
post-war treatment of his relatives 259–60
remains of 267–70
reported sightings of 257
search for remains of 241–54
suicide 8–10, 193, 211, 218–26, 252, 256
uninterested in escape 173–4, 180, 184
will and political testament 203, 210–12, 215, 229–33, 256, 262–5
political career
assassination attempts 150, 158–62, 191–2, 204
becomes Chancellor and Führer 72, 77, 97, 98
birthday party in Bunker 180–2
doubles 125–6
fan mail 82–3
imprisonment 34
life in Führerbunker 177–8
speeches 113–14
to fight to the last 184–5, 187, 215
relationships
calf love for Stefanie Isac 19
casual attachments 104–10
with Eva Braun
correspondence 166, 191
love for 195–6, 208–9
marriage 4, 194–6, 202–10, 213, 237, 261, 277, 280–1
with father 16–18, 90
with Geli 44–65, 86, 87, 88, 222
mourns her death 65–6, 70
suspected of her murder 56, 60–1
lack of friends 96–7
with Mimi (Maria Reiter) 35–44, 70–3, 87
with mother 16–18, 20, 36, 38, 90, 97, 220, 222
prefers company of women 31–2, 188
with society ladies 27, 30, 110–20
with teenage girls 32–3, 34, 35–44, 72, 92
views on marriage 147–8, 157, 194–5, 211
sexuality
erection problems 33

305

Index

Index

Index